# IT'S WHO
# I AM

**CONOR KENNY**
IN CONVERSATION WITH
PEOPLE WHO DISCOVERED
THEIR PURPOSE AND PASSION

Leabharlanna Poibli Chathair Baile Átha Cliath

Dublin City Public Libraries

Published by OAK TREE PRESS, Cork, Ireland
www.oaktreepress.com / www.SuccessStore.com

© 2017 Conor Kenny

ISBN 978 1 78119 309 9 (hardback)
ISBN 978 1 78119 305 1 (ePub)
ISBN 978 1 78119 306 8 (Kindle)
ISBN 978 1 78119 307 5 (PDF)

A catalogue record of this book is available from the British Library.

Cover design: Jeff White / Begley Hutton Design Consultants

Photo credits: Domini Kemp: Barry McCall; Liz Nolan: Frances Marshall
Photography; Pádraig Ó Céidigh: Andrew Downes.

# CONTENTS

# ACKNOWLEDGEMENTS

Book covers generally credit one person but, behind every book, there are quiet people who play their part in making it happen.

I am indebted to:

- The 14 people who shared their wisdom, kindness and stories;
- Geraldine Patten, who worked tirelessly and cheerfully;
- Grace Gallagher, for allowing me so much time off;
- Vincent O'Brien, a friend since school days, who unerringly spots flaws in logic or English;
- Mark Kenny and Jonathan Neilan, for their ideas, support and more;
- My family, for their support;
- Gary McGann, who quickly did more than was ever expected;
- Garvan Grant, for his help and meticulous editing eye;
- Brian O'Kane, for his insights, enthusiasm and constant optimism.

# DEDICATION

*For My Dad, Ivor Kenny*
*(1930 – 2016)*

# INTRODUCTION

**Maker of Dreams**
© *Finbar Furey*

*Strings of life*
*Oh, what gladness you give*
*You send my heart soaring high*
*Music of people, I adore your God.*
*He has given me the gift of life*
*Made from this poor boy who wondered*
*What am I?*
*Who am I?*

*I am the music*
*I am the man from the boy*
*I am my father's child*
*I am my mother's pride*
*I am just another keeper of hearts*
*A maker of dreams*
*I am a string of life.*

If Friday evenings overflow with euphoria and Sunday nights feel as attractive as the gallows, then you are probably in the wrong job.

I know, I was there.

Many years later, my own experience has given rise to this book and to going far deeper than exploring the over-simple clichéd question: "Are you in the right job?"

For me, a better question has always been, "Who are you?"

This book is all about just that but told through the words of 14 extraordinary people who do not separate what they do from who they are.

Life's defining moments may well come with bright lights, loud thunder and more but some are simple, silent and undeniable. They come when you're receptive and when you least expect it. Their mark is eternal and, whether you choose to listen or not, they can't be forgotten.

Mine came on a Monday morning.

I had been living in London for nine years and I wanted to come home. There was a deep recession and jobs were scarce in Ireland. I knew I was facing a battle.

It's hard now to imagine a world without Google and smartphones but this was the 1990s. Like everything, you couldn't miss what hadn't been born. You simply worked with what you had. A call home was often from a phone box and there were no online job sites. Newspapers were the only source of opportunity and they came only once a week. You sent a letter in response to the advert and weeks would pass before the inevitable "Thanks, but no thanks." You picked yourself up and started again. It was a roller-coaster with far more dips than highs.

Over time, doubt creeps in. Will I ever get a job? Am I good enough? Doubt is followed by despair and the risk of desperation. It's a predictable slide.

Running out of money and realising that London may as well have been Siberia as far as potential employers in Dublin were concerned, I decided to gamble my ever-diminishing savings on a trip home and endless knocking on reluctant doors in search of work.

It worked! In five days, I had four job offers. None appealed, but it was better than slipping further into oblivion in London.

I started with my new employer enthusiastically, despite the fact that I'd taken a huge drop in pay and status. The people I worked with were good, kind people. Within weeks, I hated my job. I hated it with a passion. I was paralysed by the beauty of being home and the dread of work. They were inextricably linked.

The canteen was a bleak, dark room, painted in a dreadful industrial green. It was an old building and everything about the room was Dickensian.

I sat alone over a lukewarm coffee contemplating which was worse, the room or the job?

I couldn't decide and it didn't really matter. My moment of peace was about to fade.

She exploded through the door, singing and whistling. Her love of the good life was plain to see. It was Monday, it was this place and I couldn't begin to understand how she loved it so much. I felt miserable and I looked it.

She ignored me for a while and I understood that she didn't want my misery to dampen her spark. But it was only a matter of time before she broke the silence.

"Cheer up, Conor. Maybe this is as good as it gets in your career."

I felt sick.

I felt really sick.

Maybe she was right. Maybe I needed to 'just get on with it'. Maybe this was to be my lot.

Maybe this is as good as it gets for you, Conor. Maybe you're not as good as you think.

In hindsight, it lit a very powerful fuse and propelled my escape from misery and paralysis into beginning to understand what it was that I wanted to do. Of course, that often starts with what I don't want to do.

And then the journey began.

Approaching his 80th year, I asked my Dad if he would give a small workshop for a chosen few. With all of his experience and wisdom, it was thought-provoking, simple and memorable. Two things stood out.

He asked me to bring a portable music player. I didn't spoil his thunder by asking what for. The introductions over, he pressed 'Play' and it was Sir Bob Geldof and The Boomtown Rats, belting out *I Don't Like Mondays*.

When it stopped, measured as ever, he simply looked at everyone and said: "Well?"

Then just before he finished, he sat in total silence for about two minutes. He wanted to emphasise the power of silence and the importance of listening. When silence settled into calm acceptance, he said, "There's no such thing as a lazy person. They are either sick or in the wrong job."

It took time to digest and then the wisdom of the apparently simple statement grew into a defining moment.

For me, these two moments changed how I thought about work, myself, purpose and other people.

I understood being trapped in the wrong job. I understood despair and dread. I understood that I was lucky to have been aware that true wisdom is often very simple.

Then, and only then, did I go in search of who I am and what it is that I was destined to do.

I'm lucky, because today, my work is exactly who I am. That created an undeniable desire to share this learning through the words, stories and experiences of these 14 extraordinary people.

❖   ❖   ❖

Writing a book, once you have finished flirting with the idea, is not negotiable.

I knew what I wanted to achieve and I knew what I didn't want.

The 14 people in this book reflect the only point I wanted to make – being who you are.

They are free from ego and see themselves as ordinary. They are universally humble but possessed of a character that is deeply and automatically engaging. They are accessible and never measure their own achievements as anything more than reference points.

They are all different and deliberately included because being who they are really matters to them.

The book does not set out to pull together common threads, bundle them into an invented conclusion and indulge in an easy form of prescriptivism. On the contrary, the importance of the book is that there is no type, no DNA that you can imitate, manufacture or buy. They simply are who they are and they sit very comfortably in that.

Perhaps the best description I can give is to say they are ordinary people with extraordinary moments and extraordinary stories.

What has been incredibly revealing is their humility and their self-awareness. Their stock question, when invited into the book, was: "Why would you want someone like me in the book with all of those incredible people?"

At one point, I was convinced the bush telegraph was buzzing brightly with certain conspiracy because I heard this question almost every time.

Everyone shared their stories without fear or favour. There were no ego trips. They were open, emotional and natural. It has been an incredible privilege to sit with them, one to one, and watch their story unfold. It doesn't take long to see the triggers, the influences, the good, the bad and the not so good. These are the stories that brought them from there to here and all of us will identify with many of the moments they describe so well.

❖   ❖   ❖

The words in their chapters are their own. Their stories flow and, in most cases, only two questions ever mattered:

- Who are you?
- Do tell me your story, from first memories, through to today.

Each conversation had a different location, the place they wanted to be. That took me on a fascinating journey into their homes, their offices, Leinster House, the headquarters of the Irish Naval Service and more. It has been a journey into daily life led by people known and people less well-known.

It is up to you, the reader, to dip into these deep pools of experience and take what you want. Every chapter teaches you something and you will be richly rewarded in your own way.

❖   ❖   ❖

*In your life's defining moments there are two choices – you either step forward in faith and power or you step backward into fear.*
**James Arthur Ray**

At the beginning of this *Introduction*, I referred to defining moments. This book overflows with them. Often simple, always significant, they change our course.

While writing this book, I was lucky – very lucky – to renew old friendships, begin new ones and meet people I'd never met before.

In life, all that really matters is family, health and friends or, put simply, people.

Not one single person in this book set out to be where they are now. Luck, hard work and circumstance took them there. They share an ability to accept the opportunities that these moments created and it's a good way to understand that life takes you where it wants to take you.

The wisdom these men and women enjoy almost always comes from hard times. Hard times can reward you – if you listen to the lesson.

In my own meandering journey through life, I have always been struck by the very real kindness of those at the top. In many ways, that's why they got to the top and stayed there.

Many years ago, I was that lost young man who hadn't sorted out his inner conflicts or purpose. It fills you full of doubt.

Defining moments are sometimes more easily understood as interventions. It's that special moment where a simple gesture, an act of kindness or a listening ear influences you for the good.

For me, that moment arrived many years ago back in England. I was lost and a big, kind man understood, listened intently, patiently and with kindness. He spoke little but what he said was powerful. His words worked and, without those words, at that moment, with that kindness, this book would never have been written and their stories never aired.

That man is Finbar Furey and he can share in the credit for inspiring me and ultimately making me who I am.

I am grateful that this book captures that precious moment and that he was the first to say "Yes."

**Conor Kenny**
**Dublin**
**July 2017**

# TOMMY BYRNE

"I'm a dreamer."

*Thomas (Tommy) Byrne is a former Formula One race car driver, who was born and grew up in Co Louth. In 1983, he moved to the US, where he raced in the IndyCar Series and Indy Lights. He now lives in Florida, where he runs a driving academy. **Crashed and Byrned: The Greatest Racing Driver You Never Saw**, his autobiography, written with Mark Hughes, won the William Hill Irish Sports Book of the Year award in 2009 and was later made into a documentary.*

**I'm a dreamer.** Yeah, I'm still trying to get the big hit. I invented the 'drift-lift' – well, it was my idea and Gary Anderson designed it for me. It's a skid-simulator machine. I sat in one for 15 years and I had an idea that I wanted to make a portable one – and so I did. That was one of my dreams, the big hit – one big hit is all it takes.

But I still dream. Not as much as I used to, but I'll always be thinking of doing something different, doing something better, coming up with something. For example, I have a shirt that says 'Say Cheeze' on the back. It's a cycling shirt with the message that anybody who is wearing this shirt on a bicycle is video-recording the traffic behind them. I would say I am a dreamer, but not quite so much any more because everything I've dreamed of has come true – just not the millions of dollars!

I was always working since I was seven or eight years of age and at one point I was working at a petrol station. There was rationing in place at the time, so I'd make a fortune giving people petrol they weren't entitled to in return for big tips. I could change tyres at 13 and fix punctures at 15. This was when you had to hit them with a sledgehammer to break them down and everything. On a Sunday, I'd put a tube in even though it didn't need a tube. I'd say, "I'm not supposed to work on Sunday, but I'll do it" and I'd sell them a tube. I was terrible, very borderline.

Growing up, I was just a little terror. I loved being on the farm. I started to go there when I was about seven or eight years old and I loved it so much I was always there. I hated school because I got beaten every day. I wasn't one of the rich kids and, of course, I didn't do my homework because my parents were always working and didn't have the time to sit down with six kids and teach them how to read and write, so my refuge was the farm. I also loved engines, cars and speed. My goal was always to get to drive the tractors! I didn't like lifting the hay bales because I was a little guy, so while I did do the harder work, I was really only there for the chance of driving the tractors.

The farm was Pete Murphy's, just down the road from my home. I remember sitting in school and looking out the window and watching him on the tractor baling the hay in the summertime. It didn't get much better for me than being on the farm, climbing up to reach the hay and riding on the tractor on the way home. As I got older and bigger, I got to drive the tractor a lot – so much so that I actually got bored with it, so I went to another farm whose owner let me do the harrowing of a whole big field.

Pete Murphy saw a bunch of kids that he didn't have to pay, but I was the one who always stayed. My brother came a little bit, but not like I did. I was there through thick and thin.

After the farm, I learned to be a welder. I was going to be a diesel mechanic, but started with welding. I loved making trailers and all that kind of thing. Years later, not long after I moved to America, I bought 10 acres of land by a lake on which I put a house. I got a tractor and I made my own equipment for it because I'd learned welding. I made my own rake the way I wanted it, the way I used to have it back in Ireland, and I made a thing for flattening the sand, for planting trees and stuff.

I rebuilt a Mini engine when I was 15 or 16; I took the whole engine apart and then rebuilt it. My auntie went to England and brought back the cams that I wanted for it. I had to do the timing and everything – and I put it all back together and couldn't believe it when it actually started up! We used to start the engines before we'd put them in the cars to make sure they ran. I then did my own car, which took about six months to complete – and I crashed on the first outing! I ran it for probably a couple of weeks and then it blew up ...

I was always doing work at home – me and my brother built our own garage. Obviously, Ma had to give us the money for materials, but I then had a garage to hold two cars. I stole the pieces from CRV to make the garage door – that's in my movie *Crashed and Byrned* – and that door is still there 40-something years later! One piece at a time, that was me, taking one piece at a time to make my stuff. I had a winch that I stole from CRV which was used to move engines around. I took it from 40 feet up in the air one lunchtime with a friend of mine helping me. That was pretty exciting, getting it out of there without being caught, then taking it home and installing it. It's still in my house today!

I was terrible; I was Dundalk's number one pilferer. I could get stuff nobody else could get. It was the excitement of doing it. I was up on a roof one day with my friends who were talking about doing a job. It turned out they were planning to steal some truck tyres. That was a big job and we had to go in there at night. I think we stole 10 tyres. These were probably 200-tonne tyres at the time – rolling them up the hill, into a waiting van, to take them away. They were all quickly sold, taken across the Border and I think my share of the deal was £10. Yeah, it was the excitement – it obviously wasn't the money!

---

## *Everything I've dreamed has come true – just not the millions of dollars!*

---

When I turned 18 years of age, that was it. Something happened and I just quit stealing stuff. But if I hadn't become a racing driver, I would probably have gone another way. Maybe. Once I stopped stealing, that was it. I thought back then, of course, that nobody else in the world steals stuff. I'd leave my car open – I still do.

Instead, I went stock car racing with Tony Sharkey. First Dublin and Santry, then up North, where the guys really knew their shit and how to make cars fast. We were riding around like culchies, white trash, from the south. We didn't know how to do cars like those guys could. Theirs were far, far faster, and the way they built the cars – a road car or for racing – was completely different to what we were doing. There was nobody in Ireland doing it. You'd go to Santry and it was ridiculous – they were driving pieces of shit around the track. Then you go to Northern Ireland and these things were beautiful. So we'd be going up and down to Northern Ireland and that's where I started. I was Tony's mechanic. I'd weld the car up when he'd break it. And even then, I wasn't going to be a race car driver, I was just hanging out with him. That's when I started to go in the right direction, I think, and stopped hanging out with the bad guys.

Tony Sharkey doesn't talk to me much any more because I wrote in my book that he was an alcoholic, who I'd taken home and cleaned up when I was back home one time. I did, but he didn't like the story. I told the truth in *Crashed and Byrned* and a lot of people didn't like it, but I couldn't tell the story without telling the truth. If Tony hadn't gone racing and I hadn't gone along to help, I don't know where I would have ended up. I'd wanted to go to America when I was 15, to be a welder. I wasn't even thinking of being a racer back then – I was always going to be a mechanic. I'd see the John Wayne movies at Christmas time with the great weather – I couldn't stand the weather in Ireland, looking out the window every morning and it nearly always damp. One of my buddies, the guy who did the big tyre heist, then went to Canada. In those days, Canada and America were the same as far as I was concerned. He sent me pictures of the big car he said he bought for $100. He basically lied – you couldn't buy a car for $100 over there. He came back to Ireland to work back in the same place again.

❖   ❖   ❖

**I decided to become a race car driver** when I first went to Mondello Park. Back then, my mother worked in a hotel where the racers used to stay when the races were on at Mondello. There was a racing car outside one time and to me it looked like a Formula One! I sat into it and thought it was pretty cool. A couple months after that, Pat McConnell, another friend of mine, went to the racing school at Mondello Park. I went up there with no licence, paid my £15, did my 15 laps in the school's Formula Ford 1600 and spun seven times in the rain. After that, I decided I was going to be a race car driver.

At that time, Derek Daly, David Kennedy, Eddie Jordan and Bernard Devaney were racing in England and I followed their progress avidly. If they'd done it, then so could I. After my laps of Mondello Park, I almost couldn't sleep until I got a racing car. John Murphy knew there was something, which I call 'the buzz'. There was a buzz around Ayrton Senna, there was a buzz around Roberto Moreno, there is a certain buzz with drivers when you see them go round the track. You take one look and you say: "That guy is good." So even in those days, you could see it. Even that day, there was a little bit of a buzz. For some reason, I just thought I was the best. I don't know where that came from. And that, thinking you are the best, helps you. I always backed it up, but it took me nearly three years to know for sure.

I didn't win a race until 1979. Well, I won a race at Mondello, but that really wasn't anything. When I really knew, and showed other people, was at the Nürburgring on the 14-mile-long Nordschleife in a car that wasn't the best out there. That's when I *knew* I was as good as I thought I was. It's the mother of all tracks, the one you go to, and if you can learn that track fast, you're the man. And if you can win there, which I did twice – in two different cars – that's when people started to say: "Wow!" I knew then that I had something different. I'd always thought that, but needed convincing, and that's when it happened.

At that time, I was driving in Formula Ford 1600. I was one of the very few people ever who got a fully funded works drive – with PRS – when going to England for their first year. Bernard Devaney got me the drive, as he'd driven for PRS the year before. I already owned a PRS, bought with borrowed money raised by my family from a field that they had. That first year, I must have done 30 or 40 races and got to race at five or six European circuits too, when usually you only raced in England.

Once I was over there, I was a professional driver. I left Ireland at the end of 1978. I went to England and had done the Formula Ford Festival a couple of times before that. When I went over there, I changed my name from Tom Byrne to Tommy Byrne, because it was thought to be more friendly. Formula Ford 1600 in those days was the bee's knees. You'd have 10 cars coming up to the chicane on the last lap, all trying to win the race! A bunch of young guys and a bunch of older, all slip-streaming, at places like Hockenheim, the Nürburgring and Silverstone. FF1600 was by far the best racing I've ever done and the best racing of my life.

In 1979, coming up to the chicane, for my first time, I'm in about third place and I'd never done this slip-streaming before, certainly not this fast. Then suddenly five cars went down one side of me and five cars down the other side of me and I'm in the middle, and it scared the crap out of me for an instant and I'm going: "Jesus, what the fuck is going on here?" I eventually figured it out, got mad and drafted past to finish in third place. But you were learning on the trot, about drafting and the like.

Today, if I got a 20-year-old kid and put him out there with no experience to draft like that, there would be a crash. We crashed all the time. Sometimes it worked and sometimes it didn't and that's how you were learning your craft. Because how else were you going to do it? Today, they have simulators so you can learn tracks and stuff. In those days, everyone was banging wheels in the open-wheel cars (when you were not supposed to) and it was just crazy – but I loved it. It was like you were half-scared yet so excited and, of course, you wanted to win. Eventually you start losing the love a little bit because you *have* to win and, if you are not winning, then it is not quite as exciting. Nothing worse than two cars drafting together and driving away – and then you are stuck with 10 cars fighting for third place. You think: "What am I doing here? There is no point in third place here. It has to be first place." These idiots would take your line away and then the leaders are gone and they'd rather fight for third place than for first.

Eventually, I got together with fellow drivers Roberto Moreno and Raul Boesel to make sure that, at every track we went to, we'd work together as a 'team' to ensure that we'd pull away from the pack and that, hey, it's either you or me at the end. At least, we were going to be going for first, not going for third. So it was all about winning, because if I wasn't going to be winning, I wasn't going to progress to Formula Ford 2000, Formula Three, Formula Two and then the ultimate, Formula One.

In 1980, I won two Formula Ford 1600 championships. Ralph Firman, of race car manufacturer Van Diemen, had given me a car and we got a free engine from engine builders Auriga, but I was a semi-works driver, meaning I didn't get everything for free. I was my own mechanic and my friends would help me when they could. Obviously, Ralph helped me if I needed assistance setting the car up a little differently.

For 1981, I was a semi-works Van Diemen driver again, but had moved up a category to Formula Ford 2000. Ralph had to pay for everything, as that year was the first year he had built a Formula Ford 2000 car. He wasn't very happy about paying for me to do everything, but he had no choice as he wanted to promote his car in order to sell customer examples. He thought I was his best chance of generating sales through results and I duly won the European and British championships. After my championships had been concluded, Ralph contacted me regarding the upcoming Formula Ford Festival at Brands Hatch. His number one driver, Ayrton Senna, had thrown a tantrum and announced he was retiring from racing and went back to Brazil. Ralph asked me if I could win the festival – the biggest showcase for FF1600 manufacturers – driving Senna's car. I replied: "Yes. It's a no-brainer. Easy." Ultimately I did win the final, but I had a huge struggle and I was actually slower than the year before. Years later, I discovered that I didn't have the special engine normally fitted to Senna's chassis; it had been replaced with a less powerful one.

> *I probably hung on 10 years too long – but my*
> *self-belief was so great I couldn't quit.*

Even though I'd just won four championships in two years, it was winning the Formula Ford Festival that made a huge change to my life. My prize for winning the festival was a free race in Formula Three two weeks later where I finished second, having very nearly won it. Murray Taylor, a former journalist turned Formula Three team owner, was running the car and saw first-hand how good I was, so he signed me for a full 1982 season even though he had no money. So, for every single race of 1982 it was the same thing: if you didn't win, you might not progress to the next level, so the fun was obviously not as much as when I started racing.

❖  ❖  ❖

**There was pressure all the time.** The chances of me getting to Formula One were so slim and yet I did, and, again, it was an accident. Frankly, I would have been better off not getting into that piece of shit, but I didn't have a manager, mainly because I didn't want one. David Kennedy wanted to manage me but I wouldn't have him around me. I didn't need a manager telling me how far to jump; I needed somebody to get me work, as that's what I always figured managers are for, not to try to change your style. Eddie Jordan was my manager for a while and he didn't try to change me. He liked me, knew I could tighten things up a little here and there, but didn't want me to change my personality.

My Formula One chance came midway through the season because of an Irish man, Sydney Taylor. He watched me win the British Grand Prix F3 support race at Brands Hatch by a mile, one of my biggest wins ever, and decided to put me in his Theodore F1 car. There was a lot more involved, however, as I'm even now still finding out. Money was changing hands without my knowledge, as I had nothing to do with money – Murray Taylor looked after that side of things for me. Rizla had given money to the Theodore team for me to drive. They had a guy called Jan Lammers driving it (Derek Daly had also driven that same car) and I was now next in line. Julian Randles and Jo Ramírez were quite happy with Lammers, who turned out to be a great driver, but they fired him and they hired me because Sydney Taylor wanted me. This all went on behind my back and I'd no idea about it until decades later when Mark Hughes was co-writing my book and interviewed Ramírez, who said: "We didn't really want him. He wasn't ready for Formula One." And I'm thinking: "It all makes sense now. I had such a hard time trying to get things done with that car and that team because they didn't want me in the first place."

I just couldn't stand Julian Randles. Jo Ramírez was okay, but Randles was very British and uptight and it was he who told me that if Keke Rosberg was driving my car, he'd be on pole position. Just stupid things that you don't tell a guy who's just won five championships, and the festival, which nobody had ever done before or since, not even Ayrton Senna.

The 1982 season became quite hectic as I was combining Formula One Grands Prix with the British Formula Three championship. In spite of missing some rounds of the latter when there was a clash with F1, I still managed to clinch the F3 title at the final round. My prize for winning that championship was a test with McLaren – a chance to sample a competitive F1 car, as opposed to the totally uncompetitive Theodore I'd been struggling with. I'd spoken to McLaren regarding the 1983 season about two months prior to the test, but there was no drive available for me because they had already signed Niki Lauda and

John Watson. At the test, I set the third fastest lap time ever recorded at Silverstone and was actually even quicker than that as, oddly, McLaren was showing slower lap times for me than my friend was recording trackside. Then, years later, I was told by a McLaren mechanic present at the test that he'd been instructed to prevent me being able to use full throttle! This was apparently because they didn't want the car damaged, yet popstar Leo Sayer drove the very same car there the next day and had only passed his driving test a fortnight earlier!

I stayed in Europe for two more years, first with Eddie Jordan who hired me to race in European Formula Three for 1983. I knew my Formula One dream was over. All those five years of leaving Ireland with no money and getting there – getting to the top of the mountain – it takes a lot out of you, and I wasn't quite the same after that. I was 23 at that stage and I knew it was over. The fight had gone out of me to an extent and so the partying started. There had not been much partying before all this went on – then I started letting my hair down. The year 1983 turned out to be one of my best and one of the most fun years I ever had, racing in Europe with the likes of Gerhard Berger, Emanuele Pirro, Pierluigi Martini and Cathy Muller. We raced all over Europe and had loads of fun. I won a couple of races, was leading the championship and still had a chance to win it – but it didn't happen.

❖ ❖ ❖

**After another fun but less successful year** competing in the 1984 European F3 championship with Gary Anderson, I finally made it to America in 1985 where I started all over again. I started a whole new career back in Formula Ford 1600 with Ralph Firman to help him win the American equivalent of the Formula Ford Festival known as the 'Run-Offs'. I started from the bottom again with the hope of going all the way to the top of American single-seater racing, except this time around I didn't have the same fight in me. I got paid well to race in Indy Lights where I won a bunch of races and got a couple of tests in IndyCar but, at that stage in America, most drivers had to pay for their drives in the premier category. At that stage I was just worn out –

opportunities of getting paid to race were getting fewer and fewer, and I clearly wasn't going to make the money I'd hoped I'd make – but you hold on because a regular job is £60k or £70k a year, and I still had a theoretical chance of earning half a million if I got into a top IndyCar team. I probably hung on 10 years too long. I should have started teaching and doing my other stuff years earlier, but my self-belief was so great I couldn't quit.

As far as thinking you are the best driver in the world, when McLaren boss Ron Dennis asks you, "How good do you think you are?", I'd say, "I'm the best" and now I'm the asshole for telling the truth. But if I'd told Ron Dennis, "Oh, I think I'm okay. I think with a bit of help and with some maturity and with some years, I could be a good driver", would that be what he wanted to hear? No. If you'd have asked Ayrton Senna if he was the best driver, he'd be disgusted that you'd even asked such a stupid question! I'd just say: "Sure I am – I've already proved it."

I used to give all my trophies away to friends. Angie, Ralph Firman's wife, has my Formula Three championship trophy. The trophy I really want to get back is the William Hill Book of the Year award made from Waterford Crystal. That's the finest trophy I've ever seen, so I'd really like to get it back.

❖   ❖   ❖

I do a lot of driving still. We have a teen school, diablodrifter.com, and I have guys who are better teachers than me. Nowadays, I'm fed up with all the travelling and I'm looking for something whereby I can be a consultant so I don't have to travel as much.

I love my mountain biking – I just want to go mountain biking all the time. I've got about six mountain bikes and two road bikes and right now, if I could retire tomorrow, I'd drive a mountain bike every day. I've had far more injuries from cycling than from racing cars: I broke my finger and my teeth and I broke my shoulder twice!

# MICK DOWLING

"I'm a happy and
contented man."

*Mick Dowling won eight National Senior Boxing titles, two European medals and competed for Ireland in two Olympic Games in a 10-year period from 1965 when he first started boxing.*

*He now coaches and commentates on boxing, as well running a sports shop in Dublin.*

**Now, at 70 years old, I'm a happy and contented man** who has had a fantastic life, made fantastic because of my involvement in sport, boxing, hurling, athletics and all of the good people I met through sport. Happy and contented because I think I've provided well for my family.

I've made a good living out of the Mick Dowling Sportsworld business and been able to provide for my family. I would hope – and I often think about this now as I'm getting older – in time, when I'm gone, I'd like people to say: "Well, he worked hard, he earned what he got. He has a nice house on Greenlea Road and a nice shop in Terenure." I often feel: "What are mums and dads for if not to provide for their children?" I was never a person who has wanted more for myself. If I did want more, it was for my family. I don't care about money for myself. When you get to our age, money doesn't matter. So you are happy to give it to your family and that's the way it is with me.

In 1970, I was lucky enough to meet a wonderful girl, Emily Hopkins, who was a well-known athlete in her day. We have four children – two boys and two girls – all doing fine for themselves, and I'm happy and proud of all of them.

❖ ❖ ❖

**My life has simply been full of sport.** For me, growing up in Castlecomer [Co Kilkenny], sport was always part of my life. I came from a huge family – I mean, unbelievably big. Sixteen children – ridiculous, I know, nowadays, but that's what it was. I had nothing to do with that. My Mam and Dad had 16 and that was it. A big mix of boys and girls. I was in and around the middle of all of those. I smile today when I hear parents who feel they must give their children each a room of their own. I not only shared a room, I shared a bed with four brothers – three up, two down! And many a night, I ended up on the floor, having fallen out of an overcrowded bed.

At the age of 14, I was out working, doing manual work in the coalmine in Castlecomer. Not down under, because you had to be 16 years old to go underground, but I worked on what was called 'the Surface'. We had a coal-carting business, so I'm sure that from the age of 12 or 13, I was already doing a lot of manual labour. It was usually a 5am or 6am start. You went out to the mines, got the coal, shovelled it into the cart and delivered it to the families of the coalminers – and you got paid for doing that. I remember well the pay I got was 10 shillings, an orange note. So work that out, whatever that's worth. We had that little business going for ourselves and we just loved doing it because we loved the work, loved to be able to make 10 shillings. Maybe go back and do a second load in a day, which was hard to do, and you'd get another 10 shillings. My brother Paddy was really very good at it. I think he showed us the way to do it. He was a tremendous worker. Of all of my family, he's one I have great admiration and time for.

I was always destined to be out working from an early age because we did not have the money to go to secondary school or go to college – that was for the sons and daughters of businesspeople, the sons and daughters of fairly well-off farmers – and I wasn't any different from a lot of other kids. We just didn't have the money in those days and, to my Mam and Dad, going on and getting an education wasn't their first priority. It couldn't be – maybe it should have been – but it couldn't be, as their children had to get out and work and that's just the way it was. My brothers and sisters as well, they were all out working young and early.

I always had a good work ethic and I suppose that stood to me when I started doing sport. As a young hurler in Castlecomer, my claim to fame is that I won two County Under-14 Championship medals. Those meant more to me later on in my boxing career when I won European medals and went to the Olympics. Those medals were as important, and I still have them and treasure them as much as I do my National Senior titles that I won here in Dublin. But I suppose having a hard childhood does prepare you for later on in life and it does prepare you in a way for dealing with competing at a top level.

I always wanted to be a winner. I was never happy to be second. When I was playing hurling, I always wanted to win. I was a fancy little hurler but I wasn't big enough and I wouldn't have been tough enough either to be a top class hurler. Hurling is a sport for real men. Like many other kids growing up in Kilkenny, I just loved hurling and if there's a better field game out there, I haven't seen it. I would gladly swap three of my National boxing titles for just one All-Ireland hurling medal.

> *I always wanted to be a winner.*
> *I was never happy to be second.*

**Athletics was a sport I loved too** and I got a love of that through my brother Paddy who was a founder of the club in Castlecomer. He was quite a useful runner himself and a good hurler – he would often claim he was better than we knew him to be – but he was very athletic. He got me into running. I was fairly successful in running as well, winning some County championships.

I competed in the Leinster Youth Championship. That was a big one to win. I finished sixth one year when I was 16 years old but I was still young enough to compete again the following year and I reckoned I'd win it. I thought: "If I was sixth last year, I'm a year older, a year stronger, a year better." But to my huge disappointment, I ended up down the field, maybe in 10th or 12th spot. I was so disappointed. That was a massive shock to the system. That was the end of my athletic career; I was heartbroken.

**Immediately after the race,** while still wiping away the tears, my brother Joe said to me: "If you start boxing, I'm telling you, in two years' time, I'll have you on the Irish team." Now I wondered how that could happen. I was then just 18 years old and I decided: "Yeah, OK, maybe I'll give it a go." But I was still thinking it was absolutely impossible to get on the Irish team in two years from the day I started.

At this stage, I'd emigrated, so to speak, out of Castlecomer, up to the 'big smoke' here in Dublin. My Mam and my older brothers and sisters saw there was no future for me staying at home and working in the coalmine, so they got me an interview in the Gresham Hotel in Dublin. I got the job. While working there, I inquired about boxing from some of the lads there who told me that Arbour Hill Boxing Club would be worth going to, as it was one of the famous clubs at the time.

I was 18 then, so I went up to the club, knocked on the door. I remember it was painted bottle green. A big man, Mr Byrne – Jim Byrne was his name, but to us he was always 'Mr Byrne' – opened the door. "Come in, son. You are welcome, son. Come on in."

I introduced myself. I started at the bags and I think they saw that maybe I could do something. It was March 10$^{th}$, 1965 the day I knocked on the door of Arbour Hill Boxing Club, the day Mr Byrne opened the door to me. He had two sons, Jim and Willie, who were both international fighters. There were a lot of good boxers in that club. The coach was Mick Coffey, a former international, along with his brother, Steve Coffey, so it was a very famous club.

I trained so hard. Everything I would do, I always did at my very best. At hurling, I tried my living best to be the best; in athletics, most certainly I tried my best to be the best as well. I had reasonable success at both of them, but I started boxing in March 1965. In November 1965, I had my first fight – a win – and then come October 1967, I had my first international fight for Ireland. In May 1968, I beat the European champion, Horst Rascher, in a Germany *v* Ireland international. That win secured my place on the Irish team for the Mexico Olympic Games.

It's hard to believe that this could be done in the space of two years. It happened, not because I was so good – yes, I had some natural ability, I had quick hands, I was very strong, from my childhood upbringing, I suppose, working with the coal, the mines and so on, manual work from being a youngster. So all of that paid off for me when I started boxing. I was strong and I knew I was very, very quick. My reflexes were very fast as well and I would like to think that I had a clever enough, smart enough brain. I was cute enough. I wasn't just a brawler, I could box. I liked to counterpunch.

I could fight and, more importantly, I could hit – and when I hit, guys didn't like that. I hit hard, extremely hard, and my record would prove that. As time went on, I had a lot of stoppages simply because I hit so hard. I was very well coached by Mick Coffey, the club coach, but more importantly for me, by my brother Joe, who was an ex-pro fighter himself. He taught me all of the skills, the combinations and the power punching. He put a lot of time and effort into my training. But I was a dog to train and no amount of training was enough.

I suppose my son Mark, who is an international cyclist, inherited that, not only from me, but from Emily as well who trained extremely hard for her athletics. She was small in stature, but my God she would train so hard and that is why she had the success at international level that she had. He inherited the genes from both of us, that no amount of training was ever enough. We were both sportspeople who were able to push ourselves to the absolute total limit – and Mark does that. My daughter Lisa was able to do that in running as well and she luckily enough got a scholarship to America for athletics. She spent two years over at East Tennessee State University. She came back and now has her own successful sports business in Dublin. As a youngster, she excelled at gymnastics and is the proud owner of a National championship title.

The 1968 Mexico Olympic Games were an amazing experience for me. Here I was, less than three years after my first fight, representing Ireland in the biggest sports event in the world. I performed well, reaching the quarter-finals where I lost on a split decision to Eiji Morioka of Japan. With the experience of Mexico behind me, I picked up my second European medal in Madrid in 1971 before heading off to the ill-fated 1972 Munich Olympics, which will always be remembered for the terror attack that left 11 Israeli competitors dead. For me, it was yet another disputed split-decision loss to eventual gold medallist Orlando Martínez of Cuba. I had the pleasure of meeting him again in 2016 at his house in downtown Havana. He looked in good shape and seemed happy with his lot in life. We enjoyed looking through some newspaper cuttings from our battle all of 44 years ago.

In 1975, I finally ended my career. I retired in the National Stadium on the night I won my last National Senior title. I had tears in my eyes walking around the ring that night. I knew that it was my last time in this ring. I had created a record, winning eight senior titles in a row at the one weight. Nobody had ever done that before.

I was finished, enough was enough. I had been on the Irish team since I was 20 years old. I was now 28 and had had enough, so I retired. The very next day, this headline appeared on the paper: 'Dowling selected to box for Ireland again – despite the fact that he retired last night.' I suppose that was an honour in itself, that I was selected to box for Ireland again.

But I said: "No, enough is enough." And I stuck with that. It was a big decision. I had gone eight years without ever losing in Ireland. To anybody, to a visiting boxer from the UK, from America, from any other part of the world. Eight years, I never lost. Sooner or later, that would go if I kept thinking: "There is one more in me." Sooner or later, that record would be broken.

I'd had enough. Ten years, 130 fights. I'd put a huge amount into boxing. It wasn't about being only 28 years old; it was all about the amount of miles on the clock. In eight years, I'd never one single time missed an Ireland international match. I was picked every time and I boxed every time. I was never sick. I was never injured. I never had a family member that had died or something that I had to take time out for. Every single championship, I was available. Every single international, I was available. I boxed them all. And I won all the nationals and almost all the international matches as well. I took two European medals and boxed in two Olympic Games. I travelled the world. I had some great trips and created some great memories. But I never really retired from boxing because in a very short space of time, I was into coaching.

I met Emily in 1970. I was running on the running track in Sundrive Park in Dublin; I used to do a lot of my training in Sundrive Park at the time. She was down there as an athlete. She happened to be injured and she was just down watching who was training on the track and she saw this little curly-haired guy, looking mad, throwing punches all over the place. She wondered: "What's this guy going around throwing shapes and punches around the place for?" And people were saying: "Ah, that's Mick Dowling, the boxer." She'd never heard of

Mick Dowling, never knew who or what I was. But I saw this girl and thought: "This is the most beautiful girl I've ever seen."

She was very, very pretty and must have had a lot of guys in the athletics world chasing her. We spoke. She said she had an injury. I said I had stuff in my kit bag that would help. I'd a particular ointment that would work on her injury. It was an ointment I'd put on my black eyes – seriously! The worst chat-up line ever! "Yeah, I'll give it to you. It'll be great for your foot." So I gave it to her.

---

*I could fight and, more importantly, I could hit – and when I hit, guys didn't like that. I hit hard, extremely hard.*

---

She had a Honda 50, the cream and red one – readers old enough will remember those Honda 50s. She had one, I had one, and I remember her on her Honda 50 with her helmet and she was the most gorgeous person. I remember thinking: "God, she's too young for me anyway." I thought she was only about 16. Then I was told she was 19, so it was perfect. On our first date to the cinema, she thought it was a bit odd – or least a bit unusual – when I bought grapes and apples instead of the usual sweets or popcorn. Maybe I was trying to impress!

We married in 1973 and had our first daughter, Lisa, in 1975, just one month after I hung up the gloves. We've lived happily ever after. We trained together so much and have gone through so many things, through her sickness and so on, a tough enough time for all of us. Like everyone else, we have our little disagreements and likes and dislikes, but to me, I'll go to my grave thinking I got the best woman in this world and I would hope she'd eventually go to hers thinking she also made a good choice.

When I retired, some people asked: "Is there a big void left in your life?" To me, there wasn't – again, I would have had family at that stage. I retired in 1975, Lisa was born that year, so I suddenly had a new interest in life. I'd had enough of my boxing. I didn't stay too long away from it because I got involved in coaching and still am very, very much involved in coaching. There are so many people who walk away from sport and give nothing back to it. I would like again that, in time, people would say: "Fair play to him! Mick Dowling has contributed back to the sport. He has given back something to the sport that gave him so much."

And it did give me a lot. In my time working in the Gresham, I met a lot of people, a lot of stars, very famous people in there. I served them. That was a time when I was doing well as an international fighter and there was really only one station, RTÉ, and Mick Dowling featured on it a lot. The newspapers covered amateur boxing a lot and to have somebody successful internationally was good news. It was good for the journalists and good for the Irish people who were reading the *Irish Press*, *Irish Independent* and *The Irish Times*. They were the three papers. There was nothing else really, only those three.

❖    ❖    ❖

**I remember somebody at the Gresham saying to me:** "Why don't you go and do some media work on radio or TV?" I never bothered, never thought of it. Then the 1992 Olympics came around and Tim O'Connor, head of RTÉ Sport at the time, rang me up and asked me if I'd go in and see him. So in I went.

He asked if I'd be interested in covering the Olympics for him. Nowadays, there are three of us sitting up there. In those days, I'd be the only one. In many ways, it was a good thing as it gave me a good profile. I'd be the one pontificating as to how the fight was going and how it should go and who should do what and so on. Luckily for me, it was a very successful debut because in the 1992 Olympics Michael Carruth won the gold medal and Wayne McCullough won the silver medal. I have now covered seven Olympic Games for RTÉ and also had the pleasure of covering Bernard Dunne, Wayne McCullough, Barry McGuigan, Steve Collins, Andy Lee and many more of our professional fighters.

Recently I was in the city with some of our international boxers and Darren O'Neill said to me: "If I and some of the other top fighters walk down O'Connell Street with you, everybody will know who you are but they won't know who we are." They all agreed that is the case, but what a pity. I really think that our current fighters need to get exposure in the newspapers, they need exposure on TV, they don't get near enough for a sport that has been Ireland's most successful Olympic sport. Yes, when the Olympics come around, they get coverage but apart from that, they don't get half enough. Coverage is good for the sport; it's good for the individual if you are in a sport that is well-covered, whether it's GAA, rugby or soccer, though they get a lot more exposure than we do. I accept we are a minority sport, as is athletics, but Eamonn Coghlan got massive coverage during and after his excellent career, and that helped him in his life with a doubt. And it most definitely helped me as well. It opens many other doors for you.

I spent eight or nine years at the Gresham. I was there during the time of two famous general managers, Toddy O'Sullivan and Eoin Dillon. And I suppose some of my workmates saw me as a bit of a celebrity. I didn't think I was but the other waiters always introduced me to the guests, whether they were Americans or whoever: "This is our Irish, European and Olympic boxer." At times, I might have had a 'shiner', a black eye, and we might have had to explain that away. What I learned at the Gresham, I put to work or it came into effect when I started doing TV and so on, because I was used to meeting people. I was used to meeting famous people and talking to them and never feeling that you were anything less than anybody else, even though you were serving them. As a youngster, I would have been shy, definitely shy. I would get a big, red face if people said anything to me. But working in the Gresham, mixing and meeting with people, that was very important in my development as someone who went on to work in RTÉ for all of those years.

Around 1971, things were going backwards in the tourism business in Ireland. The Troubles in the North were at their worst; a lot of people were not coming to Dublin. Not only were they not coming down from the North, but they were not coming in from abroad, seeing there was trouble in Ireland. Business wasn't good in the Gresham and our salaries depended a lot on the service charge: if the service charge was bad, your salary was bad. I thought it was time to make a break out of this. I wondered: "Do I go abroad?"

A man in Carlow, Seamus Hughes, saw something in the newspaper along the lines of 'Dowling thinking of emigrating' and he rang me. He had a company called Zero Ireland Limited and he asked me to meet him and his American boss, Henry. Seamus met me and said he'd great admiration for me and that he thought maybe I could be a good salesman. He hired me and I never looked back. I had seven or eight good years working for them, selling refrigerated milk tanks for farms. It was around the time when Ireland joined the EU and the farmers were getting grants to upgrade their milking and storage systems. This American company had these special tanks and Seamus Hughes was the Irish distributor.

---

*Excelling at a high level in sport is a good omen for a job or career because you would generally carry that work ethic into working life.*

---

Seamus was very good to me but again I began to think about my future, where it was going to be. Was I going to be selling milk tanks for the rest of my life? It was not really what I wanted to do. My brother Joe suggested I should be looking at a sports shop. We looked and looked and looked and eventually we found a little spot on Terenure Road North. We went and looked at it, myself and my two brothers Joe and Noel.

We bought it. It cost us very small money, about £15,000, something like that. It was only a small shack of a place but, in that little shop, we built up good custom and after about two years, I bought my two brothers out of the business. Within a year, I doubled the turnover, which was easy enough, and the following year, I doubled it again. At that stage, boxing gear, running shoes, basketball equipment and trophies made up most of our turnover. After some time, we moved out of there, five doors up, into brand new premises.

We've never looked back. That shop has provided us with a good living. I own the shop; I don't rent it. I own my house; I don't rent it. These are the things I'm proud of and as I said, if I'm going to my grave tomorrow, I won't say I'm like my Dad who had nothing to leave to me. I'll have something to leave to my children.

Dad was a very accomplished accordion player and featured on many RTÉ radio programmes in the 1960s. When he was on the radio, it was a big occasion for the people in Castlecomer. I have many fond memories of some great traditional music sessions in our house; it was a very musical house. What's interesting is my Dad was fond of a pint or two and also he liked his smokes, but I never drank in my life or smoked. If people want to smoke, if people want to drink, that's up to them. Seeing him like that most certainly had a big influence on me. I wanted to be successful as a sportsperson, I wanted to do well in sport and you were never going to do well if you were drinking and smoking. Never.

My Mam was admired and acknowledged by all who knew her as a wonderful hard-working woman, who raised a large family under difficult circumstances.

❖　　❖　　❖

There were a whole number of defining moments in my life. Moving out of Castlecomer to the 'big smoke' was a big one: it was like moving to England. As a young teenager, I would be sad when leaving home to head back to Dublin, especially when I looked back at my Mam standing at the door with tears in her eyes. To her, Dublin was a long way from Castlecomer but, as time went on, the pain of leaving home eased.

Another defining moment was the time I decided I'd give boxing a go. And when I didn't perform as well as I'd hoped in the Leinster Cross Country Championships, that would have been a defining moment. I cried, but it didn't take away the disappointment of losing.

One of the most defining moments was the massive shock in 2005 when Emily was diagnosed with non-Hodgkin's lymphoma. Someone so energetic, helpful, good to other people and still training away. I was

in the shop when she came in and said: "You'll have to close the shop."
"Why? I asked. "I'm after getting word back from the doctor and I have
to go into hospital now."

I put a note in the door, 'Shop Closed', and within one hour, she was
on a drip, her first treatment of chemotherapy. She was asking lots of
questions, especially: "Will I lose my hair?" I'll never forget that, and
they said: "Yes." "And how long will it take?" "About three weeks.
There's an address of people who do nice wigs." All of that. It was
unreal.

I spoke to you, Conor; you were the only person I spoke to. I
couldn't speak to my family, my brothers or sisters. I wasn't able to
tell my own children. But Emily was so positive about it. It was a
terrible time altogether, from being super-fit, doing so much for other
people and suddenly being struck down. It made us appreciate life a
lot more. Every year of your life that goes by, you realise you are
getting closer to your own calling day but you don't expect to get it
when you are in your 40s or 50s, young and energetic as she was.

The search began to find a stem cell match. Her brother Tommy
proved to be a perfect match. He flew in from America and went
straight to the hospital. Six hours later, the transplant was successfully
completed. I'm happy to say she has made a full recovery and I have
no doubt her high level of fitness played a major part in that recovery.
Emily was always very grateful to both Professor Daly and Doctor
Vandenberghe and indeed to all at St James's who were so
professional in treating her.

Certainly my own energy levels have definitely gone down, that's
normal and natural. I would not have the same energy now. I love
tipping around in the garden but I can't hack around in it as I used to.
I'd be a bit more careful.

Family is massively important to me. What else is life about but
looking after your family and seeing that all your family are okay and
that they, in turn, are able to provide for their families? I'd always
want my children to do well. Always. And I'd be almost disappointed

if they didn't turn out as I want them too. I think most parents are like that and should be like that. Our children are all doing very well for themselves, we're so proud of them. Luckily now, at the moment, we have five grandchildren and they are the absolute love of our lives. We love being with them and seeing them.

Mark, my oldest son, started running first. Emily convinced him to go down and help his club DSD in the National Track Championships. He ran the 1500 metres and ran 'out of his skin', as they say. We were looking and shaking our heads at the time he did.

After that, we took him to one of the world's biggest sports resorts, Club La Santa in Lanzarote, and we encouraged him to take part in a triathlon. And lo and behold, as a youngster, he finished second. He came to us afterwards and said: "I think I know what I want to do with my life. Will you buy me a bike?" We bought him a bike and it was the best money we ever spent. Well, the best money we ever spent was taking him to Club La Santa, where he saw another life that was much more attractive than the one he was living at home. That was a big, big changing point for him as he went on to represent Ireland in triathlon, before making the changeover to cycling where he's gone on to achieve some excellent results, winning most of the big races in Ireland.

While Mark is racing, there's a tension for me as a parent, as a Dad, worrying where is he, how is he doing, why is he not up there, has he crashed. I'm sort of giving out to myself. But there is nobody harder on Mark than Mark himself: he hates being second. Again, he has inherited this from his Mam and Dad. He tells me: "Second means nothing, Dad. I'm out there to win it."

Lisa, his sister, runs a very successful sports and educational business. She was in charge of the gym at Club La Santa in Lanzarote for four or five years. Then she worked for David Lloyd Clubs in the UK, where she met her husband, Sean. They now have three little girls.

Then my daughter Julie went over to work in Club La Santa. She spent five years in it and she really discovered sport over there. She has gone on to run several races, including marathons. Julie is so like Emily, a natural mother. She was never mad into sport but then discovered marathons and now has probably run more marathons than her Mam. Not as quick, though. She also met her husband, Tomas, through sport and they now have two little boys.

And lo and behold, Stephen, our youngest son, spent two years working over there, in the same Club La Santa. As we speak, he's working there. We can only speak volumes about Club La Santa. It has certainly done wonders for our family, that's for sure.

Stephen could have been a really successful boxer. He has those quick hands. He is a 'southpaw', whereas I was an orthodox boxer. He has so much ability as a boxer: quick reflexes, clever, good mover and very, very strong. Unfortunately, he had a back injury that curtailed his boxing career. I have always said he had much more natural talent than I had but injury put paid to his boxing ambitions. He is a qualified boxing coach and now he passes on his knowledge of the sport to the guests at Club La Santa.

❖    ❖    ❖

**Coaching is giving back**; taking your wisdom and giving it to the next person. Here I am still coaching at this age in my life.

Emily, since she retired, has given back so much to the sport it is unbelievable. In particular to the founding and the development of the Sportsworld Running Club, where she has put thousands and thousands of people through her hands, coaching and passing on advice as I would do in boxing.

We are trying to cut out the mistakes that perhaps we have made and make things easier for people. If you've been there and done that, you've made all the mistakes, you've had all the injuries. I love to listen to somebody like that who would coach me in that manner because they've done it, they've been there, they know in boxing terms what it is like to take a punch on the nose.

For Emily, in running terms, she knows what it is like when your legs are totally and absolutely gone, lungs at busting point and you have to push on to the finish line. Certainly, she has put an enormous amount into the club. The club would never be there if we hadn't done what we did – we don't look for thanks for it but we do look on the club with great, great pride.

Emily, in particular, put all the work into it. She has been the head coach of the running club for 30 years, as well as being a senior international cross-country runner for nine years, getting her first international vest at the tender age of 17; 14 years later she won the 1981 Dublin City marathon.

We have a race that is now running for 34 years. I have to say that I would have been the chief founder of that race, a great race, the Dublin Five Mile Classic, now renamed the Terenure Five Mile. Over the years, the event has brought many of the world's leading road runners to Terenure and has raised over €500,000 for various charities, which people don't know and sometimes don't appreciate. I'm very glad to be the founder of that race and I've now passed it on to the next generation who are carrying on the good work and doing a really good job of it.

*A defining moment was when I didn't perform as well as I'd hoped in the Leinster Cross Country Championships. I cried, but it didn't take away the disappointment of losing.*

We don't brag or boast about our successes. Maybe as you get older, you accept you've won and done these things. You don't go preaching to people. You assume people know, although a lot of the younger generation do not know. A lot of people come into the shop and the older ones would be going: "This is Mick Dowling and he won blah blah blah", and the kids are looking, thinking: "Who?" And I'd say: "Sure, you don't even care, kids, do you?"

Excelling at a high level in sport is a good omen for a job or career because you would generally carry that work ethic into working life. And if you're successful at sport, it is quite likely you'll want to be successful in business as well. A lot of time in business, it's having a bit of 'cop-on' and common sense. I've had moderate success, but there are other people who have had much more success than me and who don't have the master's degrees and all that to back themselves up – but they've been very, very successful. One of my former young boxers, Tom Ennis, has gone on to be the proud owner of 10 Spar shops. Again, he has adopted the hard work ethic and it has proven to be successful for him also.

❖   ❖   ❖

**I never got things easy as a kid.** How could you with 15 other kids in the house? So you had to fight for everything.

You wanted to work and I loved working, making a few bob and bringing it home to Mam to try to cope with the bills and looking after everybody else as well. We took great pride out of that and I think I probably carried that on into my young working life in the Gresham and later on to working for Zero Ireland and then into the sports business. We are still there today when so many other small family-owned businesses have gone under.

I am sure I will call it a day some time and ride off into the sunset. But for now, while I'm still able and still enjoying it, the shop door in Terenure remains open and my love of sport is forever ongoing.

# FINBAR FUREY

## "I'm a musician."

*Finbar Furey began playing on the pipes while he was very young – he doesn't ever remember not playing pipes. He loved the instrument and spent all his spare time practising and soaking up knowledge from other pipers who would come to the house for sessions with his father, Ted. By his teens, he had won three All-Ireland medals, the Oireachtas and many feisanna – he was the only piper ever to win the All-Ireland, the Oireachtas and the four provincial titles in the same year.*

*Finbar popularised the pipes worldwide while on tour with his brother Eddie in the 1960s. Finbar and Eddie brought a new Irish hipness to a worldwide audience that would have had no ear for Irish music otherwise and so Irish music became once again the music of youth and revolution.*

*From 1976, Finbar was the lead singer, songwriter and front man of The Fureys, who achieved international success with songs such as **The Green Fields of France**, **The Lonesome Boatman** and **When You Were Sweet Sixteen**. In 1997, Finbar decided the time was right to follow his own path as a singer-songwriter.*

*A man of many talents, Finbar has added 'actor' to his list of credits. His latest album, **Paddy Dear**, was released in 2017 and his autobiography will be published in 2018.*

**I grew up in Ballyfermot.** We were living in Engine Alley, off Francis Street in the Liberties, at the time and we got a house in Ballyfermot. Everybody was moving out to Ballyfermot and Finglas: the population was growing in Ireland at the time and they built all these houses to clear out the inner city. So we got shipped out to Ballyfermot and we'd a great time growing up there.

Me oul' fella was away at the time: he was in England when we moved out there, working, trying to make a few bob and sending money home to me mother. When he came back, we didn't know who he was as he had been away for about a year. That's the way they worked: they went away to work, put a good few bob together, then came home and bought something or invested in something. That's how they did it.

He was a mechanic for Charlie Slater's Garage. He did his apprenticeship in Kilmainham. Charlie Slater was a racing driver. He was killed in a crash. My father and Charlie went to Puck Fair together when they were only kids. That's where me oul' fella met my mother. So the father, he was always very good with cars and if anyone had something wrong with the lorry or the car, they brought it to the oul' fella and the oul' fella would fix it. He was a driver. That's what he did in London. He drove lorries, long distance.

He came home after a year and I remember we were running wild on the streets in Ballyer, and me mother couldn't control us. There was Eddie, myself, Paul and George. Everything and everyone on the street, we challenged – as kids do. We bumped into the greatest pals who have been there for life, during those days. I remember me oul' fella saying: "Right, that's it. Your days are numbered, lads." This was like a week after he got home. He brought us off swimming and everything. We did all the boisterous things we needed.

He taught us how to swim. He used to take us out to the Grand Canal, to swim. It was a good walk, a good three-mile walk from Ballyfermot. He'd have about five or six of us, all our pals. Me oul' fella was a great swimmer, an unbelievable diver. He used to dive into the '40 foot' to get into the locks and he'd take on the 'chambers', as he'd call it. He wouldn't allow us to swim there but he'd dive in and it was very deep and if he'd be missing for a minute, we'd be panicking and then he'd come up. He was just a fish in water. He taught us all how to swim and not to be afraid of water, but to respect it. Water is very dangerous, so we had to respect it. But the whole thing was if you got into trouble when swimming, never panic. "You've always got four minutes to make up your mind which way to go", he'd say, "so slow your mind up."

I remember he marched us down to the boxing club in Arbour Hill when I was about seven or eight. We met Mick Coffey and Stephen Coffey, his brother, and old Mr Byrne, who always dressed in a prim suit, but never said much. He'd just sit in a corner watching the young boxers and have a chat with Mick about who was and wasn't good. Of course, we thought we were the bee's knees, but I tell you, we were smartened up very fast. We were put into the ring with a couple of fellas our own age who could really box and, of course, we went after them fire and tongs. They hit us so many times we couldn't blink by the end of it.

We loved it and we went every Monday, Wednesday and Friday. We trained and were part of that club for years, five or six years, I think. We'd get the bus as far as the Fountain, at the top of Steeven's Hill, where Steeven's Hospital was and walk down the hill and walk up Arbour Hill and around by the back of the prison, where there was a gate with one bulb with no cover on it. It was the creepiest walk. And as you got closer to the club, you'd hear all the noise. You opened the door and the whole place was alive with kids sparring and skipping, and Mick would be in the ring.

We boxed in the Stadium, Eddie and me. We boxed for the Dublin leagues, though we were only kids. We were getting the punches in, we were fairly handy, but my father taught us about self-defence and self-control. He wanted to teach us that and the way we learned it was in the boxing club with Mick and Stephen Coffey – they were wonderful people. There wasn't just us, there was a heap of kids there and we made great friends. There was Liam Clarke, who went on to box for Ireland – a great fighter Liam was. I sparred with Liam when we were kids. So we've great memories of growing up there. It was the smartest thing I think my father done for us.

As we grew up, when we got into our late teens, we started running a bit wild and dancing and all of that and going out with the motts and the usual, as you would. Of course, growing up in Ballyfermot was not easy. You had to be able to defend yourself. You'd meet the odd fuckin' hothead who would have a go, and you had to pull back. I would never strike, never – always pulled back, talked it out. I'd very fast hands from the ring and the lads would have a scuffle now and again, but you wouldn't want to hurt anybody. We learned to back off, and that paid off. You feel a bigger man than the other guy – my father gave us the intuition to be able to do that.

*My father said to me one time: "Music is more important than food." That's what he said.*

We never had any trouble at school. We were very good. We wouldn't have been top grade A students but we were not too far off it. We were very smart. But my father wanted us to play music. We always played anyway, but he wanted us to make a life with music. And I suppose I was fairly handy with the tin whistle at the time. He bought me a half set of pipes; I think I was about seven, it was just when he got back. He got us all instruments and he got me mother a radio, which was Heaven. There was no television at the time, so it was a big radio; you could hear it all over the place. The neighbours used to come in to have a listen to the news.

He was a great teacher of music as well. I can't describe him to you. I know among the Travelling people in Ireland, among all my cousins, everybody who knew him, they called him 'The Professor', because if they needed anything, they'd go to me oul' fella. If they needed something written that they couldn't do – they could write, but they maybe couldn't put the letter together – something important, or signing a document, they'd always go to the oul' fella. My father would sit down and explain it and get them to fill it in properly. There were a few Travelling families in Ballyfermot who'd got houses and me oul' fella would have helped them fill out the form and brought them in. But the place was full of music. Ballyfermot was full of musicians. Great kids, they'd give you their heart and soul, just as we found out when we used to go over to Finglas as kids – same thing, great heart. Cabra was the same – they all loved music. The wilder the kids were, the more they were in love with music. And I'd often see them singing as kids in the backstreets, with a nylon string guitar.

There were some great singers who came out of Ballyfermot and musicians too: the Keenan family, Paddy Keenan, Johnny Keenan, all from Ballyfermot, all great musicians.

My father said to me one time: "Music is more important than food." That's what he said, it was more important than food. There was a great story told about the father by a fella called Oliver O'Connell, who wrote the book, *Free Spirits*. My father was in a place called Maam Cross with a piper called Felix Doran and they were playing music at the time in the old pub there. There was a cattle fair or a sheep fair on, or some sort of an animal fair. So the boys were there, playing a bit of music in the boozer. A fight started outside between a couple of young fellas, country lads, upsetting the whole fair. My father walked into the middle of them and started to play *An Chúileann*, right beside the two lads having a go. Eventually, they stopped rapping each other and started listening to my father playing *An Chúileann*. Then the two of them burst into tears and cuddled each other, went into the pub and it was all over. Music pacifies the savage beast within us. He just kept playing until the boys started listening. They'd have known the piece; it's a very well-known piece of music. They were not going to scrap in the middle of *An Chúileann*. So he was a very clever man, very straight, a good man.

❖    ❖    ❖

**Eddie and I were very clever, very street-wise** when we left Ballyfermot. I left home after I won the Junior All-Ireland when I was 16 – that was a young age to win it. I remember wanting to have more freedom. I'd finished now with the boxing. My father had taken me out of that, Eddie and I both, and we were doing our own thing.

Eddie was 17 at the time and had joined a rock band. They played the Gala and the Ritz. I used to laugh at him – he used to get these wellington boots and paint them silver! And then paint the trousers silver. And they'd come on with all this silver gear on them. They were called The Spartans. It was just something new and we were all screaming at the end of the stage: "Come on, Eddie!"

So he went one way and I kept with the trad music that I'd played with my father a lot of the time with the pipes and him with the fiddle. He took me everywhere – I was always the one that he'd take because of the pipes. I travelled the west of Ireland with him as a young boy and played in many kitchens and pubs late at night. I often remember being put to bed at one o'clock in the morning and being given a sandwich and a glass of milk before bed. Good memories. I can remember staying in this house; I can't remember if it was Martin Talty's or Willie Clancy's house – one of the two of them anyway. I was only very young and I was put to bed on this feather mattress. I'd never slept on a feather mattress before and I just kept sinking and sinking, and this thing was wrapped around me. I felt like I had wings and was ready to fly. Warm as toast in about 10 minutes, it was great. I just remember that sinking feeling, and any time I feel tired when I'm on the road and I have to sleep for a couple of hours, the first thing I do is imagine I'm still in that mattress and I can actually feel myself sinking and I fall asleep. Memories like that are great.

So me and Eddie moved out. Eddie moved in with Pat Dean, 'Deano', from Ballyfermot. They were playing music all the time together, so it was great. Eddie was working during the daytime and playing music at night but I was a full-time musician from a very early age. I never worked. Well, I got a couple of jobs, at Prescott's Dry Cleaners, delivering suits. I think I lasted two days. I remember my father getting me a job then working on the docks. They were building the new docks. I got a job working on this 'hammer'. After about four hours, that was the end of me working. I was back playing the pipes.

I loved music. My head is full of music. I live and I'll die music. I think music 24 / 7, whatever you like to call it. There is not a minute that goes by when I don't think of something musical. I busked with my father as a kid. We did small gigs and my father, Eddie and I and Paul won the International Folk Award in 1966. That was a big deal. We went in to win the money; we didn't go in to win the competition. We got a recording contract out of it but we didn't take it because there were too many rules in it. My father said: "Forget that."

When I left home, I was 16 and literally on a bicycle. Myself and young John Keenan, the banjo player, were like a pair of hobos, wandering around, sleeping one night at his place, couple of nights at me oul' fella's house. We weren't homeless; we had homes to go back to, but we just wanted to go on our own. We slept rough around Dublin for a while. We'd cycle out to the race courses if there was a race meeting on and we'd busk. We'd busk in Grafton Street – me with the pipes and him on the banjo – and always made a right few bob. We were never broke.

Then when I was about 17, me oul' fella met us and said: "Time you came back, and maybe win the All-Ireland Senior Championship." And I did. I went home and got the All-Ireland and won the Oireachtas the same year. So that was a great coup: to take the All-Ireland, the Leinster Championship and the Oireachtas all in a few months of each other. Then Eddie and I formed a band with Paul and young John Keenan and we started to get really serious about the music. We played in the Embankment with Mick McCarthy – that would have been 1964 or thereabouts. Eddie used to do the rock scene as well. I would work with young John as a duo, and then go on the road with my father and play a night with him. But we were not really a band; we just got together if there was a few bob in it. We never made an album.

I remember one of the nights I was booked to do a gig with Matt Molloy – Matt had just come down from Mayo at the time – and we had a great time. I think we got a fiver between the two of us for the gig and that was a lot of money in those days. Matt came back on the bus with me and stayed with us in Ballyfermot and we became good friends. Matt eventually joined The Chieftains and is still with them. Matt would have grown up in that era too. Great times.

I went back with me oul' fella anyway and won the competition; that was 1964. In 1965, we took off, young John Keenan and meself, on the bikes, because I loved his company. We were joined at the hip. He was exactly like me. We'd talk about music all day. My father used to call us 'the fairy children' because of the music. We always said there was a fifth beat in Irish sean nós music, and it was missing somewhere, so we were on a search for this fifth beat!

Then I came back in 1966 and I went to Boyle to the Fleadh Cheoil. My father was at the Fleadh with Seamus Ennis and a few more, pipers, all up there, and I got tangled up with my father again. He said: "I've put you in for the All-Ireland." And I said: "I don't want to. I've won it already, I don't need it again." Anyway, I won it and I gave him the cup. I remember he was sitting in the pub with his pals and I walked over to him and put the cup down and said: "If you need another one, win it your fuckin' self."

> *My head is full of music. I live and I'll die music. I think music 24 / 7.*

Eddie and I went to Scotland and that's a long story. We teamed up with The Corries and did a tour of Britain. We had a tough time earning a living in the folk clubs. Then the Troubles came and they were pointing the finger everywhere, at every Irish man and woman. In one way, you couldn't blame them. So we decided to go to Germany and we made a fairly good living, Eddie and I, and we started to establish a bit of a scene over there.

We came back after that and I think it was in 1975, I decided to come home to Ireland. We had just gone through a terrible time with the folk clubs and we weren't playing the folk clubs at the time. We were working more in Germany but living in England because that's where we made our base. It was easier to get the ferry because we didn't fly in those days. We got the ferry across, so it was handy enough.

So in 1976, we came home. Paul and George, the younger brothers, had formed a band called The Buskers with Davey. So we joined up together to form a group and we went back to Germany with the band and we got on fairly well in Germany at the festivals. When we came back to Ireland, we hooked up with Jim Hand and put out *The Green Fields of France* – and the rest is history. That was the turning point, cutting a long story short.

In 1987, I decided I'd leave the band. I wanted to do some of the music I'd been writing and, of course, when you have Eddie and

George who are singers as well, and Paul as well, four singers in the band, to make room for these songs was difficult. As far as I was concerned, what we'd done with The Fureys would never be repeated, we'd never top what we did. They'd always be classics and I knew that. We put our stamp on this music and this was now belonging to our heritage, and we put it there. "The well", my father called it, the "well of heritage." Your music goes into that well. The music, although you've written it, doesn't belong to you.

❖    ❖    ❖

**I went solo.** I did that for about six months, just playing pipes. I was handy enough on the guitar and the five-string banjo but it was just getting a pathway to go – you have to figure out a direction – and it took me a few years to find out which way I wanted to go. I enjoyed doing the odd cover, they are beautiful, but it is lovely to put something together, something that's a part of you, like the music I'm doing now – that's a huge part of who I am. Whereas the music I was doing with the brothers, we were sharing it. So a huge difference.

In 1990 I did my first solo album, *Love Letters*. That was the time I decided I'd leave the band, but I didn't leave until 1996 because we had contracts to fulfil. So when they were finished, I said that was it. I even hung on for another two years. I felt guilty about leaving my brothers but I had to make the break. It was a very brave act, but I had to reinvent myself.

I teamed up with Jimmy Faulkner and Garry O'Briain. They were the first musicians I worked with outside of the brothers. I'd worked with the Clancy Brothers but that was about it. But I never worked with any other musicians and it was nice to work away from the brothers. Mike Hanrahan put it nicely: "You have them now as brothers, not as business partners." And I think that's a nice way to phrase it. He was right. It's lovely now when we meet and we have a good chat about things. I think Eddie should write a book. He's the oldest brother and I always said to him, he should "put it down". He's a year and half older than me. I just look older!

I'm terrible nosy. I love listening to conversations – it's where I get ideas for songs. I love watching everything that's going on around me. I get up in the morning and I'm checking out the world – I'm one of them. Like this morning, I went to bed late last night, had about three hours sleep, then I woke all of a sudden and I was starving as I hadn't eaten much yesterday. So I went down and boiled a couple of duck eggs (I love them!) and made an egg sandwich and a cup of tea, scribbled out a few things I was still missing that I should have done before I went to bed. I went back to bed at about half seven and then woke about half 11, so it was that sort of day. I put it out there, I enjoy it. The travelling is the worst, getting from A to B. Coming back here the other day from Charleville was a long run, but we were blessed because it was Saturday and there wasn't too much traffic on the road. Sometimes, on a Friday evening, you'd get caught. A nightmare with the traffic. Not like the old days, when you'd see a car only now and again.

*The Last Great Love Song*, the winner of RTÉ's *The Hit*, we did the deal here, right in this room. RTÉ rang me up and told me about the programme. I really wasn't interested in it and that's the truth. But they insisted on meeting me, so I met them, three of them, and they said it was about Irish songwriters. And what you have to do is take one of these songs and make a number 1 out of it – you produce it, arrange it, master it and they give you €2,000 to rent a studio and put it all together. You couldn't do it with that budget – you've only got a few days of studio time to put it all together. I remember I phoned up Don Baker – Don's a great friend of mine – and I played the song for Don and I said: "What do you think?" He said the sound was very like Leonard Cohen, it's got that sort of vibe on it.

Then I got a call about a father-and-son golfing competition in Waterville, which was run by Marty Carr and his brother, poor Gerry Carr, who died about a year ago. I sang at Gerry's funeral and played the flute – a lovely guy, a nice family. Anyway, I remember going down there, and getting a call on the Sunday saying they needed the song by Tuesday, because the programme was going out on Friday. So I went back to Dublin on Monday, into the studio on Tuesday. They got me one of the greatest engineers I ever worked with – a really talented guy and a talented guitar and bass player too. We went into the studio and put it together – everything done by six o'clock that evening, in their hands. A few hours and it was done. I just knew where to go with it. I'd no worry with it and once I handed it to them, they played it and said: "Wow!"

The pipes were the icing on the cake. Nobody saw that coming. When you put the pipes on it, it was over – being an Irish song, and written by an Irish man, Gerry Fleming from Finglas, it was wonderful. It was Finglas and Ballyfermot; as I said on RTÉ, we couldn't miss. It was so lovely to see Gerry so elated and Frances, his wife, and the kids. It was very special. We had two rehearsals before the final, then straight on – so what I was trying to do was to keep the pipes in tune. The pipes are very difficult – playing with the orchestra, you can't afford to be out of tune – so I had to have them spot on. I nailed it – they nailed it, the orchestra – nothing went wrong. It was done straight from the heart, pure feeling. We fed off each other and the beautiful song Gerry had written summed it up. And when I brought the pipes in at the end, it was bang-on and the audience took off.

After that, the album took off. Number 7 on the charts at the time, and the single went straight to number 1. It was number 1 on the Wednesday. We knew it already on the Friday night but we couldn't put it out, so they left it number 2 on the Thursday before the programme went out. Which was great. It literally went to number 1 in three days. I love it, it's a great song.

We did *Living with Lucy* with Lucy Kennedy. I remember singing *The Last Great Love Song* in an Irish bar, The Auld Triangle, full of expats, and Welsh, a mixture of Celts together. I knew the Italian lad that was singing, and I got him to give me a 'D' and he played the guitar and I just sang it. The whole place erupted and loads of people came up and asked where they could get the song as it wasn't released in England. It's another *Sweet Sixteen*. I remember talking to Samantha Mumba after the competition, and her husband, a lovely guy, and I was saying to Samantha, she should sing it, it can be sung by a woman or a man. It's a wonderful song.

❖   ❖   ❖

**I went over to do** *Gangs of New York* just to sing the song, to put it as background music. I met Martin Scorsese the first day on the set. Daniel Day Lewis and Brendan Gleeson introduced me to him and we had a good chat for 15 or 20 minutes. He said the studio was all booked for me and the band were waiting. They were all Italian and they did a very simple version. I was a little bit frustrated as I wanted a little bit more 'Paddy' in it and I remember going back to Martin and saying: "Okay, I could fly in the brothers and we could really nail this." And he said: "No, it's not what I want. That would be too good for the time. This is like just after the Irish Famine, so the musicians back in them days wouldn't have been as good." So this is why he got these Italian guys. They were brilliant musicians, they were playing the way he wanted them to play it. So once we got that all over, back into the studio, and we did it and it was great. When we were finished, it was 11 verses and 22 choruses.

> *The music, although you've written it,*
> *doesn't belong to you. It goes into the well,*
> *the 'well of heritage'.*

I remember Martin saying to me: "Did you ever think of taking up acting?" I said: "No." And he said: "You should. You've a great voice and a great face. You should think about it." When I was with the Clancy Brothers years ago, Tom Clancy – Lord, have mercy on Tom – he'd say the same: "Your voice is great and it carries, so you should think of taking up acting. You've a great face and great feeling."

In the end, I got a part in the film, *Strength and Honour*. Mark Mahon was the director and producer, with Michael Madsen and Vinny Jones and Richard Chamberlain. That was jumping straight into it, my first script. It was lashing rain, thunder and lightning, when I went in to read for the part and I got the job of Papa Boss. I remember when I got down to Cork to do the first shoot, I was really nervous but I had the script off. I had the whole story in my mind and who he was and, of course, Mark Mahon comes into the bar in the hotel and says: "You are now Chosky Boss. Patrick Bergin is now Papa Boss." I was now the bee's knees who made all the rules – so meself and Patrick had great eye contact in the movie, which was a bit of craic. I didn't have to say anything – just look at him, street stuff. It was lovely to work with Vinny Jones and have breakfast every morning with Richard Chamberlain and Michael Madsen, sitting at a table, reading their scripts, going over different things. It was a whole new life – yeah, I loved it. It was great.

I got offered a part in a film they are putting together in January. It's called *Cawdor*, based around a poem by a fella called Robinson Jeffers, way back. He was a poet, a 'literary genius' the Americans call him. He stood against Roosevelt in the 1940s, as he didn't want the Americans to go into the Second World War. They said he was a bit of a hero, against the atom bomb and all that. One of the first, I suppose, environmentalists. A humanist, he believed that human life was more important than a patch of land. He was treated like a bit of a lunatic during his day but nowadays they see how beautiful he was. So they are doing this movie of one of his stories and it's a bit like *Game of Thrones*.

The bass player who was playing with me, Paul O'Driscoll, was a friend of the director's and he said: "You've got to have a look at Finbar to play the part of the blind school teacher." The director came to San Francisco to see me, to check me out and talk to me. He didn't know I was playing music. So anyway, when he came along and heard the music, he said I had to write the music too. In January or February, we'll be filming in Carmel, California, where Clint Eastwood was Mayor. The film is centred on that area, and the story is amazing. It's told in a Greek style, but set in 1920s or 1930s America. I could be there a month or two and I'll record the music before I go. Anyway, all good.

I think it's the next episode of my life: concentrate on the acting. I just turned down a part. I didn't like what was going on in the script, the story wasn't great, it wasn't me. It was a hard part, not for me. If I see something that I don't like, I just say: "I won't do that."

❖   ❖   ❖

**I went through some hairy times in my life** and I've had some great friends who'd push me and hold me up. Sheila, in particular; many a time I'd have me fists in the air and she'd pull them down and she'd say: "Come on, we'll get through this." I've given me heart to people who've broken it so many times and you'd look at them now and pity them as they could have been so much bigger and so much better, but they settled for an awful lot less.

I've grown up with a lot of great musicians but egos upset me. When I meet people with egos, we lose so much time, because we have to knock so many corners off them before we really find out who they really are – and when you do find out who they really are, Jesus, you love the ground they walk on. They are lovely people, but they hide it away for some reason to be somebody else – and I don't understand that. My father, both me parents, used to say to us: "If you can be yourself a third of your life, you'll win – just one third of your life, just be yourself, who you are." I thought that was a great lesson. What you see is what you get. That's why I love people like Christy Dignam. I enjoy Christy's company, talking to Christy, and Don Baker too, because these guys are real, no blocks to be knocked off them, it's just; "How's it goin'?" They'll just tell you how it is.

❖ ❖ ❖

**I like playing a game of golf.** I enjoy it. I was a member of Tramore for 12 years. And of Hollystown here and Bodenstown and Edmondstown. I had some great times but I always wanted to be better at the golf, get down as low as I could, to a single handicap. I'd have to give my best all the time.

I love writing. I don't do this computer stuff. I go everywhere with me notebook and pen. I'm a nuisance if I'm on an airplane and I forget the notebook, as I have to tell them I need some paper – and then they bring me a heap of sick bags! I think my life is in short stories. I love short stories that can be turned into mega-stories if you want.

We've had our ups and downs, but we try to keep them in the bin. Good times and bad times, the best times live on past the bad and sad times. When my brother Paul passed away, that was a tough time.

With me oul' fella going, that was hard. My mother passed on after that – and Paul a few years after that. Tragedy after tragedy – all the aunts went within a year of each other and the uncles were all gone. So the whole family were all taken out; within 10 years, all the elders were gone. We had a great life, they were great teachers and we couldn't have been in better hands than the people we were with and growing up in Ballyfermot was an experience.

Working around the world with different people, the Clancy Brothers, my own brothers, going off to New York with Phil Coulter for a weekend and singing at the Savoy in New York, big time stuff. Phil put a beautiful orchestra behind me and we sang *The Old Man* together. Great memories of those few nights with Phil.

We did Carnegie Hall. Me and the brothers and Dolores Keane came over to do a guest spot on the show on a Sunday afternoon at two o'clock. We took it on, when you don't take Carnegie Hall on: on a Sunday, and a summer day. It was packed. Paul Newman and Joanne Woodward were there. It was just one of those days. I remember the guy bringing us on stage saying: "I hope there's a good roof in this place as it's going to come off today with the crowd here." Albert Reynolds was in New York at the time – he was in peace talks with Clinton – and he came. He thought he couldn't make it but he got there just before we started and he introduced us on stage. The people thought we had dressed up somebody as him – they didn't believe it was really him – but it was. He had half an hour away from the peace talks and thought this was his one chance of singing on the stage of Carnegie Hall. We opened up with *It's a Long Long Way from Clare to Here* and he sang it with us. And the roof came off the place. "That was a great lookalike you had there on stage," people were saying after. But it was no lookalike, it was Albert.

It's been great times.

# JOHN HEALY

"I am John Healy."

*John Healy first discovered his love of the hospitality sector when he took a summer job in the 1980s. This led to a course in hotel management and business studies in the Dublin College of Catering, Cathal Brugha Street. Since then, John has worked at every level of the business on his route to the top.*

*John has worked in corporate management consultancy and also teaches what he has mastered in his career: how to handle every situation at every social occasion without batting an eyelid.*

*He had a heart transplant in 2012 and completed a documentary and a book, **A Perfect Heart**. John is now general manager of Suesey Street restaurant and bar and private dining venue No 25 Fitzwilliam Place.*

**It has taken me years to find out who I really am.** I suppose in the journey of your life, you come to a point when you do realise who you really are. Now I can honestly say that I am me: I am John Healy. There are many facets to me and many elements to my personality. Most of my life's work on myself has been in the last five years. Before then, I had no idea who I was or what I was doing and had no control over it either. It's only in the last five years, since the transplant, that I actually realised who I am, what my purpose in life is, and where I'm going and that I have control over it.

When I think back to how I got into the hotel and catering business and restaurant business, I've no idea why I chose it. I've no idea what drew me to it. I fell into it by accident. Both my parents are from Kilkenny, from farming backgrounds, and from massive families. Mum had eight siblings and Dad had seven, so that means I've about 110 first cousins. We moved to Naas in 1972, when I was eight years old. At the time, the family were flabbergasted as to why my father paid so much money for a house in Naas and how he was going to pay it off. It cost £18,000 at the time. He was working in Bord na Móna. He had a bachelor of science degree and was doing well. We were part of that era of up-and-coming families and we were very happy, a very close-knit family. Dad worked very hard; Mum also worked as well when she could. We joined the community in Naas, which was a satellite town of Dublin, and became that kind of upper-middle class family.

Although my parents paid a fortune for my schooling, I failed my Leaving Cert because of all the things that were going on. I think my Mum was very sick at the time as well. I didn't realise the effect that all of this was having on my life at the time. You don't – not until years later, when you realise why you are the way you are because of that kind of stuff. You learn all of that through therapy. So the abuse was very much part of the rest of my life. It mapped out the way I was going to behave and my behaviour patterns were all linked back to this period. That's why I mention it, not because of the abuse, but because that's what made me who I am.

My father then started drinking later in our lives. When we were teenagers, it was the behaviour around it that was damaging as opposed to the drinking itself. I was not aware of it but I knew there was something going on. So you act out as a kid, you look for attention. I was wild. I was perceived to be a wild one. Not disciplined, no academic background. I was very intelligent and I could get my exams but I didn't study – I hated it. I didn't hate school; I was more interested in the fun part of everything, as opposed to knowing that this is where you are going to create your destiny so, if you work hard and study hard, you'll get the right job.

Consequently, I left school and fell into the catering industry. I walked the town one day looking for a summer job when I was about 16 or 17 because my Mum knew I'd get into trouble if I didn't have a job. My Mum was wise enough to know that. She knew if I didn't get some structure into my life that there were going to be problems. I was already smoking dope and drinking and that kinda stuff, so she said: "Don't come home until you find a job." I went up one side of the town and down the other side – literally every premises – and I met someone I knew who told me to go up to the Town House Hotel, where they were always looking for staff. Pound an hour and I got a job as a lounge boy.

The Town House Hotel was on the Newbridge Road. Quite a nice place, then, little boutique-style, modern building, dining room on one side and bar on the other, with about 20 rooms. It was lovely in the mid-1970s and into the 1980s. I loved it. I loved the social aspect of it. Because I didn't have to look at me. I could entertain everybody else. I was very cute and could make a lot of money, cash. So my pockets were always full of pound coins or notes or whatever it was in those days. I remember coming home with fistfuls of money. That early on, I knew that's what I wanted to do. It was that job that started me in the business. It was the social aspect of it, having all those people around me and having instant friends and people who you could hang out with and they were all mad in that hotel at the time. There were a couple of girls there who were crazy people and subsequently I found out that half the restaurant and hotel businesses have crazy people working there. You have to be, it's part of the required personality!

I went back to school to do my final year and failed my Leaving Cert. So I started working with my father. He had a warehouse, a wholesaler business before the B&Qs and Woodies and all those were in Ireland. He was a wholesaler for garden and horticulture stuff, garden tools, furniture, barbecues and all that kinda stuff. With the money I saved working in the warehouse – I had saved about £500 – my parents made me pay to repeat my Leaving Cert in the Institute of Education on Leeson Street. It was probably the best thing I ever did, but it was horrendous at the time. I got it, of course – and then I got a job. I decided I wanted to do hotel management, having got that job.

❖　　❖　　❖

**I wanted to become a hotel manager,** where I didn't have to take orders from anybody. I knew that early on. My Mum tried to get me to change my mind as she knew what the business was all about as she'd been working in the business a little bit, like helping out in the kitchens, as she was a very good cook, and she knew how hard and gruelling it was all going to be. But no, I decided that was going to be it. So being from Kilkenny, they helped me to find a job in Leighlinbridge in Carlow with James Kehoe, and I went and worked in the Lord Bagenal Inn for the summer for about four months. James' and Mary's son, young James, was just born, so that would have been 1982 or 1983. I learned the art of multi-skilling there. It was so busy that place and organisation was part of its success.

*I think it is your training ground when you are young, in your early 20s.*

I worked behind the bar in the Lord Bagenal and I loved it. I lived with my aunt and I got to know the chef and the other guys and picked up a lot of stuff. One particular guy, Sean, was very clean-cut, very sharp. I remember looking at him compared to the rest of the barmen and I wanted to be like him, to have that image. Sean was brilliant. I learned from him how to serve 10 people at the same time behind the bar. I loved it. I worked 80 hours a week, no bother, day in, day out. My work ethic was set from an early age.

I applied through the CAO for Cathal Brugha Street and I didn't get it. I was devastated. So I came home to Naas after the summer; my contract ran out or they didn't need me for the winter. I worked in Lawlor's in Naas as a waiter for a while in the restaurant and I reapplied for college, and I didn't get it again. But I was on a waiting list and so I phoned Brendan Keyes every second day for three weeks. Years later, he told me he got so sick of me ringing him that he let me in. I wanted to do it. I knew if didn't get it, I would have no qualifications to do what I wanted to do and, for some reason, I knew that there was no way I was going to succeed in this unless I had qualifications. I needed to go to college, I needed to learn, I needed to be taught the background of it. It is interesting that I had that insight. I don't remember being that kind of person at that age, when everything else in my life was chaos. I don't remember being that wise or that sharp. It just happened.

So I got in, and during the three or four years I was in college, I went abroad in the summers. I went to Canada the first year. My uncle was in Toronto and I worked for him. I couldn't work in a hotel because of the visa restrictions at the time, so I worked in a warehouse for my uncle driving a forklift. The second year I needed to go to France, as my French was so bad that I wouldn't get my finals if I didn't do something about it. I was really bad at French, I couldn't string two words together. So I went to France with a crowd from college on a wing and a prayer. I got a job in La Résidence du Bois. I don't know how I got the job, but I do remember walking around Paris with a bunch of CVs in my hand and going to all the five-star hotels and getting turned away – as you would do, if kids came around here. I was desperately trying to get a job somewhere so I wouldn't have to go home.

I was also trying to find somewhere to live. Our gang ended up living with the guys who ran La Ferme Irlandaise, which was Myrtle Allen's restaurant. Two of the gang had jobs in the restaurant and I ended up washing up dishes in the restaurant for a while. Then I got the job in La Résidence du Bois, which was a boutique hotel. I was chamber-maid, luggage porter, room service, the whole lot, all rolled into one. I loved it. I must have had a huge determination and perseverance, which I never really realised. I must have been driven. It happened in Naas, happened again in Paris, and the same thing happened when I moved to London, but we'll come to that later. It was probably preparing me to move to London, because I went back then and did my finals and got my exams.

I always worked. I always had a job. I always had money and I paid my own way and had my independence. That time, in the 1980s, there was a huge recession on and things were very bad. I remember sitting with my parents and saying: "If you pay for my college fees, I'll pay for everything else and I'll look after myself, socially and whatever." So I worked every weekend when I was in college – in Lawlor's Hotel in Naas, every Friday, Saturday and Sunday. I worked during the week too, one or two days a week, in the Burlington Hotel, in the bar with Mary, which was the best part-time job in the city – certainly, the best paid at £5 an hour. I saw all the great and the good. Rugby weekends were good, great money to be made there. You only had to work maybe two days and you'd have enough money to pay your rent. I'd enough money to live on. My rent was £26 a week. You'd get nothing for that today, but I had enough money to go and socialise, to go out drinking and go partying and to live. So that was great.

College was great. I had a great time in college. I had a great time in Dublin. I had a great time running around and working. I was a bit mental anyway, unhinged and flamboyant, but I hadn't yet 'come out'. I had a girlfriend and all that kind of stuff and still kind of maintained that lifestyle and went away for the summers and came back. Every time I came back, there was something different about me.

I remember when I came back from Paris, I had lost two or three stone and had shaved my head and changed my fashion image; I absorbed the culture and the environment I lived in. It was the chameleon kind of thing where I absorbed the attitude of Paris. My French was fantastic; I spoke almost fluently when I came back. We lived down near Les Halles, so we saw all the fashion. Michael Rath was a chef at the time and he was very into his clothes and shoes and music. He was one of my influences of that era; I admired him and the way he dressed, and his independence and the way he presented himself. So I developed my style on the back of his, spending money on clothes and shoes and getting my hair cut properly and all that kind of stuff. It was totally about perfectionism. I had seen it in Sean, I suppose, in the Lord Bagenal Inn, that clean-cut image at work, so I was developing a style throughout those years.

After I did my finals, I ended up in the Royal Marine Hotel in Dún Laoghaire. I was 20 years old, I was the night manager, my first job in there, the most horrible job in Ireland. Connie Rothschild was the restaurant manager. After the training, I found I was actually quite good at figures and accountancy. So it was no problem to me to do the books, the revenue and the VAT and all that kind of stuff. I flew through it. In fact, the accountant and myself developed this quick process that we used to do from the computer system that we had, which was antique. I would work everything out and know where the money was going, coming from and anything that was missing. I could figure it all out and the 30 per cent and one third of room rates and the breakfast charge and the supplements and all that kind of stuff. I was taught that by someone else and I picked it all up very quickly. I loved the accountancy side of things and, if it wasn't hotel management I was going to do, it was going to be accountancy because I could balance the books. I was good at that.

The first night I was on my own, three cars were stolen out of the car park. I was hanging over the desk, the big marble desk they had, trying to get the registration numbers of the cars being driven through the gates. I'll never forget it, it frightened the life out of me. That's when I became friends with the gardaí in Dún Laoghaire. I knew all the cops – who was on duty and what schedule they were working – because of the cars being stolen from the car park. Never was it more secure after that, they were always around. I used to have them in; they'd come in for drinks at four o'clock in the morning before they'd finish their shift. They'd come to the bar and I'd give them pints.

I knew very quickly who the important stakeholders were to make my life easy, safer. Safer because as night manager, I was completely exposed. You had to have a bit of street cred and know what's happening. I suppose, because I was abused, I always wanted to know what was going on on the ground. I always wanted to know about the seedy side of things. I wanted to run everything. I wanted to know back and front. I remember running Magnum's Bar in the hotel and I knew there were drugs being sold in that bar and I knew that would be dangerous for the hotel. So I called the drug squad in as I knew the gardaí. They came in in plain clothes and we figured out where it was coming from and who was doing it. I was very quick at solving all that kind of stuff, without anyone getting exposed or caught – just discreetly done. I wouldn't put myself on the line. I think it is your training ground when you are young, in your early 20s; that's a massive training ground in your life to discover what is actually going on. There is no fear there and you know, when you do move around in different circles, and this comes out later, there was no fear of what the consequences of anything. I moved to London quickly after that and that was the biggest move of my life.

❖    ❖    ❖

**There were a couple of reasons I moved to London.** One, the reason that was prominent in my conscious mind, was because my career had come as far as it could in Ireland. I was too young to go any further and too experienced to continue doing what I was doing and I needed to get out and discover something else. That was one reason. The second, personal reason was because there was a girlfriend who wanted to marry me and I didn't want to get married. I didn't know why but I didn't want to get married. I was too young to be married, so off I went. One of the girls from the hotel had moved to London and she said: "Oh come over and stay with us and you'll be fine. Sure, there's loads of work over here." So I left after my 21st birthday.

---

*Five-star hotels appealed to me because that's where you make a career in the hotel business.*

---

I flew over to Luton, probably because it was cheaper, and got the train down to St Pancras and met Geraldine, a friend of mine from college. We went to where she was staying but she never told the girl who owned the house I was coming, and so I was back on the street. Within two hours of arriving, I was homeless and the training I got from being on the street in Paris looking for work kicked in again.

Although London was a massive place and I didn't know how to get from A to B and I had my suitcases in my hand, I got a job at the end of the first week. I was working in a gentleman's club in Pall Mall, which was very central, but I still had nowhere to live. That took me a month. I'd say at least a month. I stayed two consecutive nights at the airport. I spent a lot of time in the Bunch of Grapes, trying to hook up with Irish people and, God help them all, they felt so sorry for me. I suppose I had an innocent look on my face and they were: "No problem, come stay on our sofa." It was a very difficult period. To try to get accommodation, it is a bit like it is here now, you have to have a deposit and a month's rent in advance, and the rooms were very expensive. One of the girls had moved over from the Royal Marine and we ended up getting a room-share together.

I changed jobs. I got a job in the Hyatt in Sloane Street as a commis waiter. Five-star hotels appealed to me because that's where you make a career in the hotel business, that was where you could make something of yourself. I knew then that this was where I wanted to be. So I was aiming for the top the whole time and I was going to do whatever it was going to take to get me there. So I got the job as a commis waiter. I will never forget my first day on that restaurant floor, walking into the luxury of the restaurant and feeling completely intimidated and scared of even approaching a customer, never mind serving a table. I hadn't a clue what I was doing. Cappuccino – I hadn't even heard of it and I couldn't make one. So I literally taught myself everything about restaurants.

I ended up making a lot of money there and running the restaurant very quickly because I had very good talent and it became second nature. Being Irish, I had the gift of the gab and a personality that I knew that was going to help me get to where I needed to be. Professionally, I was very self-aware because I knew I had the personality to be able to do it. And I knew that I could talk to people and I was funny. Very quickly, I picked up a lot of the skills. I had the basics; I just needed the skill of being able to work tables.

There was a restaurant manager who was Spanish and was completely over the top when someone came in. He was, "Oh Mrs So-and-so, look at you, looking so fabulous, lovely to see you. My God, mwah, mwah, how are the little ones and how is the husband?" and on and on. I'd be like: "Does he fuckin' know them or is he playing? What's the story? Has he slept with her?" But, of course, that was his show and that was the theatre of it. There was an old English man there as well, who knew everybody that there was to know in that area, Belgravia. Everybody, especially the Arabs, because they were the ones with the big pockets and that was where the money was. And the tips alone in that restaurant that we were making were £1,000 a day on average, which was mind-blowing stuff. So quickly, I made a lot of money.

I remember Michael Davidson – he is dead now, God rest his soul – a fantastic man, East Londoner, very sharp, street-wise, who knew exactly what was going on. He could tell when people were coming to the door who was real and who wasn't and where the money was and who was genuine and who wasn't. You learned to read people very quickly – he was teaching me who were gangsters and who weren't. I never wanted to be in a position where I didn't know what was going on. It was because of the abuse that I needed to be in control and I always wanted to know what something was like, what it was going to cost and all that – no surprises.

I did drugs and I did the partying. It was the summer of love in 1989 when I came out – eventually came out. There was a gay roster in the restaurant, you couldn't but come out in that restaurant. And I remember, because of the abuse, it was the first time I admitted to myself that there was something different about me in that I was actually gay. The guy who I spoke to is still my best friend to this day. He was so self-assured and so comfortable in his own skin. It was the comfortable and delicate way that he handled me that made us friends to this day. I lost two stone. I became like a butterfly, it freed me completely of the shackles of my life. To admit to someone that you are actually gay, it was just rebirth.

It was still illegal in Ireland. There was no such thing as a gay bar or a gay club in Ireland and the only homosexuality that I knew of was the abuse that I'd experienced, behind closed doors, or in dark rooms or toilets or whatever. This was a different life. There were gay bars and when you come out like that, the only place you want to be is around gay people, in gay bars or gay clubs, only in gay bars. I wouldn't go to any straight places for a while. And I became very comfortable with it very quickly. I was very young still so it was quite easy for me to do that. I lived this gay lifestyle and became very flamboyant at work, even more camp than I already was. I suppose everyone around me knew I was gay except me. It gave me the confidence to know who I am – and I made a fortune with people, because they loved my sense of humour, loved the fact that I was Irish.

The Irish who used to come in were absolutely beautiful people and I still know a lot of their families today. I remember Mr and Mrs Purcell, Gerry Purcell's parents. Mr and Mrs Purcell used to come in and she was wonderful to me because I was so homesick. She used to give me hugs and kisses and say, "How are you?" and I'd say, "I want to go home". It was all new – it became almost surreal.

I moved over in March and I came home in July. I'd come out. In three months, a lot had happened. I'd come out, got this job and eventually moved out of the apartment I was in to a bigger apartment, so I became very independent and I became very secure, and I was earning a lot of money. So I came home and I told my friends and my family that I was gay, and that was a coming-out period of mine for about six months which was really the unfolding of me into my current personality.

My sister came over to London, and I told her, and she went ballistic – yeah, for reasons that I understand now. I phoned my mother and she was always so cool. I think I said something like: "I've just realised something that you've probably always known, Mum. I'm gay." And she said: "Are you sure?" I said: "Yeah." And she said: "Okay, why don't you come home and we can talk about it?" So I did, I flew home the next day. I went into work and told Michael: "Michael, I've just told my parents I'm gay." He replied: "Get on the flight and go home." He understood. But I was already very sought-after in the restaurant as a waiter and I became a chef de rang very quickly, controlling a section and running it, taking the orders and that kind of stuff. It's a very skilful job in itself and what I learned on the floor in that restaurant, I still have today and I teach everybody else. Anyway, I came home.

I never wanted to move home again. It was the anonymity of being in London and nobody knowing who you are. You could be your own person. That was very important to me at that stage in my life and very important to me in my coming-out stage. Plus the fact that I was earning a lot of money, which gave me a huge amount of security. I wasn't pinching and scraping to save and all that kind of stuff, so when we did the parties and the drugs and all that, we did it in style; there wasn't any sordid backstreet kind of stuff.

*Volume is an art form. Volume is turning tables and handling hundreds of people coming in and out of a restaurant. It's a completely different ball game.*

I developed a circle of people around me that were very solid and Gary, the guy I came out to, was one of my best friends at the time. The nucleus of the group was him and a couple of others, and it grew and grew and we are all still good friends today. All of us. We partied together and we explored together. We were all the same age and we explored life and what was available at the time. We were going to Ibiza and going to New York and travelling and moving around the world and having the money to do it. It was a very privileged kind of lifestyle that we lived and we worked very hard and played very hard.

Not that you necessarily needed to play, but it gave you the opportunity to do that. There was so much happening for young people at that time. London was exploding and it was quite an exciting place to be. The music industry was exploding, the night club scene was exploding so it was all very much the Woodstock of the generation that was happening and we were in the middle of it. We saw it happening around us because of the jobs we were doing. We were very much on the ground and all of us had different jobs in different parts of town, on different levels, so we knew what was going on in every aspect – music, theatre, City. There was a lot of different things going on. There were a couple of fashion designers in the group, so we knew what was in and what was out. We were very much part of the crowd.

When I left the Hyatt, I went to New York for a year because I got a green card. New York was only a short stay, only a year, and I worked with Hyatt again when I was over there. But because I couldn't make the money I was making in London – and I needed money in New York – I came back. Now what I learned in New York was that I hated being on my own, without a crowd of people around me. I was drinking very heavily and I knew there was going to be a problem with that and I knew I'd have to sort it out. I remember standing in the middle of Gramercy Park with a friend of mine, who is still my friend today. He goes: "You are going to have to sort that out." And I remember saying: "I know, but I actually like it. So until there is a problem, I'm going to enjoy it." And I did for another 20 years. I put the glass down slowly. I was aware of my alcoholism then, that there was a problem and that there was going to be a problem but I continued to use it. For as long as it functioned for me, I was going to keep drinking. We partied and we moved – and then I moved back.

❖    ❖    ❖

**I went back to the same hotel in London.** David Loewi, the food and beverage director in the Carlton Tower at the time, took a job with Terence Conran as the GM of Mezzo, which was about to open. Mezzo was going to be the largest free-standing restaurant in Europe. It seated 350 downstairs and 250 upstairs and I was asked to do the downstairs restaurant. The whole thing was based on a turnover system: you gave a return time on tables. So we were doing 950 or 960 covers on a Saturday night. We had 100 staff so it had to be orchestrated and controlled. You had to make sure you knew what was happening in every aspect of that restaurant at all times. It was a massive responsibility and I was taking over the restaurant from the manager who was there. I was part of the management team of seven managers.

The decision I had made was that I loved the restaurant floor and the social aspect and the people aspect, but I didn't want to do an office job. To become food and beverage director, you needed to take on the office job and I didn't want to do that. That didn't appeal to me at all. In fact, I hated even sitting down, so that wasn't going to work. So that's where Mezzo came in. I didn't know what I was going to do: "Where do I go from a five-star hotel, making £2,000 sterling a week? What am I going to do now? Open up a place of my own?" That could have been a thing. But David Loewi called me and asked me to go for the interview.

That's when I met one of the biggest influences of my life: Wendy Hendricks. She ran Quaglino's and was a total bitch: totally fabulous, but totally insecure. She interviewed me and she liked me and she didn't like me and she liked me and then she didn't like me and she couldn't make up her mind whether she liked me or not until she saw me work the restaurant floor. That summer of 1995, the heat was 100 degrees, a fabulous summer – and we were trying to open this restaurant. We didn't know each other from the restaurant floor, we knew each other from an office and I'm not good in an office. I don't sit well on a computer – I like to be standing up. So there was a lot of friction and we were fighting with each other and she was going to get rid of me until we opened and that's when I switched. I watched her do the floor and I thought she was on drugs the amount of energy that came out of her and the amount of control that she'd have. I wanted what she was doing and I wanted to learn that. I wanted to be that person, to have the control she had. She taught me how to do it, how to control a room, how to do volume.

Volume is an art form. Volume is turning tables and handling hundreds of people coming in and out of a restaurant, as well as controlling a vast number of staff. I mean, running restaurants is one thing and it's fine. A normal restaurant of 100 seats is fine, but when you multiply that by three or by 10, it's a completely different ball game. The style of your floor management changes: you don't talk to the customers when you do volume, you just talk to the staff, because customers are numbers. There is a hierarchical system always when there is a problem on a table. There were systems for everything: undercooked, overcooked, too hot, too cold – straight back into the kitchen and back out again. Nobody even dealt with it; it was just done.

Each section of about 40 seats or thereabouts had a waiter and a head waiter. The head waiter did not leave the section. The waiter ran. The head waiter took orders and cleared tables and called them away.

Each half of the restaurant of six sections had a first head waiter. Last, there was a restaurant manager: me. So, if a problem came to me, it was very serious, it meant the head waiter couldn't deal with it and the first head waiter couldn't deal with it. Too hot, too cold, undercooked or overcooked was the head waiter's problem. The first head waiter dealt with more serious complaints with a glass of champagne or prosecco or taking something off the bill. But if it was a really serious complaint, I got it. Of the 900 covers we did, we'd always get 10 per cent complaints – always. And doing volume of that size, you always will. Of that 10 per cent, 10 per cent would be my problem. So I'd get nine serious complaints a night. That takes a lot out of you. When you are faced with a serious complaint from some mad person, on drugs or half-drunk, you learn very quickly how to solve problems. You also learn very quickly how to distinguish between somebody taking the piss out of you or being serious and how to defuse a situation. So I learned a lot on that job about complaint handling right from the word go, and Wendy taught me an awful lot of it.

I remember the first time Wendy told me, "Go and move that table", I was thinking: "I can't move a table. It's a five-star hotel, we don't move tables." She just said: "They had a reservation. Their reservation time is now over. The table is due back to the restaurant at 8.45. It is part of your responsibility as a manager of the floor to go and move them and turn all those tables around." So you'd a list in in your hand of all the tables that came in to the restaurant at seven o'clock and that were due back to the restaurant at 8.45 and you had to make sure that they were back, because at nine o'clock you'd another 50 covers coming in to sit at those tables.

So I learned very quickly: "Hi, good evening. I hope everything was okay for you. Your table is on a return time. We need the table back. There is a reservation coming in, so we have to move you to the bar – NOW." You learn very quickly how to deliver your message to somebody without them arguing with you or coming back at you, saying: "We weren't told this when we made our reservation." Yes, you were. We told you. I had to have faith in the system; it has to be bulletproof, that everybody does the same thing, at the same time, with every reservation.

The turnover of staff was huge because it burnt out people very quickly. We were open until three o'clock in the morning. It was a gruelling, gruelling place. I took over the restaurant from Wendy. She was phenomenal to work with, but didn't like the job because the hours were ridiculously long. I burnt out a couple of times in there but I kept going back to it because I was an adrenalin junkie and completely addicted to the adrenalin and the buzz of the whole thing – completely. It was an octane level that I'd never seen before. Plus the fact that I could walk into any restaurant in Soho and get a table and the best service and free champagne anywhere I wanted because everyone had either worked with me or had come through Mezzo at one stage. There was a period of about two years in London where I was a well-known restaurant manager, running one of the biggest restaurants. So that brought with it a kudos, a street cred. We played hard, we played very hard.

---

*Two rehabs, two heart attacks, a transplant, four years of therapy and the death of my father – all in 10 years. That's too much.*

---

But there's an expiry date on everyone. So when I got to 34, I applied to go to the Sanderson Hotel and a few other places, because it was time for me to get out of Mezzo. I was just tired. It was getting very messy and sloppy around the edges. I was becoming very worn-looking and losing my shine. In the end, someone came to London and poached me to come home to Dublin. It was to La Stampa.

❖    ❖    ❖

**I came home to run La Stampa.** It didn't last long. The owner thought he was getting somebody who was going to change his restaurant into an incredible, money-making thing because that's what we did in London. We were turning £50k sterling a day in Mezzo. But you needed the whole machinery around it – the PR and general management and the purchasing and the buying, a meeting structure and so on. I did my best but we eventually had a big row and I ended up leaving. Beautiful room, a stunning place and I loved the size of it and the staff in there I'm still friends with today. Declan Maxwell was there with me as my assistant manager and he and Karen Noble now run Luna.

When I finished that job, I broke down completely. I was burned out, just worn out. I had to take time out for myself, so I took the summer out for myself and I kind of did nothing for the first time in my life really. I moved around and went home for a while. I didn't realise that I was actually as bad as I was and I was about to go back to London because I couldn't find anything here. When you've done something like Mezzo, it is very hard to come to the B class – to economy. But even if you look at the business in London *versus* the industry in Ireland, they were worlds apart: it was like coming from a five-star hotel to a two-star hotel. The attitude wasn't there, the experience wasn't there, the set-up wasn't there, the professionalism wasn't there. So it took me a while to actually find something that I wanted to do. I ended up coming into the Four Seasons, now the Intercontinental.

But first I worked for MasterChefs. I was going to open Fire restaurant for them in the Mansion House. I was with them for about a year and I ended up doing the race courses and football stadiums. That was the lowest point of my entire career: standing in the middle of Fairyhouse on a Sunday morning wearing a Gucci tie and a Cartier watch, wrapping cheese and ham sandwiches, in white bread, on a plate, with cling film, thinking to myself: "Something has gone wrong here." I'll never forget it. I resigned, just left without anything to go to.

I was about to go back to London when I met John and Michael Brennan and Gerard Denneny, who I was in college with, at the opening of the Morrison. They said: "Come up to the Four Seasons and see John before you do anything." I'd been out of hotels, so I was thinking: "I'll go and talk to him but I don't want to go back into hotels again." I was now identifying myself as being more into restaurants than hotels and it's different. Especially in London, you have to be horrible to people to get what you want, and that's the difference between a five-star hotel and an independent restaurant. In a hotel, the customer tells you what they want – that's the difference. I met John and he told me about the restaurant in the Four Seasons, and what they were going to do. It was very much like the Rib Room in the Carlton Tower. I said I could run it with my eyes closed, so he goes: "Do it then." I said: "Okay."

It was kind of like a challenge to me, to make it work, to make a hotel restaurant in this town work. Hotel restaurants in this town were shocking and were not perceived to be good places to go and dine in. So I ended up taking the job and I didn't really like it at first. I didn't like the whole ethos and structure and the hotel wasn't open; we were stuck in an office. Back to the office again, which I absolutely hated, trying to come up with a manual and policies and procedures for the hotel, which I fucking hated. It was just awful. I used to work down in Diep Le Shaker at the weekends because I was addicted to the floor and I knew then that this is what I loved and this is where I belonged.

Anyway, I ended up going to LA, where I worked for the summer in the Regency Beverly Wilshire Hotel LA, now the Four Seasons Beverly Wilshire. And that's where my drinking took off, completely. I had gone from being a big drinker to being a spectacular drinker. The gallon of gin, the gallon of vodka you can carry on one finger, with the cranberry juice in the other hand, from the off-licence from just around the corner. LA is a boring place when you've nothing to do and no money, and I'd no friends there.

So I came back 10kg heavier than when I left, and I now had a bit of a problem. Alcohol does something to you – to your motivation and to your enthusiasm for what you do and to your zest for life. It takes all that away from you. You become depressively apathetic and you have this negativity about everything around you and you've no interest in anything around you and you've no drive to do anything and no motivation. Of course, my colleagues here saw this and suggested I go into St Pat's or lose my job. So, that was tough, but it was actually the kick in the ass that I really needed in life to stop drinking.

I kind of welcomed it because I was tired. I was tired of it all. I was tired of the stuff that was going on in my head that I couldn't control and I was tired of the inability to function without drinking and the inability to do my job without looking forward to that drink at home.

And I knew what the problem was: the Gramercy Park euphoria moment I had in New York was now coming to fruition. I had predicted this so I welcomed it with open arms. I packed my suitcase and went in and threw it on the bed and said to myself: "Welcome to the rest of your life. It begins here and now."

❖   ❖   ❖

**That was another moment in my life** when I knew my life was going to change and I loved every fucking minute of that hospital. I was in for six weeks, loved it. Because every day of my life I drank. Throughout my whole career, I drank every day – not too drunk, but just drank every day. This was the first time that I actually didn't drink. Brilliant! It was like: "OMG, who is this person? Who are you?" I didn't know who I was! To take away all those pressures of life to focus entirely on myself – it was the first time I'd ever done that. And I welcomed that. I met this person that I'd never met before and I dealt with the issues that I needed to deal with. I came out of hospital and stuff started to happen in my life.

I went through this counselling procedure where the Jesuits contacted me through another friend of mine, and we all went through this healing process together, which took me to a place where I could live with myself. I was getting treatment for child sex abuse and all that kind of stuff. So it was the start of something fabulous. And I just went with it. I didn't change it. I didn't try to do anything with it. I just went with it. It was something that was happening for me to me and it was the first time in my life that somebody was giving me something. And the guy, Gearóid – he has actually left the priesthood since then – was amazing in his knowledge and his insights of abuse and what had happened to the person and I'll never forget that.

When I came out then, I went back on stage with full lighting, plush elegance. I felt like a new person, like I had been reborn. My personality came back, the whole show came back and I took over that restaurant and ran it like as though it was my own. The TV show started the year after. Yes, that happened as soon as I came back. It was almost like God gave me a gift. Do you know what I mean? I see those things as a gift. They don't happen and you don't orchestrate them; they were given to you as a reward on the work that you've done on yourself.

---

*It is impossible to separate your work from who you are. Your work is part of you.*

---

What you don't see is what you give out and what I was giving out at the time was pure positivity and pure enlightenment. That was purely as result of what I'd gone through. People who have suffered are very humble. People who have been through wars are very patient. So, the destruction that happens to you as a person when I went through what I had been through, the reverse of that happens immediately when you come out, and that's what you radiate. Plus there is a spiritual enlightenment and a whole thing that goes on with it between you, your psyche and your spirit and the cleanliness of it all. That comes through in all aspects of your life. My work life improved, my personal life improved and everything got cleaner and got better.

I don't know anyone who has been through as much as I have. Two rehabs, two heart attacks, a transplant, four years of therapy and the death of my father all – in 10 years. That's too much.

In 2007, when I had the heart attack, I couldn't believe it. I was far too young, far too fabulous to be having a heart attack. I didn't understand it at all, but I knew instantly it was true and what caused it – instantly. OMG, it was because of all that. Of everything. And then I realised, even through rehab, that I was always running from myself. Everything made sense to me, when the heart attack happened, that I was running away from me, I was running so fast that my heart gave up.

It is impossible to separate your work from who you are. Your work is part of you. You spend eight hours of your day there minimum and you talk about it and you are the person at work – it's who you are. Be it in private, a quiet person, working on their own, working on a computer all day, with figures or whatever, that's part of who you are, regardless of whether you think it is or not – it is.

All these traumatic events in my life, I think, made me more honest with myself and in my work. When I started being honest with myself about what was really going on with me, I started admitting to the problems that got me there in the first place. I started becoming able to handle stuff emotionally and psychologically, I began to understand me and the way I behaved. My behaviour. I learned more about myself.

I had a heart attack, went back into rehab, had another heart attack and then I went to Portugal and when I came back from that, I went on the transplant list.

The second heart attack happened in November and I moved to Portugal the following April, so when I was coming out of the illness phase, you go into a heart rehab. Your body takes a year to recover from a heart attack and the medication takes a year to kick in and all that kind of stuff and the doctor said to me that I really needed to think about having a transplant. Now I didn't really know what that meant. I was like: "Okay! It's bad, isn't it." "Yes, it's serious." I was just kind of sick, tired and that was kind of like a seed planted and he did it very subtly, just planted a seed there.

I went off to Portugal. Everyone was freaking out, but I felt fine and when I was in Portugal, I wanted to live in the sun, wanted to get some sunshine. I wasn't going to work very hard. I got someone else to drive my car because I felt so sick I couldn't drive, but yet I was going, and there was no question about me not going. Nobody could stop me. I was going. We drove down to Portugal, opened a guesthouse in a villa I had leased and I'd people come down and help me. They flew down and stayed with me. I met the guy who owned the villa recently and he said he was freaking out at the time because he thought something was going to happen to me and he'd have to fly me back. I found a cardiologist or a surgeon to make sure I was okay and I was fine. I knew, I just knew I was going to be okay. There was a divine intervention in my life at that time that took me to a level that I knew I was going to be all right. I instinctively knew.

When I came back to Dublin, I did the Marker Hotel. You take bites of what you can do and do little bits of it. I made some limitations as to what I would do, but I had to do something. I always need a purpose in my life. You have to have a purpose in your life. I'm not a person who could do nothing. If I won the lottery, I'd still work because I'd need to get up and do something. I know we all have these fantasies about not having to work, but I realise that I need to get up in the morning and do something. Your day off is a day off and a holiday is a holiday, but I need to be able to get up and do something and earn some money and get out of my own head. Whether it is exercise or running or yoga or a job, but I have to get up and do something. It's in my nature.

❖   ❖   ❖

**I'd have to be really old to hang up my maître d' shoes**, because I think I'm going to do this until I can't do this any more. Literally until I can't do it any more. And when I can't do this any more, I'd like to learn to be a yoga teacher and do yoga. I do a lot of yoga since my transplant. I've spent the last four years doing yoga and really found it very helpful to me. Whether it is running or yoga or the gym or whatever, you release all that tension in your body or stress in your life and you balance everything out. I never realised that when I was working. Now I do. When I started working in the current restaurant, I had to stop yoga because I was working 12 or 14 hours a day. But now I'm going back to it again and I realise that I should have kept doing it. So I'd probably end up doing something like that. Something holistic. I don't ever see myself doing nothing or retiring to do nothing. I don't think I'm the kind of person to do that.

I've a week off this week and I've been flat out, booking things and getting stuff done, teeth checked, eyes tested. When I was ill, recovering from the transplant, I had to teach myself to sit and do nothing. It took me a year to be able to say to the doctor: "I'm doing nothing." He said: "Well, thank God." And it wasn't easy. The hardest thing I've ever done in my life was doing nothing. I think it is part of who you are.

# DOMINI KEMP

## "I'm all about saying: Yes."

*Domini Kemp was a showjumper before training as a chef at Leith's in London in 1996. She then returned to Ireland to co-write* **New Irish Cooking** *– the first of her five books – and to work in the Michelin-starred Peacock Alley in Dublin.*

*In 1999, the Kemp sisters opened the first Itsa on Abbey Street. Since then, the company has grown to include five brands and over 100 employees across 14 locations, as well as a catering and event management company.*

*After her breast cancer diagnosis in 2013, Domini drastically changed her eating habits and to coincide with this change of direction to low-carb, healthy fat eating, she created the health, juice and whole foods store, Alchemy Juice Co.*

**My parents met out in the Bahamas.** My father was married twice before, so our Mum was his third wife. She came out to the Bahamas from Dublin – a very glamorous, very beautiful woman – for a life full of adventure. She was of the generation of Irish people brought up to accept religious belief without question. She lived on Eglinton Road – a wonderful place to grow up in the early 1950s. It was tree-lined, winding and bright on the south side, forbidding on the north; same as it is today.

They met in Nassau, which was the place to be in the 1960s. Dad was Scottish, from the Isle of Skye. He was an accountant in what was to become KPMG. The Bahamas was – and still is – a tax haven, so there is no income tax. As a result, about 800 banks have their headquarters there on this tiny island. There is a lot of accounting to do in a tax haven, so Dad had a very successful career out there. He nailed a famous financier and drug dealer called Robert Vesco; similar to the whole Al Capone thing, he got him on tax stuff.

Mum was completely horse-crazy ever since she was a child, so our entire childhood was spent between the beach on crazy ex-racehorses, and spending summers here in Ireland on fat ponies. We had the best of both worlds really, in many respects. The Bahamas is an idyllic place to grow up in when you are very young, but once you get older, you really need to be sent away to boarding school. Being on an island that is only 21 miles long meant that young folks got into all sorts of tragic mischief. We were all raised with the idea that we'd be going to boarding school from the age of 10 or 11. Peaches was in boarding school in the States when Dad became very unwell. He spent about six months going back and forth between Miami and the Bahamas. As you can imagine, in the early 1980s, the hospitals in the Bahamas left a lot to be desired. After six months, he died but Mum was left quite comfortably off. I was about 10 then.

Mum, a relatively young widow with two kids, was trying to figure out what to do and really the only thing for her to do was to come home. Her mother and brother were both over here and so, after a brief stint in the States, we came back and she bought a house down in Co Meath. I went to Headfort boarding school and that was that. I never looked back and had no interest in going back and settling in the Bahamas. It was very much a case of: "This is my home now."

I think my Mum was probably born a generation too early. She was incredibly fun, horse-crazy, so enthusiastic and encouraging, and she wasn't very strict. She did a load of things: she was an actress for a while and had an affair with Robert Mitchum years ago when working on one of his movies. She was an adventurer and I think that the life of being a housewife in the Bahamas probably didn't suit her as she got older. When she arrived back here, she was able to enjoy her horses, had the freedom, wasn't anybody's wife, and had a great time. I suppose it was just very nice being back here with her Mum and brother and us being young enough to make good friends here. It was nice to be settled. It was nice to be home.

❖   ❖   ❖

**Headfort was great, but it was a big change.** I remember being horribly homesick, though, for the first term as well as being horrified at how cold it was. We'd spent summers over here, but never a winter. So that was very, very tough. If you say it nowadays – that you are going to send your kids to boarding school – people look at you with horror, but that was what was done back then. It was that whole British thing. My half-brother and half-sister were sent to boarding school at the age of seven. And they didn't come home except for holidays. At least with Headfort, I was weekly boarding. But it was definitely tough. I remember being dropped off on the Sunday evening and running down the driveway, chasing after the car, desperate to go back home – really awful stuff. But it was the making of me in a lot of respects.

I think by the second or third term, I really started to enjoy it. I toughened up hugely and that terrible neediness that you probably have as a young kid when you're taken away from home slowly subsided. I found my groove and made friends and life felt better once I got over that terrible homesickness. But it's a funny thing that still afflicts me and I suffer from it. I fret about going away and I hate leaving home. I'm a real home-bird! I can't wait to get back home when I'm away.

My early teenage years were brilliant because I was hugely into horses. I competed internationally for Ireland in hunter ponies, then graduated to showjumping after that. Sport is such a good discipline. Early starts, long hours and never a day off, a bit like farming. The animals come first. You have to care for them completely, so you learn a sense of duty and discipline. You can't just lie in and hope they feed themselves. It was a good way to learn that you get out what you put in. You had to clean your tack and polish it, pack up for horse shows; you had to be prepared. That's a great thing for any young person to learn. If they are into sport, it's an important thing to learn and it stays with you forever. Even now, I can chalk up a good or bad result as to whether or not I was prepared or if I was a bit lazy or not. The jobs you do best are the ones that you've prepared for, where you've left nothing to chance. And I think that lesson has always remained with me: if you fail to prepare, then prepare to fail.

It was a great time growing up in this country. I think Ireland's schools are brilliant. I made great friends and I've been friends with them since I was a young teenager; we are still great friends. They became an extended family and my mother was very much a central figure in their lives as well. She was terribly close to a load of my girlfriends. I think it was because she was so liberal and very fair and supportive. We never felt that there was any problem that we couldn't go to her with. She never judged us.

---

*The jobs you do best are the ones that you've prepared for, where you've left nothing to chance. That lesson has remained with me.*

---

But my goodness, she really despised the Catholic Church and hated the nuns ever since she was sent off to convents as a youngster – and from which she regularly got expelled. Really, to the day she died, if she saw a nun she felt a real surge of anger. Some of them were very cruel. When she was much older, she tracked down one of the nuns who had taught her and had been horribly cruel to her as a child. She wanted to meet and talk with her . . . maybe see if there was some atonement to be had? It was a great dawning, because sitting there she thought: "This is the person who really made my childhood a misery." She felt nothing but pity for the woman then. I think it was a good moment. She understood that it wasn't really personal, it was just the way it was back then.

She had so many great stories. There is one very funny one about when she 'mitched off' and got into the sick bay at school and discovered the most amazing marble and tile bathroom she had ever seen. She later learned it was the 'Bishop's Bathroom' to be used solely by His Grace, the Bishop, when he came to officiate on the Day of the Annunciation. Extravagantly pink, it had mirrors all over the walls and a massive bath. A cornucopia of soaps and lotions stood on the shelves and a gleaming electric razor stood proudly by the basin. As the ceremony progressed, Mum (meant to be convalescing in the sick bay) ran herself a luxurious bath and used all the lotions and potions set out for the Bishop. Unfortunately for her, she got totally busted by the nuns – who were understandably outraged – and was thrown out of the convent. It is a great story. She was definitely rebellious.

My father would have had that same streak, too. He despised snobs, as do I. Both of our parents had a bit of rebellion in them, though it was probably more to do with a sense of injustice. We lived on an island that was 98 per cent black. We lived there year-round, but for a lot of the white people, it would have been their second or third home. We had cleaners, gardeners, maids. That's the way we grew up, but if there was ever a sense that we were taking advantage or being spoilt brats and not being respectful, we'd have been killed.

The sense of right and wrong was very much ingrained in us, although it was never a thing of having to be 'nice' to people because they were doing a subservient job. As an adult, I do plenty of 'subservient' jobs. Work is work, and everyone has to work if you want to get ahead. But I think at that time there was a lot of corruption in the police force and there would have been a lot of racism even amongst blacks, a lot of Haitians coming in illegally. Mum would have been very good to a couple of people who worked for us and got into trouble and ended up in jail with families to look after; she'd have helped bail them out or lent them money. Our parents were always decent in that sense and that was very much instilled in us. She would have always been on the side of the underdog to some extent, and I think that's definitely something that has stayed with me. I hate bullies, absolutely hate them.

Years ago, in Nassau, we used to do this walkathon in school to raise money for charity. Of course, so many people down there were so loaded that they'd sponsor you to the tune of $10 or even $50 per mile. Literally, about the equivalent of about $1,000 now. My best friend and I were eight or nine years old at the time. After the race, I had to collect the money pledged to me for completing the six miles, but I had an excess of about $15. So, instead of handing it all in, I took the $15 and went down to the supermarket with my best pal and bought sweets and a kite, loads of stuff. The manager of the supermarket was understandably suspicious, so he called Mum. I'll never forget: we were around the back of the supermarket, stuffing our faces, having the time of our lives when we got caught by Mum and the manager. I was murdered, absolutely murdered. I had to 'fess up to the school headmistress that I'd taken the excess money and had to write an apology note to the orphanage saying that I'd taken the $15. The humiliation never left me – oh, that feeling of shame and having done something so terribly wrong. It was a good lesson.

Going to Alex [Alexandra College] was a piece of cake in comparison to Headfort. Headfort was such a beautiful – but rambling – old building, with a slightly eccentric headmaster. We were not allowed to wear tights. The food was dire. There were 15 or 18 of us in a dorm – blankets, no duvets – and only one shower or bath a week. Really quite Dickensian, so Alex felt like Disneyland in comparison with its central heating and vegetarian options at dinner time!

I'd come over from the Bahamas, from the American system, which is way behind us, and was plonked into Headfort where they were following the common entrance exams for UK schools. When I started in Headfort, I was horribly behind where I should have been for my age in terms of education, so I really struggled. But I did very well – mainly because of the great teachers there – and caught up. So, by the time I got to Alex, I was breezing through. Everything came far too easy those first few years. I was getting great marks, because Headfort was so far ahead in terms of its education. So I had lots of time to doss, make good friends and have fun. We had a great year. We are all still terribly close. My friends very much became my extended family and still are to a large extent.

I breezed through, did the Inter Cert, and as I got to fifth year, I really took my foot off the gas educationally. I kind of thought I could cruise along as I had done. I didn't bother my arse for fifth and sixth year. I got very bad results. I was having too much fun, was having a great time. And probably in those final years, I'd started to get less and less interested in the horses and competing. My attention turned to boys! I started to stay up in Dublin at the weekends, so I was less interested in going home and mucking out the horses. I totally took my eye off the ball.

It was such a different time. Alex had a secretarial course stuck beside it. I think the idea for many of us was that you went to Alex, you potentially married well, or you could go to the secretarial course if you really wanted a 'career'. Very, very different. I don't know if I ever thought much about what I was actually going to do in life. It just never really dawned on me that I had to have a plan. I didn't really like studying. I found classes very boring, so I would often challenge a lot of the teachers. I loved science, but I hated the idea of learning things off. I found studying and all that area very, very dull.

The night before my English exam for my Leaving, I was reading Jilly Cooper's *Riders*, whilst giving friends a crash course in *Castle Rackrent*. I loved reading and was always a bookworm, but I just couldn't be arsed studying. I did terribly in my Leaving. Nearly failed it, as I got an E in 'business org' – which I was disgusted about, as I was always quite good at that – so I demanded that it got remarked and got it put up to a D, which got me over the line and was a great lesson: you don't have to accept a first offer.

The assumption was that I'd repeat and do better, but I'd no plan – no real plan – and was just a bit lost as to what I was going to do. I spent the next three months faffing around. I got a job in Buck Whaley's night club for £20 a night, handing out cocktail sausages and chips and ferrying dirty glasses down to the kitchen to be washed. It was pretty hideous. But there were not a lot of jobs in Dublin at the time, so to get 20 punts – in cash! – for 10 hours work in Buck Whaley's was great!

*The weight of responsibility, at 19, was madness
– but it gave me huge trust and faith in myself.*

I think at that stage Mum got a bit fed up with me and felt I needed to
do something. I was booted off to the States to my godmother who
worked over there and lived down the road from a Grand Prix
showjumper who had a beautiful stableyard, just outside Princeton.
He was, and still is, incredibly charismatic. He ran a yard with about
50 horses there. They had a very active lesson programme, and a
bunch of top showjumpers that were on the US circuit. I was about 18
or 19 and was getting paid $200 a week. I lived on the property with
a group of Mexicans, which was often terrifying, because they'd
regularly get completely drunk and melancholy, so there were many
nights that I'd lie awake thinking: "I hope they don't burn the house
down!" But they were good guys and we were all there working
illegally, although sadly, it was always clear that their situation was
much more precarious than mine. I was white and Irish. I wasn't
sending money home to my dependants and if I got caught and booted
back to Dublin, it wasn't the end of the world for me. For them, it was
potentially a disaster for their extended families. Completely unfair,
but that was and still is the reality.

I think it is really important to get a work ethic somehow. I got it
in my time in the States because I was given so much responsibility. I'd
been faffing around being a pain-in-the-arse teenager for the previous
year – doing nothing – and I suddenly found myself teaching about 70
lessons a week and running the business. After a year, I was as
indispensable as anyone can ever be to a job. I learned how to manage
different personalities. How to keep the clients happy. How to increase
business. My boss was a real wheeler-dealer. He could charm any
potential buyer into parting with a lot more than budgeted for. He
was an unbelievable salesman. He was great to see in action but he
was always getting into all sorts of problems. He put a lot of trust in
me. I had a good, strong, professional relationship with him and it was
so refreshing to be given all that responsibility. I'd be driving the horse-
truck – I barely had my driving licence – from one end of the US to the

other. He just dumped responsibility on me and I had to either sink or swim. I really thrived over there. I loved it, absolutely loved it.

He had been to Poland buying horses and had done really well out of it. It was 1991, when I came home, and I said to Mum: "We are going to Poland. We're going to buy some horses. We'll get them cheap as chips and sell them really well." So we went to Poland. We got to the Holiday Inn in Warsaw and managed to get a driver to bring us around. We went to all the studs and imported three horses back from Poland. A crazy road trip but it was brilliant, absolutely fantastic. We brought three young horses back, two that sold well and one that was a bit of a dud but competed okay. I then opened up a tack shop in Kill – my first business at 21! – bringing in all the stuff from the US. Probably, I was a bit before my time: it was all very posh, all custom-made stuff. I had the exclusive European rights for all these amazing things like hand-made chaps, riding boots and rugs, all things I had seen on the circuit there. And that was great, my first taste of business. Concurrently, my sister Peaches had done a Cordon Bleu course and was doing a bit of catering, so I helped her whenever I could. Food and horses hovering simultaneously in our lives.

I was still in my early 20s. We then moved to England with all the horses, so I could start competing on the circuit there. I was hoping to eventually start competing at Grand Prix level and to get on a team, but it's tough at that level. I reluctantly came to the realisation that I was never going to be good enough. Never going to be where I wanted to be. Always going to be feeling like I just hadn't 'made it'. I had a real desire for success, but I knew I was just never going to be tough enough with my horses, that's my honest opinion. You have to be really tough in sport and I loved my horses too much.

❖   ❖   ❖

**I was now in my mid-20s.** I hated studying. I was going to struggle to work for someone. What was I going to do? So I thought I'd go to cookery school and get a piece of paper because I could always make money cooking. It's easy to find work when you can cook, so I made the decision and, while still competing, started to make moves to sell the horses. I loved cooking, absolutely loved it. I thought, "With this, I could also write", which was something I also loved and was always good at. I felt there were loads of directions I could go with it.

I did the year diploma in Leith's in London and started working in a few restaurants in London. One chance weekend, I came home and met Conrad Gallagher, Lauren's dad. We got on incredibly well. I think we both saw a leg up, as it were, in the other person. He needed someone like me to come and lasso everything and take control of his interests and I saw him as: "Oh great, I don't have to work as a commis chef and work my way up. I suddenly have a restaurant to run. Happy days!"

I blame my sister, it's all her fault! Peaches had been in Peacock Alley for dinner. Conrad had opened up first in Baggot Street, to rave reviews. Everyone was talking about him. He had just moved to South William Street. I had been out in Atlanta during the Olympics, cooking for the head of Speedo, for all their directors. I'd been out there for two weeks, cheffing away, wondering where to go next. Peaches had said: "You should meet this guy. He used to work in Monte Carlo." I was half-thinking of going to France and working in a good Michelin star restaurant over there, so I said: "Grand, I'll see if I can make some contacts and get a steer." I also remember thinking: "I don't need to meet yet another dick of a chef." But we met, clicked straightaway and he came down to a party she was having on the Sunday. And that was it: I didn't get the flight home the following day.

So I moved back to Dublin and, initially, I was viewed as the bit of totty – no one really took me seriously – but I just bided my time. I was doing a bit of everything, down the kitchen a bit, learning 'front of house', wherever needed an extra pair of hands. I'd never worked front of house, I had always been in the kitchen, never out front, so I hated that because I was suddenly plonked into what was going to become a Michelin-star restaurant and trying to manage that room and the inevitable difficult customers. It was really tricky because the reservations gal – although lovely – was hopeless at managing bookings, so we'd suddenly have 100 people at half eight on a Saturday night and there would be endless delays on the food. Anyone who was a Peacock Alley customer in that era will remember waiting for nearly two hours for their main course on a busy night.

I was 24 or 25 and just didn't have the confidence or know-how to deal with a room that felt like it was on fire with customers' rage. We used to have a system that only one person would take the orders for the whole room, to ensure good timing of orders going down to the kitchen. So I'd take the orders for the whole room, trying to ensure a docket went down to the kitchen every 15 minutes. But what used to happen was that the other waitstaff, desperately trying to ignore customers' pleas to have their order taken, would finally cave in. So they'd take the orders and stuff the dockets into my pockets as they were far too scared to go down the stairs to put up yet another docket and hear Conrad's roars. It was awful. Great learning, but awful!

Conrad was a real perfectionist. I learned so much from a food point of view – how to get the best out of flavours – and we collaborated well. He was unbelievably charismatic and charming, but he used to drive us insane. We'd be failing to pacify a really difficult customer and he'd just breeze in and deal with them in two seconds. I kind of resented that as well, the fact that he could put out the flames with some charming remark. I'd be seething inside, thinking to myself: "You little bollox!" There was a clash of egos, without a doubt. It was perfect in so many ways because, for a while, we were a great team and we wanted to get a Michelin star. But you do get resentful of somebody getting all the glory when you know you are the one actually holding up a lot of the support, so that used to bother me. It crept into the relationship, without a doubt – working together is hard. I think it is about giving credit where credit is due. Maybe that's a better way of describing it. I think it's about being fair: you have to acknowledge what people around you have done and I think that was definitely an issue between us.

It was such a mad time, a great time, but a mad time in so many aspects. Conrad had got himself into such a hole financially and I was very much out of the loop and then I was pregnant. Staff at time would probably say I went from being quite nice on the floor – and possibly pliable? – to a raving lunatic, which I am sure a lot of pregnant women can relate to! A customer might say to me, "Could I have that fillet steak well-done?" and my eyebrow would raise, my lips would snarl and I would hiss, "No!" There was terror on the floor for a few months, as the bump grew, so I think when we got the book deal, there was a collective sigh of relief as I was banished upstairs to the office.

---

*They'd no classification for bagels in Customs*
*& Excise – no one had ever heard of bagels.*
*They thought we were importing dogs.*

---

So I started writing the cookbook, which was fantastic. And again, it was: "Like, write a book? Eh, how? OK, I'll figure it out." It was quite a big deal doing that in your 20s when you actually had never done it before and the level of support and information was patchy at best. No info or how-to on the web! We were children basically, dealing in a very adult world. I think that – definitely – I'm all about saying "Yes" and then I'll have a fleeting moment of panic before I figure it out.

I really credit my first boss – probably my only boss – in the States for that. I can't tell you the responsibility that was dumped on my plate from literally the first month. He could see that I was hard-working and wanted to learn, so it was like a magic combination. So he was like: "There you go." When you've been plonked in those situations, you can fall back on them. You think: "Okay, I have driven six hours from Palm Beach to Tampa and back again, with about three million dollars' worth of horses in the back and I only have a normal driver's licence. I shouldn't even be driving a truck!" The weight of responsibility, at 19, was madness, but it gave me huge trust and faith in myself. It gave me the ability to say: "I can do this".

So I said: "Write a book? I'll figure it out." Sometimes we need to give ourselves a metaphoric slap across the face and say: "Yes, I can." Just do it. And sometimes it's great not to have the choice to say "No" in a professional sense and just have to get on with it. You remind yourself that you have been in worse situations, scarier situations, that it's not rocket science. You figure it out and just break it down into pieces. I'm good at that: figuring out a way to overcome obstacles and to solve problems.

It was great experience writing the book. Hilarious, going to the chefs at the time and saying: "Give me the recipe for this and that. Write it on a piece of toilet paper for all I care, just give me the basics. Just give me the ingredients, I don't even need the methodology – I'll go from there." Half of them are just appalling, you can barely read their writing, scrawled on scraps of paper. But one of the lads dropped me up an A4 piece of paper, beautifully typed up – ingredients, methodology, order of food as it appeared – and I thought: "OMG, I love you. Heaven!" I read on and, word for word, I realised he'd copied a Marco Pierre White recipe from a book! If something looks too good to be true ...

But it got to a point where we were so screwed financially. The book was about to come out. I was six or seven months pregnant. I was thinking: "OMG, I've got myself into such a hole here. We are in big, big trouble." We were being told we'd have to shut the doors. Literally, it was that bad, and I was annoyed that I didn't know how bad it was.

But there were a couple of things that I did that were smart: we didn't get married and I never became a director of the company. I was always reluctant to do it, though I was always being pushed to do it. However, I was never going to do it unless I had full control of the finances – and, thank goodness, I didn't. I called a friend who was an accountant. I'd known him a long time, a real gentleman. He came in, had a look at everything and said: "Right, you are fucked!" And I said: "We just need to hang on till September. We've a shot of getting on *The Late Late Show*. The book is about to come out. Is there any way ...?"

This was about July 1997. He was great. He stemmed the blood flow, as it were, and made a few calls to suppliers, the landlord and other key creditors. So we hobbled on for the next eight weeks and *The Late Late Show* came down to Peacock Alley and did a little filming of Conrad during service one night. I remember the show so well as I was sitting in the audience, about eight months pregnant, gripping the chair, hoping that it would be the good publicity we so desperately needed for the book and the restaurant.

Conrad was a huge fan of Gay Byrne's, but for the first minute of the interview, he was so nervous that he completely clammed up with the impact of being on live telly. And then they played the little clip of him in the restaurant, roaring in orders, in his domain, and suddenly he clicked into his persona and they had a fantastic interview. From that night, the phone didn't stop ringing, morning, noon and night – the restaurant was jammed. By the following summer, our problems were over financially – it was a huge coup to turn that around. It was definitely down to persistence, having the right supports, a great team and working our arses off.

It paid off but then it all came apart again a year later but, at that stage, we were starting to go our separate ways. We had three years together. We'd incredible people working with us during that time, many of whom went on to have great careers. It was a huge learning curve. A 'What not to do in business', and to a large extent for me, that was better than any college course. I got to write a book, run a Michelin-star restaurant – we got a Michelin star during that period – to write articles (under Conrad's name), manage all the marketing and PR and start an outdoor catering division. Three years earlier, I had no clue, but I was always trying to learn. We'd no money to do anything, but we figured it out. I used to nick headed stationery from our solicitors and use it to write 'legal' letters that we couldn't afford to have done professionally – you do whatever you can when you have no money! We were young, fearless, and we were so determined. We worked really hard as well. It was a funny time but really exciting. I wouldn't change it for the world.

So, I was pretty heartbroken when we split up. I was terribly upset and had that feeling of being a real failure and so sad for Lauren. Of course, women change so much between their 20s and 30s. The idea that my daughter now would have a baby and be settled down in five years' time, I'd be: "What? NOOOO! You're FAR too young."

❖   ❖   ❖

**But heartbreak can be a great catalyst for change.** I had been out to New York about six months before we split up and started speaking to people out there who made bagels. I had felt very unhappy with the balance of the business and thought we needed something day-time –

some bread and butter, no pun intended. We needed something that was a day-time business which I could get stuck into and put my stamp on. So I'd gone out there, started making contacts. Conrad and I split up a few months later and I thought: "He isn't going to do anything with this idea." At that stage, Peaches had split up with her husband and I said to her: "For years, I was your teenage slave-labour. We always said we'd love to open up something … but now is the time, because I'm unemployed. And so are you!"

I needed to do something the opposite of what I'd just been through for the past three years. I wanted to be home at night. Lauren was only about a year and a half old, and working nights when you have a young child is tough going. I wanted to treat people the way that they are not usually treated in catering. I wanted to be in control of that and to create something a bit different. So we were very committed to those ideas and still are in a lot of ways.

Conrad and I had bought a house out in Newcastle, Co Wicklow. I thought: "I'm never going to stay down there on my own." So I sold the house. He was off gallivanting. I got £50k profit from selling the house and, for me, that was like faith money, not something I earned, so I never felt attached to it. I put it into the business, and that's what Peaches and I used to set up Itsa. Then I bumped into Stephen Caviston one day and he said: "Oh, I hear you are looking for premises. There's this lovely place, an amazing food hall." It was on Lower Liffey Street, 256 square feet, a little triangular-shaped premises – that's where it all started.

I went over to H&H in New York and asked: "Can you export?" They said: "Yes, you can either take 40,000 or 80,000 bagels. Your choice." We said we'd take 80,000 and had the frozen container shipped over. They'd no classification for bagels in Customs & Excise – no one had even heard of bagels. They thought we were importing dogs: "No, they are *bagels*, not beagles." It was mad. We imported them, and then I suddenly thought: "What if this doesn't work?" We hadn't done a small shipment to see how they thawed out, we just ploughed straight in. Anyway, it was fine. We figured out we needed to spray them with loads of water, then put them in the oven and they'd be grand – there is always a solution.

*A little serendipity and a bit of luck came just as our world was falling apart – and then suddenly the company was on fire.*

When we started, business was slow. It was kinda dodgy around there in those days. One day, *The Irish Times* rang. It was Louise East and she said: "Oh, I hear you are bringing in bagels from New York." I told a few porkies in the interview about how people were walking all the way down from Baggot Street, down to the Epicurean Foodhall, because the bagels were so amazing! She wrote up a fantastic review of Itsa, and from that day forward, we had a queue out the door, 20 deep at lunchtime – and that was fantastic. Going from turning over £80 a day to £300 one day, jumping up and down, and thinking: "This might work." This was the tail end of 1999.

It was a teeny tiny spot. There was Marc Michel's organic veg store, Caviston's, Momo who ran the most beautiful bakery, a wonderful cheese shop, a wine shop – amazing stuff. But you'd have people coming in saying: "Whaaa? Feckin' two quid for a carrot?" It was the wrong time and wrong place. The security guard had to walk us to our car at night it was so dodgy, rough as anything. But a great starting point, as we did everything on site.

In 2001, we got Dún Laoghaire. In 2002, we got a third premises. A commercial kitchen after that, then Feast Catering – and it just started to grow nicely.

❖   ❖   ❖

**I suppose what we started to see was the decline of carbohydrates,** in the mid-2000s. In 2008, probably around then, we started to look at the market a bit more closely. Our focus changed as business opportunities came and we started to see sales fall in certain areas and then the recession came. It was a difficult time for everyone but a couple of extra grim bits happened to us: Mum passed away, we lost a big contract, my husband Garvan took voluntary redundancy from his job and I got diagnosed with breast cancer. We lost the big contract with only three months' notice and that was nearly 25 per cent of our turnover. There were not huge amounts of overheads that we could cut in keeping with that, so Peaches and I came off the payroll, and it was a case of: "Shall we fold or not? What shall we do?" And everything kind of happened within those three months in 2013. At some point, you have to look above and say: "Are you fucking serious?"

I hate to use the expression 'dig deep', but that's kind of what happened. A little serendipity and a bit of luck came just as our world was falling apart – and then suddenly the company was on fire. Three really good opportunities came, one after the other. One I completely pulled out of a hat and it was great. That was Joe's Coffee. It was gun to the head stuff: "Here's a space. What would you do with it?" And I had a lightbulb moment, back-of-an-envelope type stuff and away we went. It's been a wonderful concept to develop and has got better and better over the last few years.

Hatch & Sons, our Irish kitchen restaurant in St Stephen's Green and the Hugh Lane Gallery, was a little different. In 2012, I kept coming back to the question: "What could we do in a recession that is reflective of how people are changing and how we now want to grab our sense of Irishness through food?" During the recession, we realised how important it was to promote Irish artisans, whereas in the Celtic Tiger, it was: "Ooooh, unless it's French or whatever, I don't want it." Hatch & Sons was such a lovely thing to create and develop and to bring the four directors into a sister company and say: "Can we do this? We've brilliant restaurants – like Chapter One – doing it at Michelin star level, but what can we do in daytime that's like a showcase of Ireland and all our amazing suppliers, and expressed in a really simple way?"

A lot of it stemmed from a Bord Bia report that I had been given which said Europeans found we had amazing raw ingredients but no food culture of our own. I was furious when I read it and thought: "Well, feck that, we need to 'pride up'." And that was the lightning bolt moment for Hatch & Sons: "I'm going to fix this." It was one of those lovely things that just kind of happened.

The name came about because we happened to be in the Little Museum of Dublin and there was a milk bottle there from a dairy called Hatch, just off Leeson Street, along with this wonderful story of Mr Hatch, his sons and his farm. His great-granddaughter got in touch with us recently, sending us more photos and background, and it was just a lovely brand to work on and create. It also fit so well under the Little Museum of Dublin and they were hugely supportive of what we were trying to achieve.

Back to 2013, like many breast cancer patients, I went through chemo, radiotherapy and then had a mastectomy. I was extremely frustrated and really disappointed with the dietary advice on offer: namely brochures of the food pyramid, the implication being that nothing you eat is going to have any kind of impact in the same way the chemotherapy or radiotherapy would – and I found that really disheartening and thought: "Fuck that!" I wanted to know: "What can I do? How can I contribute to my well-being?" So I delved into the latest research and really tried to figure it out. It was that rebellious streak again.

I was asking: "Why are we being told to eat this way? Where is the proof for this? Can we do better?" And, sadly, the answer is yes, we can do a lot better. And we have to do better because financially we can't afford healthcare at these levels. There must be greater focus on prevention. If everyone was doing their bit with regards to diet and exercise and keeping stress levels down, the end result would be much better regarding prevention. But so many healthcare professionals fight about what the best course of action is, much to the detriment of patients. So doing all that research, then writing the book, *The Ketogenic Kitchen* with my co-author Patricia Daly, was so important to me. During my treatment, I came up with the idea of a café for people who believe in all sorts of food 'religions', as it were, whether it was low-carb, ketogenic, paleo, wheat-free, dairy-free, vegan, sugar-free, raw food or juicing. There could be something for everyone focusing on whole foods. I wanted to take something from all these food religions – and that's Alchemy Juice Co. That was the thing I was most proud of. I love all our brands but the Alchemy range is my complete baby.

When I was first diagnosed, I let colleagues know very early on. I sent an email out to all our partners, suppliers and staff, basically saying that I had breast cancer but that it was business as usual. Head down, end of story – and it just cut out a lot of that awkwardness that people feel. For me, it was the right way to do it; others might want to lie on a couch and watch box-sets and eat crap – but that wouldn't have worked for me. I saw such an upside, mentally, from being in a better place physically and by throwing everything I could at it. I couldn't have sat around and hoped for the best. It isn't in my nature. I do believe there is always a solution – I'm such a fighter and it's very rare that I'd give up. But I was only 41 when I was diagnosed. Getting a cancer diagnosis at 61 would be a completely different struggle.

There is a lot of good support for people with cancer. Support groups, yoga for cancer patients but, with all due respect, it wasn't for me. There were often days in the chemo ward that I would be literally bawling crying, because I just needed a good cry. The amazing nurses would come up to me and say: "Are you sure you don't want to go and talk to someone?" And I'd say: "No, I just need to have a cry." And that was my way of dealing with it. But someone really smart said to me that you can't always speak to people who have a stake in your life and therefore sometimes it is good to speak to someone outside of that. Whether it is somebody who has been through cancer or someone who you don't even have a friendship with. I thought that was really wise because when you are given a diagnosis, the doctors bandy around terms like 'survival' and 'outcome' – they are not nice words. I remember hearing the word 'survival' and thought: "What? There is a question mark over my 'survival'?" I was horrified.

So I would protect my family from those words because you need time to digest what you have been told and you then translate it for them, once you've kind of localised that information. I remember I let it slip one day to Peaches and mentioned something about 'outcome' and she burst into tears. They are horrible words to hear when you are facing cancer. But with people outside of your immediate circle or who have been through it, you can have frank conversations and you don't have to protect them from your fears. You can't necessarily do that with your loved ones. They need minding!

❖   ❖   ❖

**I was always quite organised.** Possibly because my mother was a little disorganised – or because I was such a control freak! – so from a young age, I used to do all my entries for the horse shows and organise everything. I'm like that now with my kids. If they want to do something, I'll push them to do it and organise it for themselves. I feel very strongly about that. You've got to raise independent, good citizens; and they have to care about stuff. Lauren is working in the business now. She was in DIT, doing business and Italian, so she took the year out and she's going back to college in September. I think everyone should work in hospitality for six months, the equivalent of military service or something! It gives you such insight into people and teaches you confidence around dealing with difficult people and tough situations. She's learned so much and it's great for her. It's a hard slog but I think hard work is really good for the soul. It stays with you.

I recently started an entrepreneur programme in Wheatfield Prison with prisoners. There was an article in *The Economist* a few years ago, about a prison entrepreneur programme that they started in Texas and they managed to reduce recidivism rates because of this course. It just really resonated with me. Some career criminals have the same traits as entrepreneurs, such as risk-taking. But it's about harnessing these traits and steering them towards positive enterprises. I really liked the sound of this Texan thing and I looked into it a bit and into what was going on here. It costs around €70k a year to house a prisoner in Ireland. I was frustrated when I read that. It seems like such a waste if most prisoners are going to end up back in prison. What if they could start their own business?

I went and met John Lonergan – lovely man, good fun – and said: "Do you think there'd be any interest?" He said: "Sure, give it a go." So I met Michael Donnellan, director general of the Irish Prison Service (IPS), and asked if I could run a pilot course. For a large organisation, the IPS is incredibly forward-thinking. I couldn't believe it actually – I thought it would be a case of 'computer says no', but no, they said: "Give it a go."

> *I'm not a proper teacher, but I love teaching,*
> *really enjoy it, and hope I'm good at it.*

I started with a class of 17 and then whittled it down – yes, you always have a few messers. I taught them how to set up a business. I'd bring them articles from *The Economist* and we'd discuss them. Then, eventually, we got down to writing a business plan and teasing out their ideas. These guys went from not being even able to tell you what their business ideas were – suspicious, lacking confidence, not wanting the others to hear their ideas – to, by the end of the course, being able to give a three-minute pitch *Dragons' Den*-style and showing samples of their work. They wrote their own business plan, completed a cash flow, and they were able to answer tough questions about their business idea. They dressed up in business attire that their families had sent in for the final. It was transformative. Absolutely transformative. I'm not a proper teacher, but I love teaching, really enjoy it, and hope I'm good at it. And to actually see these guys change and to have helped them potentially start their own business gave me a great feeling.

At the start of the course, they would complain: "We can't get online to do our market research." I'd say: "I don't give a damn. You've got visitors each week, get them to do it and do your market research for you. Use your phone calls wisely." I'd talk to them in a blunt manner because I really hate whingeing. "This is not impossible. It's what entrepreneurs do. This is an entrepreneur's course. You'll face much tougher challenges when you get out into the real world. Landlords are not going to want to rent you a premises. Banks are going to be reluctant to give you a loan. You're going to find it hard to get insurance. Get on with it." So they did.

And I know it's trite and clichéd, but we had a ceremony at the end of the course. I was bawling, such a proud moment. There was a level of respect for the course, the process and the final competition. I got more out teaching it than you can imagine.

So we've just finished the first year, the evaluation has been done and we are trying to find a way to roll it out. For many in prison, crime is the only way to survive financially. It's survival, you know, and definitely, if I was born into similar circumstances, there is no way I can say that I wouldn't have ended up in similar situations. Mentoring wasn't a big thing when I was in my 20s and anyway I probably thought I was so brilliant I wouldn't have needed mentoring! But when you get older, you realise the value of all those things. Even the short time I had learning from the great man, Ivor Kenny, things like that, they resonate. And that's all it was with some of these guys doing this course in prison, somebody to say: "That's a really good idea. That's a potential business. You can do this."

Sometimes that's all people need to hear. It's that whole thing of understanding where other people are coming from – and you often can't do that unless you've worked beside them or have truly tried to see things from their perspective. I see it a lot with accountants, for example, saying things like: "You've got to cut your wages by 5 per cent." And I'd be saying: "It's very easy to sit behind a desk and to do that. You go down and do the work with 5 per cent less staff or 5 per cent pay cuts and see the dent in morale." I don't think it is right that people can make those kinds of decisions unless they've really grasped the impact of those decisions on the world around them. Yes, that always frustrates me. It's easy to send people to go fight wars. Not so easy to pull the trigger yourself.

❖     ❖     ❖

**To create a company that had good morals and good standards,** was profitable but not ridiculously greedy, was where we started. Then to have survived the recession without cutting the arse out of the company or demoralising people, taking pain personally, and not putting it on staff ... people could – and have argued – that we were fools! But you have to be able to put your head on a pillow at night and know you've done a good job and you've done your best.

I would rarely say, "I've done my best" and give myself a pat on the back. I am much more likely to say to myself that there is room for improvement and that I could have done better. I suffer from professional, chronic dissatisfaction! But as I've got older, I'm beginning to realise that you have to be a bit kinder to yourself as well. I'm not as neurotic and crazed as I was in my 20s and 30s and that's good, because I exhausted myself. So, now, I try to be a little more relaxed and to look at all that we have accomplished in work. To remain grateful and to thank my lucky stars for my kids, Lauren and Maeve, my husband, my sister, the rest of my family and friends. And to give myself an occasional kick up the rear!

# BOBBY KERR

"I am a liver of life."

*Bobby Kerr is the chairman of Insomnia coffee and a weekend radio presenter on Newstalk 106-108FM, where he presents **Down to Business** and **Bobby's Late Breakfast**. He was one of the original 'dragons' on **Dragons' Den** for the first four years of the series.*

*A popular business, entrepreneurial and motivational speaker, Bobby is actively involved in raising money for several charities, including the Special Olympics, Habitat for Humanity, St Luke's Hospital and Blackrock Hospice.*

**I grew up in Kilkenny** and I'm still very proud and passionate to be associated with that city and county. My father was in business – he owned the Newpark Hotel. It was in our family for 50 years. I was the second eldest child. I've an older sister and a younger sister and two younger brothers, so I'm the second oldest of five. We lived in a 400-year-old house beside the hotel, in a kind of an idyllic scenario with an orchard and wandering fields, even though it was only two miles from the city. And because they were almost on the same site, home life and business life were very intertwined.

My father would have been one of those proprietary-types of leisure hoteliers, where service was everything, recognition was everything. He knew everybody. He used to go to the afters of funerals and to wakes with cooked turkeys every week for customers. He wouldn't tell anybody his politics because he wanted to get all the dances from Fianna Fáil, Fine Gael, the Labour Party, so he'd play this game with his customers. But he was a very clever guy. He was probably a marketer before his time. He had all sorts of gimmicks and gadgets. On First Holy Communion Day, he used to have all different colour-coded envelopes in his pocket whereby, if a child came in with his parents, depending on the frequency of their visits to the hotel, he had £1 in a yellow envelope and a fiver in a red one. All this stuff going on. He really was a great guy for customer standards; he really 'innovated' stuff in hospitality, but in an uncomplicated and honest way.

When I was growing up, he would have been sort of set in his ways. I'd have had my differences with him, particularly when I was about to leave school. It's funny when you are that age, 18, and you think you are the polar opposite to your father: you can't agree with anything that he says or any advice that he gives you. Then as the years go on, you realise how alike you actually are. People say it to me now. I walk like him, I talk like him – and I never thought we had anything in common. What I would have learned from him was the value of absolute hard work and dedication to your craft, your profession. Good customer service and making sure that you work through people. I didn't think I had picked that stuff up but I definitely had. Having had a few rocky years on the relationship front with my Dad during my teenage years, we went on to have a great friendship and I loved working with him. He died in 2001 and was a huge influence on what I went on to do.

I was an average student. I went to CBS in Kilkenny and then Castleknock College. I loved boarding school. I went aged 12 or 13 to Castleknock. An interesting place, I loved Castleknock. My father had gone there, as had my grandfather. So I was the third generation, and both my brothers went there as well. And it's funny how you reflect on your learnings there: I learned how to get on with people. I learned that my true friends and people that I'm still friendly with to this day are guys that I was at school with in Castleknock. These are people that I might not see every week, but there is a gang of about 12 of us that still to this day go fishing, sailing, do all sorts of different things together. And it's funny because, in Castleknock, there were two types of characters. There were the ones who went to work straight after school and the ones who went to college – the friendships diverged then. I ended up living in flats in Rathmines and Rathgar with all the guys I was with in Castleknock, who were also from the country. Fellas from Cavan, from Sligo, from Kerry. There was a double friendship then, not only the Castleknock thing, but we went on to have a friendship of four years in bedsits and all sorts of horrific places. I remember my mother and father calling to a house I had up in Rathmines and my mother refusing to get out of the car and sending my father in. She said: "I'm not going in there." I think back at those times with very happy memories.

I boarded for five years in Castleknock. I left in 1978. I did a very average Leaving Cert, to the point that I actually repeated my Leaving in the VEC, 'the tech', in Kilkenny in 1979. I almost did worse the second time I did the Leaving than I did the first time! But I just about got enough points to get myself into DIT in Cathal Brugha Street.

❖   ❖   ❖

**When I went to college, I got a part-time job.** I had worked at a number of jobs part-time as a kid in the hotel in Kilkenny. I'd worked in the bar, sorting bottles, landscaping, and I actually worked in the kitchen for two summers. So I kinda had an interest in food and food production, basically because I loved the atmosphere that was evident in a busy kitchen environment. So I managed to get a job in what was the Peppermint Gardens out in the South County Hotel and worked there a couple of nights a week. The busy nights were Friday and Saturday, but I was too busy having a good time. I used to work Sunday, Monday and Tuesday and we'd work till 2am and I'd go into college the next day and wonder why I was falling asleep all day. In that kitchen, I learned that this is something that I really enjoyed. I enjoyed the creativity part of actually being part of a team, that provided a function and what you produced ended up on a customer's plate and it was something you wanted to be proud of. And the banter, the humour, the pressure cooker environment that it is, really appealed to me.

So I graduated from DIT in business and management and I decided that I was enjoying the kitchen work so much that when I was at a rugby match over in Edinburgh – we'd go to the matches in those days and I was playing rugby in Bective Rangers – a guy I met in a bar in Edinburgh asked me what I did, I told him I'd just graduated in catering and business from DIT but "I kinda work as a chef". And he said he was the operations manager for ARA Offshore, which looked after all the catering on the rigs in the North Sea out of Aberdeen. A huge business. He said he was looking for chefs. If I was interested in working for them and could start the next day, they'd give me a job!

---

*If I saw an opportunity or saw I could enhance my reputation by way of taking on a challenge, I was kind of up for it.*

---

So from the rugby match, I went straight to Aberdeen and did my first two weeks offshore on the Beryl, a sister platform of the Piper Alpha that blew up, just a few miles over the sea from that. I worked out there for two and half years, two weeks on and two weeks off. I used to live in a flat in Rathgar with my mates from Castleknock and fly out every two weeks, work for two weeks and come back. I really enjoyed it. Total school of life. Working with hardchaws, Glaswegians, Geordies, rough diamonds.

I worked with some tough guys and I remember to this day there was one other Irish guy who worked on the rigs with me. He was a Red Hand of Ulster man from deepest loyalist Shankill and I remember – and this is absolutely true – going to Belfast to get the boat, because sometimes we'd spent too much money and we'd end up getting the cheapest way back, which was train to Belfast, Larne to Stranraer, train through the night right across Scotland to wake at Aberdeen at 5am. Anyway, I got friendly with this guy because we were the only two Irish guys there but he was a staunch loyalist. He brought me to a British Legion pub in Belfast right at the height of the Troubles. We went in; we had five or six pints. He said: "I'm bringing you in here. Just keep your mouth shut and everything will be fine." And I went in with him, had the pints, with all his mates, with Red Hand tattoos all up their arms, and off we went then, the pair of us, out to Larne. Because I was with him, when I spoke, it was cool. Now when I think about it – what was I doing? – but there you go. That's what you did back then.

That was in the construction phase of North Sea Oil. We were on rigs with 800 or 900 men on them. Our job was to feed them. There might be four or five people tasked with feeding this number of guys and the food had to be good. No women, no booze, so food was where it was at and because the money was good, you ended up having a lot of Michelin star chefs from all over the UK working out there. The big joke was that we had five-star chefs and one-star customers, which was kind of true. I really enjoyed it but towards the end of it, I felt that, while it was great and the money was great and I was spending it as fast as I was earning it, I'd better look at my career and get on to doing something that I was supposedly trained to do.

I suppose in those days, I'd have been a bit impulsive and I reckoned there was no downside. I didn't really have a plan around what I was going to do. An opportunity presented itself and I said: "You know, I'll take this and I'll see what I can make of it." And then I made a good fist of it. I ended up working very hard and being all-consumed by it and got promoted there and eventually I managed to persuade the company that I was working for to transfer me into a management role in their Canadian operation. That's how I actually got out of it. I didn't leave, I just changed to a different country – same company, different country.

They transferred me to their Canadian equivalent, which was called Versa Services. When I went over first, Versa Services were doing the food services for the World Ice Skating Championships in Ottawa and the chef was a total disaster. The guy who met me off the plane said: "I've a problem up in Ottawa and I need you to go up and sort it out." So I went up there and got dug in and as far as he was concerned, I sorted it out and he looked after me for another three years on that basis.

Next, I worked in catering management in an amusement park in Fort Erie, about 11 miles from Niagara Falls. I was the assistant manager for about 12 catering concessions, from pizza to ice cream, and it was a busy place. Seasonal – we only worked from May to September – but it was really good experience. Then I worked in the CNE [Canadian National Exhibition] Stadium in Toronto, where the Blue Jays played, for another six or nine months. We did rock concerts and we did all the bars and catering.

My father was always of the view that you should always work in good places. Always work in places that have standards. On the rigs, the standard of food was really top class. The company that I worked for in Canada again was a high-end, very professional company that gave me lots of opportunities, so I was working in good places. When I think back, I've only ever really worked in three places, even though I did lots of different jobs in between. So I consider that as my first incarnation between Aberdeen and Toronto and Ottawa.

Then I nearly stayed in Canada, but didn't because I used to have real instability every six months around my visa. I never knew if I was going to get it or not and that insecurity of not being able to think beyond six months made me decide to come home.

So I came back from Canada and took a job in Jury's in Ballsbridge, doing work that was very mundane, given the responsibility I had been given in Canada. I almost saw this as a step backwards, even though I enjoyed working in Jury's. I was duty manager. You went around with a bunch of keys. You were basically the only guy there and when the shit hit the fan at 4am, in the Coffee Dock, you had to call the Gardaí in Irishtown – but it was all right. I remember the salary. I was paid £6,750 per annum and that was in 1985, I'd say. So it was hard to live on it.

❖    ❖    ❖

**I then applied for a job advertised for offshore supervisor** with Campbell Catering on the rigs off Kinsale. I was being considered and I think I'd actually got the job, but then they said there was a problem in UCC, one of their biggest contracts, where there were eight different food outlets and a bar and they'd no manager. They wondered if I'd go in and look at it. So I went in, it was a bit of a mess, I was the manager, it was losing, I think, about £90k a year which was a lot then. I got dug into that and completely commercialised it and, within about 18 months, I had it making about £200k, by opening new outlets, closing down outlets. At that point, I realised I was able to do the stuff, that I had the confidence in order to run a place. It was a unionised environment, but a nice place to work, in a nice part of Cork and it just needed sorting.

So I sort of turned that around and then got promoted to run the area of Cork, Kerry, Waterford for Campbell Catering. I ended up with 30 different contracts and I had a dual role of managing and selling, like winning new business and operations. I was 26 or 27 at that stage. Again, I made a good fist of that.

My wife Mary and I had been going out on a long-distance basis since my last year of college. She worked in the ESB and then Marks & Spencer's and she got a job in Cork in Marks & Spencer's for the opening of the Merchants Quay Shopping Centre, their first site in Cork. So Mary worked in Marks and I worked in Campbell Catering, and we lived out in Monkstown. We started in a flat in Montenotte, then lived in Monkstown and we had five or six really happy years there.

Then I got promoted to that regional job and next I was asked to move to Dublin to take on the director of sales role for Campbell Catering. I'll never forget moving to Dublin. Our first baby, Meghan, was born in Cork, and we moved to Dublin and I started a new job all in the same week. We had lived in a lovely, big, six-bedroom house overlooking the sea in Monkstown and we moved to a one-bedroom flat that an aunt of Mary's owned up in Dartmouth Square. I remember thinking: "What in God's name are we doing here?" It should have been such a happy time with the new baby but I remember thinking: "I've made a big mistake here." It was all because I had this ambition: if I saw an opportunity or saw I could enhance my reputation by way of taking on a challenge, I was kind of up for it.

*It was never really front and centre to me to do my own thing. I was more interested and consumed with the content of what I was doing and whether I was doing it well or not well.*

So we moved to Dublin and I did that job for about two years. I kind of enjoyed it. Campbell Catering had bought Bewley's back in 1986, around the time when I started with them in Cork. There was a bit of a reshuffle and I was asked to take on the role of managing director of Bewley's, which I did in about 1992 maybe. I did that until 1997 and again Bewley's was a different business in those days. We'd 50 shops. I ran the shops, the cafés, the bakery, the franchise company. Big business. I would have been young enough. I made a success of that. The business was profitable, growing, and I really enjoyed it. That's where I cut my teeth around property, dealing with management issues, growing a business, opening new shops. How to open a shop: how to fit it out, get it right, all about coffee. So I did that and was blissfully happy doing it, even though it was a very busy job and quite a demanding job.

I had a few share options in Bewley's but was never an equity partner. I sort of ran out of rope in the sense that I felt that I was getting to a point where I was becoming unfulfilled. Not that I was ever desperate to do something for myself. I wasn't actually. As long as I was happy in the role and working well and achieving something and the thing was going well, I was reasonably happy to keep doing that. But I felt things were starting to change.

I ended up being moved from the CEO role to a group function, which to me didn't have the autonomy of running all the cafés and the shops but was more a strategic type of position. I did a lot of work overseas. I looked after exports. I was involved in the development of the hotels, which was all good but a little bit left of centre. I did that for my last two years in Bewley's but at the same time I was looking at what was happening in the marketplace. I saw up close what was happening with the likes of Starbucks, Seattle Coffee Company, all that stuff, and I could also see that the footprint of the Bewley's 25,000 square foot café, with the rent doubling every five years and selling cups of coffee for less than two quid, wasn't going to work much longer.

❖    ❖    ❖

**My thinking then was I'd do something myself.** I actually decided I wanted to come up with something that was coffee because of all that was happening with coffee, the specialty coffee in particular. Bewley's was black or white coffee, that was it. So perhaps I could do something with coffee and also maybe take-out food. Almost no one walked down the street with a cup of coffee in their hand in the mid-1990s. It doesn't seem like that long ago but it was only starting to happen. My thinking was that I would open something such that half the business would be taken off the premises so that it would have a much smaller footprint with a lower rent.

It was never really front and centre to me to do my own thing. I was more interested and consumed with the content of what I was doing and whether I was doing it well or not well, whether it was for me or not. Maybe subliminally or in the background, it was there and it was always going to happen at some time, but I didn't go out on my own until I was 38 years of age, having had very much a corporate career. I'm 19 years in business this year, so there's been a whole other life since then. But I think I went into business on my own having learned, having made mistakes on someone else's watch – not that I didn't make any of my own.

When I decided to leave Bewley's, I'd a small few shares I managed to sell internally, which was quite difficult. I remortgaged my house and I actually went into business with Fitzers, an Irish family business that operates high-end restaurants. They had 50 per cent of my first entity, which was called Perk. I ended up buying them out after a couple of years. We were 50/50 partners and we opened our first shop on Grafton Street underneath Laura Ashley. I nearly went bust a couple of times; we were totally undercapitalised. I opened one then on Dawson Street and Baggot Street, all on a shoestring. And I mean a shoestring.

My father had said to me back when I left college, "There's no job for you here" [in his hotel] because he was of the view – and I'd be of the same view with my own kids – that you need to go and work outside the family business. Handing me a business when I was fresh out of DIT would have been the worst possible thing that could have ever happened and he was dead right. So I said: "Grand, I'm off so." But the downside of it was when I went off and did my own thing and got my own business going, he needed somebody to hand over to. Even though Suzanne, my eldest sister, went to Shannon, she had ended up working in a childcare business and was married in Limerick and wasn't interested. One brother was in the bank and another brother was an accountant and my other sister worked in the bank, so none of them were either qualified or interested. So I was the only one who have had any interest and it's funny what actually happened.

I think I'd five shops when my father got sick and he needed somebody. The hotel business in Kilkenny was very profitable. I was barely able to pay myself a wage – it was hand-to-mouth stuff with my five shops. So I ended up for seven years working in Kilkenny one day a week, going down on a Tuesday night, working there all day Wednesday and coming back up then. It's funny how you can do things: I worked totally differently in that business. I had a structure of good management with David O'Sullivan and people who worked with my father and I worked on a hands-off basis with them. They'd tell me what I needed to know when I came down. I worked with them on Wednesday and they knew I'd be back the next Wednesday. No customer saw me. I wasn't front and centre in the way my oul' fella would have been in the place.

Dad died in 2001 but we continued to develop it, added on more bedrooms, built it up very nicely. In 2007, I decided I had to do one or the other and I said to my mother: "I think it might be time to go." Talk about luck: we decided to sell the hotel and sold it within four weeks of the recession actually hitting. It was the last hotel to be sold pre-recession – we were steeped. All the brothers and sisters got paid off. There were 13 shareholders (some non-family) and everyone did nicely out of it. We were lucky.

I got Perk up to six units. I had it running in the black, but only just. Insomnia started at the same time as Perk. It was a competitor of mine and there was a third company, Bendini & Shaw, which was a sandwich company. Bendini & Shaw was bought by Insomnia, which gave them 13 shops in total. They then came to me and said they wanted to buy me, so I sold Perk to this conglomerate. Harry O'Kelly, who was the MD of Bendini & Shaw, said he didn't want to be the MD and asked me to do it, so I sold my business and then reinvested almost the same week. The money I got I had for about three days. I put it back into the business and became the MD of Insomnia with 17 rebranded units. John Clohisey of BWG Foods, which operates the Spar and Mace convenience store brands, also invested in the business at this time. Harry, John and I bought out the original investors in Insomnia and have had an equal three-way partnership for the last 15 or so years.

We now, as of 2017, have 150 shops, with 400 concession units in Spar and Mace – and that's taken us 19 years. It's been an amazing journey from great highs when 50 per cent of the business was bought out by an Icelandic company that gave us €8 million to huge lows when the Icelandic company went bust, and another high when we bought their shares back again. We've had recessions and booms but we've managed to run the business according to the marketplace. We've also managed to grow the business each and every year.

In the recession, I renegotiated with all the landlords. I went to visit them all personally and believe it or not, the landlords, with the exception of institutional landlords, which thankfully we only had one or two of, were actually very pragmatic in terms of reducing the rent or potentially getting no rent because that was what was facing them. We came up with a marketing campaign that involved 'bundling' products as a way to try and increase sales during the recession. We managed to market the proposition of the €3.50 coffee and muffin and the €5 sandwich, which we kept for nearly seven years, effectively reducing prices by 28 per cent if somebody bought two things. It was very successful but things were tough. We had to close a kitchen in Rathmines. We had to take vans off the road. It was painful, difficult and we weren't sure that we were going to come out the other side of it, but we did. That marketing campaign saved our bacon.

---

*I'm a big believer in partnerships, provided you've the right partners. They've always worked for me.*

---

We learned a lot from those days. We learned the value of customer loyalty. We learned you had to price your proposition according to the market. I'd have got involved during that period, I suppose, in driving the brand. My own association with Insomnia, and going on *Dragons' Den* and doing what I did there, helped give Insomnia a kind of a national recognition that it hadn't got up to that point. People thought we were an American franchise, they didn't know what we were. So driving the brand with my personality worked with where we were in the marketplace. The good thing about a recession is it really allows you to take excess fat out of a business because if you don't, you'll just go bust. Survival is the greatest driver. In other words, if you are looking death in the face or extinction in the eye, there is nothing like it to spur you on to doing the right thing.

❖    ❖    ❖

*Dragons' Den* **came about through a friend of my wife,** who worked in Bank of Ireland. They approached me and said they were doing this thing – they were the sponsors and they were looking for individuals. I don't know how I qualified, because on paper I wouldn't have had the financial means to be some angel investor, but we were growing the business, we were doing well and I was at the cutting edge, I suppose, of a business that wasn't really there 10 years previously. I had a bit of a way about me that they liked and they thought I was an interesting enough character. I was a complex enough individual and so I said, "No" first and then I thought about it and realised it could be really pivotal to moving my business and what I was doing to another place. And it was.

I was there for the first four years. I invested in nine things. I went through with them all. I lost money on loads of them. I broke even on a couple. I made small money on one or two. Overall, if you look at it in its purity of financial investment, in nine different propositions, I lost my shirt. But if you take where it brought me and put in context what it did for Insomnia, what it did for me personally in terms of my own profile, in terms of the stuff I've done since, even my introduction into radio came out of it.

I liked the idea of it being something different, something I hadn't done before, and I'm still enthused by stuff I haven't done before. I've often done stuff that I haven't done before. I sailed around Ireland. I've done *Strictly Come Dancing*. I've done lots of stuff. I am somebody that probably does get fatigue over a period with the mundane, the *status quo*, and I am up for doing something that pushes me out of my comfort zone – and I always have been. I felt that *Dragons' Den* would be a bit of craic. I also had enough money to go in there and speculate without borrowing a penny. It was money I had and I had a kinda relaxed enough attitude to it. And I enjoyed it.

I enjoyed working with the individuals, the buzz of the whole thing. But I got tired of it after four years. I felt the calibre of what was coming through wasn't as high. There was a lot of bullshitters coming in and I could see where I had spent my money, and again it was time to do something else. Was it good for me? Yes. Was it good for the brand Insomnia? Yes. Would I do it again? Absolutely.

There was a perception around the fact I was a dragon. I'd still be very friendly with people like Niall O'Farrell, a great friend and a great character. And I think it was great that we were all very different. There was certainly a chemistry in those early years, with Sarah Newman, Norah Casey, Niall O'Farrell, Sean Gallagher and Gavin

Duffy. All very different, but it kinda worked. Different people with different skill sets and attitudes. It was good. There was great banter, all sorts of highs and lows, take it for what it is. It was genuinely competitive but, at the end of the day, for the people making *Dragons' Den*, their first and foremost quest is to provide entertainment. So they don't give a toss if Bobby Kerr loses 50 grand, as long as it's funny or entertaining or somebody cries, so you have to go in with that sense of realism.

❖    ❖    ❖

**Interestingly enough, I knew I wanted out of *Dragons' Den* but** wondered if there was a platform that might be similar. There is always a time to get out, and I felt my timing of getting out of *Dragons' Den* was also on the money. I'd been there as one of the original contributors and I felt I'd been there long enough after four seasons to have made an impact on it. I felt it was time to go – and it was, I was right. As it turned out, I was right.

So I went and did a radio course with Terry Prone, which lasted about a week. She did a mock show with me and I said I'd give radio a go. So I persuaded the MD of national radio station Newstalk, Frank Cronin, who is a great character, to give me a whirl at 9am on a Sunday morning when no one was listening anyway. When I think back, I was absolutely appalling, I know I was, and I found it really difficult to make the transition.

*Dragons' Den* was prerecorded, a highly edited piece of TV, and this was a move to live radio. I didn't realise the difference; there's little or nothing in common between the two. So anything I'd learned on *Dragons' Den* was pretty much irrelevant. Anyway, I approached it like I approach anything else. I knew I was shite, but I really got dug into it. I reckoned the key was to get good guests. I did all sorts of things to get people in to talk to me at 9am on a Sunday morning. In 2010, there were about 22,000 listeners at that time of the morning. I managed over the years to slowly build up my radio show *Down to Business*, to give it a bit of personality and to appeal to the ordinary bloke in business.

Then it was moved to Saturday and extended to two hours because an hour was never enough to do all the stuff I wanted to do. There's a listenership of over 100,000 now. It's highly sponsored, so it always paid its way. Commercially, as a proposition, it's always worked. Even if you are shocking, some fella would have known you because they'd have seen you on *Dragons' Den* so you are low-risk in some sense – people maybe are more forgiving because they'd have seen you somewhere else.

But also, 9am on a Sunday morning, back then, was a graveyard shift, so for the station, they didn't need to worry, it was low-risk. Unless you completely screwed it up, no one was going to notice. I'd have thought I was shocking, but Frank Cronin believed in me. Where there might be a talent deficiency, I'd certainly do my best to override it with brute force and slog it out. I would never be found wanting in terms of putting the effort in to try to make it sound as good as it could be and I've still got that attitude today.

So it's been great. One thing I like about my life and my business is that it is all so varied. I'm long enough around to know that probably a broadcasting career is not going to pay the bills the way it should, but I've been very fortunate that I've been able to develop my own business with my two partners, Harry O'Kelly and John Clohisey. Again, I'm a big believer in partnerships – they've always worked for me – provided you've the right partners and we've been a threesome for 15-odd years.

Again, I found lots of things very difficult over the years in business. I found it very difficult to stop going to every shop every day. To not know every employee in each shop that I had, to not know all the customers the way I had in the early days. I found that very difficult but I knew that if I didn't make the transition, the business was never going to grow beyond three or four shops. I was clued in enough to see that thankfully. My father had great vision but he never wanted to run 10 or 15 hotels. But he wanted to keep developing the hotel that he had. He was great: every time there was a few spare quid, he came up with something else or he built something else, or he built more rooms. I had a vision when I started my coffee shops first that I might get to 25 shops. Never in my wildest dreams did I think we'd have Insomnia in nearly

500 locations. So it's funny, stuff can happen beyond your wildest dreams.

❖    ❖    ❖

**I've always been a liver of life.** I've four lovely daughters, Meghan, Emily, Rebecca and Michaela. I'm blissfully married to Mary for 29 years and whatever about my passion for my work, my passion for my family is absolutely foremost. I live for the girls.

---

*The reality of getting sick for me was that there are only three things in life that matter: your family, your friends and your health.*

---

Meghan is gone to Canada and Emily is gone to New York and I find that very difficult. I still do. I was used to having them around over the years and the two of them left the same week. Half the girls went and the house changed overnight in terms of the dynamic. So I do miss them terribly but I see Emily working out there for a great restaurateur, working as a photographer part-time, and Meghan working in a marketing department in a bank. They are learning stuff, they are out there, seeing the world. They need to do it and I need to let them do it. So unfortunately, that's the way. Hopefully, we'll be able to get out and see them and get them home the odd time. You just hope they'll come back!

Strangely enough, the younger two, Rebecca and Michaela, are both studying retail and business in DIT. I hope retail remains around long enough to give them both a career and that everything doesn't go online. In my view, retail will change but there will always be retail.

❖    ❖    ❖

**So in 2015, everything is going well with the business.** Newstalk is going well. Bang, a restaurant I co-own with Joe and Anne Barrett, is also going well. All the public speaking, lots of different things all going well. I was down in Kilkee in August when I felt a small swollen gland in my neck. I said I'd a bit of a sore throat and my third daughter, Rebecca, said I'd better get it checked. I was kinda: "Yeah, yeah, yeah ..." She actually rang the family doctor and booked an appointment for me to go to see him. I probably wouldn't have gone otherwise.

I went to him and he does the usual: "Yeah, it looks fine but we'll get a biopsy on it." I go into Vincent's to get the biopsy done and I got the call from the guy to say: "You need to come in and see me." I remember going in, although deep down knowing there was something up here, still being flummoxed when he said: "You've got cancer." I'd head and neck cancer. I didn't know what it was. I didn't know and this is the difficulty of those early days, when some guy says that to you, you don't know if you are going to live or die. You just don't know and, in those first three or four weeks, I found that bit of not knowing how sick I actually was really difficult.

Then I went to James's and was sitting waiting to get a CAT scan when this guy comes in to the waiting room with a can of Dutch Gold and says, "Howya, you're the guy on *Dragons' Den*" and I said, "Ah no". I'm feeling like shit and I just wanted to go away and die. I just didn't want to talk to anybody. I said to the guy in James's: "If I'm going to be sick, I don't want to be sitting in waiting rooms talking to people about *Dragons' Den*." So he said I could go to St Luke's, it's much quieter and they could give me a programme up there. I did seven weeks of chemotherapy and radiotherapy in Luke's but got pretty sick in December and was hospitalised for four weeks. I got out two days before Christmas, feeling like absolute death. I lost, over the process, about four stone and I felt like shit. I didn't eat for something like three months.

But gradually, with the support of Mary and the girls, my own brothers and sisters, my mother, the guys in Insomnia keeping the business going, I got myself into a better place. I was able to go away and get better and I was hugely grateful to the people around me to allow me to do that.

So I thought then I'd go back to work on January 15th, 2016. I'd been off air, as the doctors wouldn't let me broadcast for 10 weeks. All the lads at Newstalk filled in and kept the show on the road. The night before I'm due to go back on air with *Down to Business*, I went on *The Late Late Show* and told the story as it is.

I got a massive reaction. Talk about a good news story for the HSE! I felt I was well looked after, not quite better, but I thought I was on the mend and I was able to try to make something good out of something bad. The reality of getting sick for me was that there are only three things in life that matter: your family, your friends and your health. And you almost have to take one of those away before you realise how interdependent the three are.

I look at it now and think: "If Insomnia goes in the morning, if I have my family, friends and my health, I can go again. I don't owe anybody any money – so." Sometimes we complicate life hugely. We make things really, really complex. We fall out with people. We bring all this hassle and stress into our life, but if you distil it back to those three things …

❖    ❖    ❖

**I've always been a liver of life,** somebody who has fun along the way. I've never regretted anything I've done, be it corporately or family-wise. I'm blissfully happy in the 56 years I've put in so far, but being sick has given me a realisation that there is still another life to be lived – and I intend living it. There are still lots of things I have to do. At one level, I want to calm things down. I want to spend time travelling, see my kids, stay involved in business even though I don't need to be front and central to every business decision and I'm happy to work with others, so I want to stay in business.

But I also want to develop my broadcasting career. I've started a new show on Sundays now and, even though people say, "What are you doing working seven days a week?", I'm trying to take time off now on a Monday, when I work Sunday. Even though I'm up early, I'm home by 12 o'clock on Sunday. I don't miss that much. The kids are only getting out of bed at 11, so I don't feel like it's even work.

The diversity of what I do, in all the different places that I get to do it, really keeps me energised. I don't do the same two things in any one day. I suppose I do in terms of Newstalk, but every week we've different guests, different content, something different and new. It keeps me close to business in a way that I really, really enjoy. I'm right on the pulse of what's happening and I get to speak to the most amazing people. I'm naturally kind of curious, and while I don't consider myself a terribly eloquent broadcaster, I do have a genuine curiosity about what it is somebody does, why they do it and what it has resulted in and I go along in my own crude way, doing that. I'm enthusiastic about stuff. I'm never going to lose my enthusiasm for business, for people, for life. And hopefully that'll stay with me, so the radio is a great channel for me to rebottle that enthusiasm and try and keep close to things I'm really interested in. I don't want to work in broadcasting on a full-time basis but it is a very enjoyable and important part of my working week.

I did *Along Home Shores* last year, which was a maritime television documentary that brought me around the coast and inland waterways of Ireland. The sea I absolutely love, I'm a competitive sailor. That was massively special for me. To do something that touched all parts of my life – the sea, business, people and again the wonderful maritime geography of Ireland that I enjoy. To be places by the water that I hadn't been before. I want to do more of that. So I love radio, but don't want to be working for 'The Man' 9 to 5, five days a week. The way I'm pitched at the moment, two shows a week, two two-hour shows, is probably as much as I can handle, given all the other stuff I have on.

I've always been active, even though I was totally overweight for years. Before I got sick, I was over 17 stone. I think I might have been almost 18 stone at one stage. But believe it or not, I've always been active. I had been going to the gym. I'd been doing some running, even though I was carrying far too much weight – but I hated running. I hated running before I got sick, but running then, when I reapproached it, having lost four stone, became a totally different experience to me. Now running is part of what I do and what I am and I don't even consider it a sport. It is something that is almost part of my work, because I find it very good for my mind.

*I remain optimistic, energised, happy and fulfilled. I will continue – as always – to have one eye on the next big adventure.*

I've always been an early riser. I'd be up at 5.30 every morning and I just love the peace and solitude of being out there, running along Dún Laoghaire pier, seeing the same very few people at that hour of the morning, getting my head straight, listening to music. The sailing is a different thing. That's a sport, a team thing I do with lads that I've been sailing with for years. The running is a solitary thing and I'm not a very solitary person. I'm somebody who likes to be around people and enjoys other people's company, but I find the running to be instrumental in getting me better. I can't say that with any medical sincerity but I definitely think it has helped get me through the very difficult health period that I had. I'm going to continue to do it. I think you need to keep driving on, and I'm sorta thinking whether I'll do a marathon. But if I get out for an hour three times a week and I enjoy doing what I'm doing, why do I need to be doing a marathon? I don't think I need to. I've run in different cities, 10km of a place, and it is a great way to see a city. All you need is a pair of runners. I feel bad myself if I don't do my three runs a week. I feel I've let myself down. I don't like letting myself down.

❖   ❖   ❖

**For the future, I think we can bring Insomnia to a whole other level.** We are 'internationalising it', there are big opportunities in the UK, Germany and the United States. I want to be part of that as well, because I've been central to the development of our brand for so many years. Even though I may not be the day-to-day driver any more, I'm still very clued in and very much part of what it is we do and where we go – so there's unfinished business there.

Yes, the broadcasting. I think between *Down to Business* and *Bobby's Late Breakfast*, we can really push the boat out and be something people want to tune into over the weekend. People who have an interest in business, but there is more to life than business. That's why I'm interested in culture and food and all those things that we are trying to do on Sundays now – another challenge. So a lot of unfinished business there too.

I probably want to invest in some other businesses, because I think you've got to stay close to businesses, and one of the ways to stay close is having some skin in the game. I wouldn't say I'm not absolutely driven by money. But while money can be a contributor to overall happiness, it's only one small component. I don't need a lot to live on. I'm driven to a point where I am happy and comfortable and can provide for my family. As they say: "You can only eat one breakfast." I'm not the type of person who wants to keep rolling the dice. So I've become a bit more risk-averse as I approach my late 50s. I don't intend frittering it away at this late stage but I don't want to leave a big inheritance for my children – it's been hard enough won and it's my intention to spend most of what I can accumulate.

The work environment has changed. I think you do different things in different ways, but I don't ever see myself not being busy. I think we are all working differently now. I think there is probably more of a fusion between work and home life. I can be on my computer at 10 o'clock on a Friday night just as easily as I can be seen walking on Dún Laoghaire pier at 11 o'clock on a Tuesday morning. I think that it's a 24/7 world and, for me, it is a bit less structured. I still do the work when it needs to be done, but I see retirement as being a different type of work being done in a different way.

I remain optimistic, energised, happy and fulfilled. I will continue – as always – to have one eye on the next big adventure.

# PAUL KIMMAGE

"I'm afraid."

*Paul Kimmage was born in Dublin in 1962. A talented cyclist, he was a double National Road Race Champion and represented Ireland at the Los Angeles Olympics in 1984. A year later, he finished sixth in the World Road Race Championships in Italy and, in 1986, he turned professional and completed his first Tour de France.*

*In 1990, after four years as a professional, he became a journalist. A former Sportswriter of the Year in Ireland, he was shortlisted five times for Sportswriter of the Year in Britain and is a five- time winner of the Sports Interviewer of the Year award at the British Sports Journalists' Association Awards.*

*He has written for the **Sunday Tribune, Sunday Independent, Sunday Times, Observer** and **Daily Mail**. He has also presented a sports magazine programme for Setanta TV and was an analyst for Al Jazeera TV during the 2012 London Olympics.*

*His first book, **Rough Ride**, is widely acknowledged to be the most honest account of life in the professional cycling ranks and won the William Hill Sports Book of the Year award in 1990. In 2000, he was shortlisted for the same award for **Full Time: The Secret Life of Tony Cascarino**. In 2011, his fourth book, **Engage: The Fall and Rise of Matt Hampson**, was the British Sports Book of the Year and the William Hill Irish Sports Book of the Year.*

**Who am I? It depends who you ask.** I heard Gavin Duffy describe me on radio once as a "man who would darken any room", which was interesting as I've never met Gavin or shared a room with him. And if I had a pound for every time I've been described as 'bitter' or a 'failed cyclist', I'd be a very wealthy man.

Who you think you are and how you are perceived by other people is often very different. Two years ago, a lawyer who was helping me defend a libel action in Switzerland, said: "You are a really complex person." I said: "No, no, no, I'm simple. Black and white." But when I started thinking about it, I *am* a complex person. I think it's important to listen to what others say and to learn. And what I've learned in my 55th year is that I haven't quite figured who I am; I'm still working on it, still finding out. It's funny but the first word that came into my head when you asked the question, was 'afraid'. I am afraid. Yeah, I'm afraid. But don't ask me to explain that.

❖   ❖   ❖

**I am the eldest son of Christy and Angela Kimmage.** I'm one of four boys: Raphael is two years younger, Kevin is five years younger and Christopher is 11 years younger. My Dad was from Cabra and my Mum was from Kimmage. They met through cycling. My Dad had left school at about 15, my Mum at 14 – no education really. They lived in a one-room flat, opposite the Mater Hospital on Eccles Street, which they shared with about four other families, with one toilet on the second floor. I've gone back there. It is unbelievable. It's now a doctor's practice and the secretary's reception is where we used to live.

Mum went straight from school into a sewing factory. Dad got a job welding in the Volkswagen factory on the Naas Road. Then he got a chance to work on outdoor advertising signs for Carrolls cigarettes: maintain them, clean them, fix the lights. Dad didn't have a clue about electrics or anything like that but he brought a sign home, took it apart on the bed with my mother's help and they tried to figure it out: "Okay, well this does this and this does that." So that's the essence of them really and the essence of me I suppose: "This is a chance for us now. Let's try to figure this out." They did not lie down.

My first childhood memory is of my father racing. Dad was a great cyclist, a really great cyclist, and I grew up watching him and listening to people talking about him. For most of my life, I have always thought I followed his footsteps because I loved cycling and wanted to be a winner like him, but it wasn't that at all. It had nothing to do with that. I was on *The Marian Finucane Show* about five years ago when the penny dropped. We were talking about Dad and my career as a racer and it suddenly dawned that I had been driven not by a love for the sport, or for winning, but by affection. My father's affection. I craved my father's affection. Everything I had ever achieved on a bike was driven by the fact that I wanted him to be as proud of me as I was of him. And I'm 50 years of age when this suddenly drops on me. I'd never considered it before, but that is the absolute truth.

The key to it all was my brother, Raphael, one of the most gifted young talents the country had ever seen. I would go to bed and my parents would start talking downstairs about the race that day and how good Raphael had been. And I'm listening to this – my father glowing about Raphael – and I'm festering: "Was I not good? What about me?" That's where it came from, the drive that shaped my racing career. And I only realised this as I'm talking to Marian, which is quite shocking really ... well, not shocking, but a real "Oh! Wow!" moment. So when you ask who I am, that's what I mean when I say I am still finding out.

Here's another example that I should probably keep to myself, but it comes back to: "You're a complex man." We have lived in north County Dublin, where my wife Ann grew up, since my cycling career ended in 1990. Our daughter, Evelyn, was born in August that year and we have two fine sons, Eoin and Luke. My parents moved out a few years later and built a small bungalow on the plot of land beside us. It was great having them so close and they were happy and content in retirement until my father passed away suddenly two years ago. The loss was crushing, particularly for my mother, and I've really struggled trying to help her to fill the hole.

Anyway, I'm going away for a week and get on to the boys about cutting her grass – she has a huge garden – but they protest that they've got plans of their own and I absolutely rip them: "I don't give a fuck! Make sure you get it cut." Ann is fuming. We go to bed and she rips me for what I've said to the boys and we have this massive row – the worst in 30 years of married life. There's no issue here as far as I'm concerned – the boys should shelve their plans – and I'm lying there, fuming, for about four or five hours before I realise I'm wrong and admit I've made a mistake. I apologise and the wound is healed but afterwards I think: "How could you have been so stupid? How could you get that so wrong?" So again, a 'work in progress' is the phrase.

---

*Brother Breheny gave me an orange one day*
*for a story I had written in English class.*
*It felt like a million dollars.*

---

I think a lot of people don't look at themselves – or have the ability to look at themselves – and hold themselves to account: "Did I get this wrong?" That has always been important to me but I think it comes later rather than sooner. Things are much simpler when you are younger. When I was a pro-bike rider at 25 or 26, I had no idea how long I'd be retired. It's astonishing, all you can see is the next tour, the next race, and you live with a sense that it will always be like this. It's later, much later, that you realise: "My life hasn't even started yet."

We lived on Eccles Street until I was five years old. I often have flashbacks: a little park in Phibsborough we used to go to; the Garden of Remembrance; getting a bun and milk as part of your lunch at school, little things like that. I've a vivid memory of being brought into Temple Street hospital with a nose bleed and having to get that cauterised – it was my first night in hospital. I still remember that very well. And I remember being afraid. There was a woman, I don't know if she was sleeping rough or if that happened then, but I was terrified of her. And my mother tells a story of waking up one night with a guard banging on the door, looking for a prostitute who used to live there.

We moved to Ballymun in 1967. It was a beautiful flat with underground heating on the eighth floor – the top of the building – but we were only in the door when my father said: "No. We are not staying here." Each flat had a balcony and he nearly freaked one day when he caught Raphael climbing on it. And one time he had to carry a washing machine up eight flights of stairs on his back because the lifts were broken again. But I liked it. There was a H Williams supermarket across the road and they used to throw all the vegetables out the back and burn them, and we'd be there picking up burned carrots and eating them and thinking: "That's gorgeous!" But Dad wasn't for changing and, after a year in Ballymun, we moved down the road to Coolock.

Our new house, a three-bedroom semi on Kilmore Avenue, must have felt like a palace to my parents but as kids, home was home. Our new school was St David's primary school on Ardilea Road. It was a Christian Brothers school, in the bad old days of corporal punishment and we were ... no, not battered – battered is too strong – but there was a threat of being beaten there with a stick or a 'leather' and I was often afraid. We hear all sorts of horror stories about how cruel these brothers were – and there were some right sadistic bastards – but there were some good people too. I remember Brother Breheny gave me an orange one day for a story I had written in English class. It felt like a million dollars.

I would have been 10 maybe when it was noticed I had a talent for writing. Michael O'Braonain – one of my closest friends now – was the first to pick up on it in fifth and sixth class and was a big influence. Michael says he always knew writing was my talent. I didn't see it. I left him in sixth class and went up the road to St David's secondary school and it was almost like I shut down. I did not enjoy secondary school. A couple of the teachers were fucking animals and my only goal was to survive. It was an all-boys school and there was a lot of bullying and fighting. There was one kid in our class who was bullied terribly and picked on all the time. I'd love to be able to say I stood up for him but I was afraid: "Fuck that! It ain't happening to me."

I got two honours in my Leaving Certificate – a B in history and a C in Biology – and haven't stopped hearing about it from Ann and the kids. I am, by some distance, the least educated person in our house! So I left school with these two honours not knowing what I wanted to do other than to be a professional cyclist. Obviously my mother wasn't having that: "You're going to get a qualification before you do anything else." A friend of my dad, Reggie Kearns, was an electrician in Dublin Airport. There were some apprenticeships going in the plumbing department there and Reggie got me an interview. I sit down with Jimmy Kiernan, the plumbing supervisor. "What do you know about plumbing?" he asks. "Nothing," I reply. And maybe he was impressed that I hadn't tried to spoof him because he offered me the apprenticeship.

So I spent four happy years in the maintenance department at Dublin Airport and qualified as a plumber in 1983. There wasn't an option to stay – they trained you and sent you out – but I was one of the best amateur cyclists in the country at that point and was keen to pursue my dream.

❖　❖　❖

**The first step was a trial with ACBB** – Athletic Club de Boulogne-Billancourt – one of the top French amateur teams. I left for Paris with Raphael, who had just qualified as a diesel mechanic, in January 1984. We went straight to a training camp on the Côte d'Azur and were surrounded at the dinner table each evening by 18 French men. It was a ruthless business – we were all chasing the same goal – and I'm not sure I'd have got through it without my brother's company. After a slow start, I began to find some form and was selected to travel to Los Angeles for the Olympic Games in July.

It was a big deal back then to be an Olympian. It wasn't what it should have been, because my goal wasn't the Olympics – it was to ride the Tour de France – but it was still a significant milestone. We didn't walk in the opening parade. We had the road race next day and the team time trial four days later and had to leave a couple of days after that to get home for the National Championships. And a week later, as John Treacy was racing to the silver medal in the marathon, I was racing to the National Road Race title in Carrick-on-Suir. Because again the focus wasn't on being an Olympian and having a good time, it was on getting to the Tour de France and being as good as you could be.

This will tell you how dedicated we were. When we were teenagers, living in Coolock, we were in bed every night at half-nine. We trained after school and raced at weekends and there was no time for discos or chasing girls. And it wasn't a sacrifice. We were getting so much joy from what we were doing – going off for weekends, making friends, talking about racing and telling stories – it was just brilliant. And it gave us great discipline.

In 1985, after a year of being treated badly in Paris, we left ACBB and joined another club near Lille, the CC Wasquehal. The people were much nicer up north and, after a string of good wins and a sixth place finish at the World Championships in Italy, I was offered a professional contract for 1986.

The Tour de France started in Paris that year in the suburb of Boulogne-Billancourt and it felt good to come back and give two fingers to the club that had rejected me. But I was also nervous. The race started with an 8km time trial, and I remember sitting in the start gate and gazing down at the crowd and almost falling as I kicked down the ramp. Nothing prepares you for the madness of it.

We started that year on a Friday afternoon, then there was a split stage: an 85km road stage around the streets of Paris on Saturday morning, followed by a 56km team time trial in the afternoon. By Sunday morning, I'm already the worse for wear, and it's absolutely hammering down. We have a 214km stage to Liévin on the menu and an old tour rider, standing under an umbrella at the start, smiled and said: "Well, Paul, only four more Sundays to go." And I thought it sounded absurd but he was absolutely right: we had four more Sundays to race before we'd see Paris again. It was brutal, just brutal. Then you reach that final stage – 255km from Cosne-sur-Loire to Paris – and that first glimpse of the Eiffel Tower and the enormity of what you've done hits you for the first time: "Wow! I'm going to do it. I'm going to finish the Tour de France!" And it's the greatest thrill of your life.

I've seen footage of an interview I gave to Channel 4 straight after it – and this goes back to the 'Who are you?' question – and it was actually quite shocking for me to watch. I'm standing there talking to Phil Liggett and my face is just a portrait of joy. I was so, so happy. And I remember seeing this and thinking: "What the fuck happened to me? What happened to the sport?" It was really sad.

❖    ❖    ❖

I raced in three Tours – 1986, 1987 and 1989 – and in the 1989 Giro d'Italia. But my 'sliding doors' moment, the day that changed my life, happened two years before I left for France in 1982. It was a Sunday afternoon in June. I'd spent the week racing in the Isle of Man and had gone to the Phoenix Park to watch the finish of the 'Rás' – or Rás Tailteann, as it was formally known. I'd had an okay week in the Isle of Man, but not great, which is probably why I'm thinking about a girl. She's the sister of one of the guys riding in the Rás and I know that, if I go to the park, there's a chance she'll be there. The race finishes. I spot her in the crowd, go across and start chatting. Ann Nolan has spent the week on the race, taking notes for a journalist from the *Irish Press*. "He's here," she says, "I'll introduce you." And the moment I meet my wife is the moment I meet David Walsh.

---

*We were getting so much joy from what we were doing – going off for weekends, making friends, talking about racing and telling stories – it was just brilliant. And it gave us great discipline.*

---

Four years later, we've become really good friends when I ride my first Tour de France. David is covering the race for the *Sunday Tribune* and has a feature to write for *Magill* and decides he would like to interview me on the rest day. He seems enthused when it's over and does something unusual – well, it was unusual at the time. He decides to write the interview as a first-person piece: By Paul Kimmage. So David has done the work, but I'm getting the credit. Soon he is planting a seed in my head. "I think you could do this," he says.

In 1988, when I didn't make the Tour de France team, he had a proposal to soften the blow: "Why don't you write a piece about what it's like watching the Tour from the sideline?" So I wrote three pieces about the race for the *Sunday Tribune* and the reaction was positive.

Then, at the start of the following season, he suggested a weekly diary on life as a professional cyclist. So I start these diaries for the *Sunday Tribune* and Gay Byrne is flagging them on the radio and five months later there was an offer from Vincent Browne: "There's a job here for you as a sportswriter whenever you decide to finish."

The month was June 1989. I had just finished the Giro d'Italia and had a short break before the Tour de France. I spoke to Ann about it – we were two years married at that stage – and decided I was going to accept Vincent's offer and retire at the end of the season. I started my final tour three weeks later and was going okay until Stephen Roche – my friend and the team leader – abandoned in the Pyrenees. Once he was gone, I thought: "What am I doing here really?" And two days later, during the 13th stage from Toulouse to Montpellier, I got off the bike and decided that was it. I knew the moment I stopped that I was not going to race again. There was an option to keep racing until the end of the year but, in my heart, I was done. In hindsight, I probably should have finished the tour and raced in the World Championships but this door had suddenly opened – an opportunity to be a sportswriter – and I was ready to move on. So I spent the next six months writing a book, *Rough Ride,* and started with the *Sunday Tribune* in January 1990.

The first months were interesting. I had won Sportswriter of the Year and got so much praise for my racing diaries that I thought I'd fucking invented writing! I really did. I had been parachuted over guys – really intelligent people who had gone to college and studied journalism for years – and I had no idea why they might have been pissed that a plumber had been given this job. It took me six years to become a journalist and I'm still learning today, but at the time I thought: "This is easy." And then the reality started to bite.

Some days, Vincent would call me into the office after taking a red biro to the piece I had written on Sunday: "What the fuck is this?" Then he would shred it and give me an absolute coursing. It was brilliant training. There were guys who didn't like it and couldn't handle him but I loved him. He was brilliant. Unique. Who else would have given me the opportunity? And it wasn't just me; there were some other guys in there who hadn't gone to university either. It was almost a thing with him: "No, that's not where journalists are made." But if he saw something in you, he was prepared to give you a chance.

He was great. He *is* great. I've huge admiration for him. I've a photo of him over the door of my study at home – 'Abandon all hope ye who enter here' – but haven't spoken to him for a long time. I've followed what he's done with *Magill* and *Village* and the TV show and keep thinking: "Jaysus! Why does he never call me? Why has he never asked me on? Maybe he no longer rates me!" It's a bit like the affection I once craved from my father: if only Vincent loved me. That's probably the highest compliment I can pay him.

After four years at the *Sunday Tribune,* I joined the *Sunday Independent* in 1994. There were some real heavyweights there at the time – Eamon Dunphy, David Walsh, Gene Kerrigan, Tom Humphries – writing some really brilliant stuff and it started a period when I had a real crisis of confidence. I wanted to be like them and write like them and might have sunk without the support of the sports editor, Adhamhnan O'Sullivan, who encouraged me to be myself. But again: who am I?

❖   ❖   ❖

**There's a perception that I'm this fearless crusader** who has never taken a backward step in the pursuit of truth, which is extremely flattering but not how I see it. It started with *Rough Ride* in 1990, the book I had written to highlight a cancer of doping that was eating away at the sport. It was an uncomfortable truth to tell but I was doing the right thing and felt sure that, when the book was published, people would applaud. But that's not how the world works. The sport turned its back on me. I was dismissed as an embittered loser by friends I had raced with and a public who didn't want to know. The injustice almost drove me insane. "What the fuck!" I thought. "You are fucking kidding me."

Six years later, just as I'd started to calm down, it happened again. Michelle Smyth had just won three gold medals at the Atlanta Olympic Games and there was a lot of disquiet in swimming about how it had been achieved. When I addressed some of the questions being raised, the reaction was the same as *Rough Ride*. The backlash was horrendous. The public just did not want to know. And that changes you. It changed me. I thought: "Fuck this! I don't care what it takes. I am never going to stop dumping the truth on your parade."

It was the same thing with Lance Armstrong. Another fairytale. The same besotted fans. "No, no, no, no, no. I am not having this!" But if there wasn't that backlash against *Rough Ride* and there wasn't that backlash against Atlanta, I would not have become this person. It takes an acorn to make an oak tree and those were the seeds that changed me.

---

*I'm really proud that, when the pressure came on, I was true to my profession and to myself.*

---

I was also lucky. What if I had made the transition to sportswriter and not written *Rough Ride*? What if I just moved on and conveniently ignored the doping problem in cycling? What kind of a hypocrite would that have made me later when it arose in other sports? I'd have been screwed. The point I'm trying to make – and the reason I was lucky – is that there was no forethought about what was coming down the road. I had absolutely no idea. But what if I hadn't done it? What would my reputation be then?

Another story, same theme. In January 2012, I lost my job at the *Sunday Times* after 10 years in London. They called it 'redundancy'; I called it 'the sack' because I had won more awards than any other writer in the section but I was the one being cut. The injustice was poison. I remember standing on the platform of the train station one morning after they had put me on notice, thinking: "If I step out in front of the next express, those fuckers will have to pay Ann what I am due for the rest of her life!" The hardest part was that I did not see it coming. One moment I was this great journalist, one of the best sportswriters in Britain, and the next I was signing on at the local unemployment office. And for the seven months that followed, I did not have a single commission.

Then Bradley Wiggins won the Tour de France – the first Briton ever to win it – and I got a call from the *Daily Mail*. I said: "Listen, I'll write a piece. It may not be what your readers want to read, but I'll write a piece." They said: "Yes, just tell us what you think." So I wrote a piece that raised reservations I had about Wiggins. The *Daily Mail* pays well. I hadn't worked for seven months and I was getting about two grand for this piece, which wasn't bad when I hadn't earned for seven months.

So I write it and send it in and get a call an hour later from the sports editor, Les Snowden. "We can't run this. You're saying he's doping," he says. "I'm not, Les," I reply. "I'm saying there are some valid questions being asked. Read it again." Ann is listening as I take the call. She's upset; this is not what she wants to hear. I step outside to take some air and I'm thinking: "You fucking idiot! What the fuck is wrong with you? Why didn't you just write a 'glory glory Rule Britannia' piece and earn a few quid?" But I couldn't do it. I couldn't do it. The phone rings. It's Les. "No, you're right, Paul," he says. "It will probably cause a shit-storm but we're going with it. It's good." There have been a lot of questions about Wiggins since but I'm really proud that, when the pressure came on that day, I was true to my profession and to myself.

A year later, in August 2013, I returned to work at the *Sunday Independent*. It had been a rough 20 months. I remember, shortly after I was laid off, Luke got very upset one night. It was brutal, like a dagger in the heart. I walked over and gave him a hug: "Don't worry, son. Everything will be okay." It was a moment that really fortified me. I thought: "I will not let this kid down." It's been said that what doesn't kill you makes you stronger – and I get that now. I think I'm definitely a better person.

❖   ❖   ❖

**People automatically assume there is loads you want to do** but writing is torture for me. I've been doing it for 27 years and it has not got easier with time. I've been asking myself for years: "Can I keep doing this?" But oddly, in the last couple of months, I've thought, "I can, and I will" – and more importantly – "I want to".

I'm looking at a couple of projects at the moment that could be fulfilling. I've no idea where they will end but I'm determined to enjoy the ride. I still enjoy being a sportswriter. It has always been about people for me. I enjoy people. I am curious about people.

"Who are you?" It's a great question.

# MAEBH LEAHY

"I'm me, I'm Maebh."

*Maebh Leahy has been chief executive of the Rutland Centre since October 2015 and is responsible for all aspects of the organisation, from strategic planning to daily operations.*

*For six years prior to this, Maebh was chief executive of the Aer Lingus Social and Athletic Association (ALSAA), a large sport, fitness and hospitality business based at Dublin Airport and catering for over 5,000 members. Maebh joined ALSAA from the Westgrove Hotel in Clane, Co Kildare, where she worked her way up from assistant leisure club manager to deputy general manager of the hotel. In her early career, Maebh held management positions in the Dunshaughlin Community Centre and the Leixlip Amenities Centre.*

*Maebh has a bachelor's degree from Waterford Institute of Technology (2000) and an MBA from DCU (2012). Maebh also holds a diploma in addiction studies (2016).*

**I'm me, I'm Maebh.** I'm the same person here as I am at home, as I am with my family, with my friends. I currently work at being chief executive of the Rutland Centre. I don't think that defines me, but I don't think any job ever has. I think I've always been me, going through my different career changes and moves. I am a daughter and a wife. I'm a sister and a friend. That's how I see myself, how I would have seen myself.

I had a great childhood. I know that I'm very lucky to say that. Particularly in the line of work I'm in now, I know that anyone who can say they had a great childhood is blessed. I grew up in Leixlip, in a semi-d. My Dad worked in Revenue all his life. My Mum stayed at home after she got married. I've two older sisters, a younger sister and a younger brother. I'm in the middle, so it's always a good joke at home: the middle child. We were always very close growing up. We were very sporty. Dad was from Tipperary, a big GAA fan, so we were big GAA supporters as a result and travelled the length and breadth of the country supporting the Tipperary hurlers. My poor Mam is from Dublin and I think she felt a little sidelined that we were not all Dublin supporters.

It was a very normal childhood, very balanced. My Mam and Dad worked hard to make sure that we had everything we needed. They worked hard also to make sure that we were balanced and that we were not spoilt. But we knew that we could do anything that we wanted to do and they'd support us in it. They certainly never ever put pressure on us to be a certain person or try and make sure we went down a certain career path. They were always really supportive of our individual choices and passions and what we wanted to do. My Mam and Dad were brilliant.

My grandparents lived quite close to us and they only passed away in the last few years. I could see the same relationship going back through the generations, and my grandparents would always have been the same, really supportive, really loving, whatever we wanted to do, once we worked hard and were genuine about it. The work would have to come from us, nobody would do it for you.

Whether it was Junior Cert, Leaving Cert or college exams, you had to take responsibility for what you were doing. All through school, certainly secondary school – there would have been no pressure in primary school – we definitely would have been well-behaved. Well, most of us, not all of us – and not all the time, I might add. But they definitely kept a tight unit in terms of keeping us all together and making sure we were all in school and finished school. But once we got to a point where we were approaching being adults, I think the responsibility was very much on us to know what we wanted to do and it was up to us to work hard to get it. That is still something that I would live by and I'd like to think I'll pass down to my own children some day: a strong work ethic and personal responsibility.

In childhood, at the time, I don't remember any defining moment or trigger, but in hindsight, looking back and seeing how hard Mam and Dad worked, and how hard my aunties and uncles all worked, across both wider families, on both sides, I think that defined the direction that we all took. And even if I look at cousins and siblings, everyone is in employment, everyone is part of a strong family unit and I think that has certainly shaped our wider family and definitely has shaped me.

I think seeing my Dad work really hard up through the ranks in Revenue, that has been a big influence on me. It lit a spark in me: if you work hard, you would progress. And it was something they were particularly proud of wherever it happened but it wouldn't be something that was shouted from the rooftops. I always got a feeling that there was a sense of accomplishment there but it was intrinsic: it didn't need to be shouted from the rooftops.

When I was a teenager, I just thought my older sister Niamh was the bee's knees. She paved the way for the rest of us: she did all the hard work going to discos, having boyfriends, ahead of the rest of us. Niamh was always a brilliant sports player no matter what she turned her hand to and she went on and made a career out of that. So when I was in school, I saw the life she was having and I saw that she worked really hard, but she had loads of friends and she was off on holidays and she was doing really well at work and Mam and Dad were so proud of her, and everybody thought she was great.

I was five years younger than Niamh, so she'd have been leaving secondary school as I would have been coming in, so through those influential years, I'd have been watching her and thinking: "She's great. I'd love to do all that." And I think that is what kind of shaped me, going into sports and fitness first, really because Niamh was doing it and I thought: "That looks good and I'm really sporty. That sounds great." I never had a vocation and I really don't like that word. I never had that defining: "I definitely want to be … a nurse or a teacher or a certain title." And still I don't have that. I'm just me and I like working at something I enjoy and at that time that's what drove me. I really enjoyed sport, I really enjoyed fitness, I really enjoyed the thought of being in that area or industry, and that's what I went with as I thought that's what would make me happy and what I'd be good at.

*You need to open your mind, be more objective, make a more conscious effort to see what's around you and consider other views. What you know now isn't all there is to know.*

I went to Waterford IT to do my bachelor's degree. I remember one lecturer, Paddy Bergin, saying to me one day: "You need to open your mind. You need to look further than what you are seeing." The class was very small so we got to have these one-on-one conversations. It struck me at the time that maybe I wasn't learning all that I could from people, and maybe I was very narrowly focused and that has always stuck with me: you need to open your mind, be more objective, maybe make a more conscious effort to see what's around you and to consider other views.

That's one of the great qualities my husband Kieran has: he always challenges me to look at things differently and to consider other points of view and I learn a lot from him like this. What you know now isn't all that there is to know. What you know now is actually a minuscule part of what there is out there to know.

I was in my third or fourth year in Waterford then, and up to that point I'd been having a great time. I was living the dream, student life, having a great time. However, I realised that I had to go home from college after four years, that my Mam and Dad were after scraping to put me through. I wasn't really study-focused but I always passed my exams. I never failed because I didn't want to let my Mam and Dad down as I knew how much of a sacrifice it was for me to be down there, paying rent, having to survive, pay books and fees and all those bits and pieces, so I hope I always balanced the two and made Mam and Dad proud. Definitely towards the end, I was thinking: "What's next? What am I going to do next? Where do I want to be?"

Paddy Bergin's comment definitely stayed with me. I didn't take it as a criticism – it probably was a criticism, but it was constructive. I think I had handed in a couple of assignments that surprised him how they were done and maybe caught his eye that year. I can't say it was more or less than anyone else in the class, but he's probably one of the few teachers or lecturers in college up to that point that I would have felt any kind of a bond with.

❖   ❖   ❖

**My first real mentor was a guy called John Kenny,** who was a manager in the Leixlip Amenity Centre for years. He took me on as a part-time fitness instructor though I was also cleaner, receptionist, birthday party organiser and mini-soccer organiser – whatever was needed to be done. As I was going through there working part-time on my way through college, he gave me the role of duty manager, which was basically a weekend supervisor. That was my first taste of responsibility and my first taste of: "God, I can do this." I liked it, I really liked it and got on well there, with John.

He moved on subsequently and I moved with him and worked part-time in another community fitness centre in Celbridge and did little bits and pieces there. When I left college, I got a full-time job in the Arklow Bay Hotel, in its leisure centre, which always makes me smile because I still have great friends from there although I was only there for about six months.

I don't really remember the interview but I remember going down on my first day and I heard: "Here's the girl with the master's." And I was: "Hold on a sec, I don't have a master's. Is he after mixing me up with someone else?" I was panicking then to myself and didn't say anything. So I spent the first couple of weeks feeling like a real fraud thinking: "Everyone here thinks I have a master's and I don't." I was young at that time, only 21, and a master's seemed, wow, huge. So I really thought I was a fraud. I actually said it to the manager: "You know I haven't got a master's, just in case you are expecting me to do something, or be something that I'm not." It turned out that he didn't realise the difference between a bachelor's degree and a master's. So I had a giggle to myself about that.

I haven't been afraid to take a chance on something. I've changed career direction and industries more times than you could shake a hat at, for that reason. I think that's just me. Maybe when I was younger, I thought everyone else had it figured out and they knew that they wanted to be a 'whatever', and I didn't – so maybe, in my earlier years, I was trying to get to that point. How do I figure out what I am. "Am I a teacher, nurse, architect? What on Earth am I?"

Maybe that's what drove me: a need for identity, trying to identify with something or relate to something. Whereas now, I'm me. I know what I'm good at. I know what skills are transferable. I know the types of organisations that I would like to contribute to. So I'm less concerned about a title, less concerned about a vocation. I'm more concerned about whether it's an organisation that I want to be involved in and whether there is a 'fit' for me and less about a label or title or about what anyone else thinks.

When I went to Waterford, I didn't have a clue where Waterford was, where I was going. I was so naive. I had just turned 17 and off I went. And I know Mam and Dad were nervous because I was young. I was younger than my classmates all through school. They dropped me at the digs and there were two other girls who had just been dropped off at the digs by their Mam and Dad as well. We ended up getting on like a house on fire. And all through college, I moved house and shared with different people, and it was the making of me. Before I went to Waterford, I was afraid of my own shadow in school and at home. I wouldn't say "Boo" to a goose! I wasn't confident in my own skin, was always the quiet one sitting at the side or the back, didn't speak up unless I was pushed to speak up. Waterford was the absolute making of me. I came out of my shell. I remember my Mam even saying to me the first Friday that I got the bus home that I looked like a different person. And that stuck with me.

I even felt like a different person, so going to Arklow wasn't that big of a deal. I was seeing a guy from Wexford, so in my head, I was thinking, "I'm half way to Wexford", and that made it easier. I got a room in a house, with a couple, Beth and Brian, who'd just moved over from Texas. Beth is still one of my best friends. They had a dog and a cat – we'd never had a pet at home – so it took me ages to get used to the dog and the cat around the house. We had a blast, had a ball. Beth eventually got a job with me in the hotel. I don't think she had a visa at the time, so there was a bit of shenanigans going on trying to get work. We partied and I worked away and got the train home at weekends when I wasn't working or mid-week if I wasn't working, and just figured it out.

I have a vivid memory of walking from the house that we shared in Arklow into Arklow town and I'd money in my pocket, because I was now getting paid a weekly wage. I'd paid my rent and I'd money to spend. There was a little shop, like arts and crafts, for the house – you'd see them everywhere now, but they weren't around really back then. I remember going in and buying something like a CD rack and a candle-holder and thinking: "Isn't life great? Isn't it great?" When you look back now, it's so simple, but I thought: "Isn't this brilliant?"

I got a call from the amenity centre in Leixlip, from the new manager there, who I had worked with all through my part-time work and was great friends with. I still am great friends with him today. He was the manager now and needed an assistant manager, which was quite a step up at that time for me, but he offered it to me. So I jumped at it, because there weren't going to be opportunities like that in Arklow. I knew that, after four years in Waterford, I did not want to be a fitness instructor. I wasn't any good at it, being honest, and it wasn't something I had any passion for.

I learned around that time that there is a difference between enjoying doing something as a hobby and making it your work, your career. So this opportunity came up and gave me a chance to get in and be more of the organiser, the co-ordinator, managing different pieces of a business. There were still parts of it that were very hands-on, doing summer camps, teaching kids and teaching gym circuits and lots of variety, but I was learning a lot as well about how to manage people, and managing teams and the complexity that comes with that and it wasn't as easy as it looked.

---

> *There is a difference between enjoying doing something as a hobby and making it your work.*

---

And it was probably my first introduction to accounts, having to be accountable for money coming in and out. Very basic-level stuff but I loved it, I thrived on it. I loved the organising.

I used to think I was a perfectionist, but when I look at myself more and more, maybe it's just as you get busier and you get more comfortable in your role, you become less of a perfectionist, maybe that's it. But yes, maybe at that time, I would have thought that everything had to be perfect rather than sometimes 'good enough is good enough' or sometimes 'done is done'.

I suppose, at that time, my priorities would have been quite low level in terms of management. I didn't go to board meetings, I was the runaround to the manager, and I did the shifts that he didn't want to do – but I loved it. It was my first time really having to be in a position of authority or responsibility.

I learned a lot in Leixlip about people. At the time, I probably didn't learn a lot about myself or maybe I didn't sit back and look at how I was with people, or didn't take the opportunity to reflect – that came much later. I think I just went into work, bulldozed through and did whatever I needed to do. I was assistant manager after all: they had to listen to me.

It was only much later that it struck me that, if you are asking people to listen to you, you need to have something really worthwhile to say or you have to say it in the right way. I put it down to a little bit of naivety and over-confidence and a learning curve. You are just 'doing' and more concerned about your life outside of work than anything else. So you don't really take that time to reflect, until you are a bit older. It's not until you are a bit older or you move into more senior roles that you realise how important it is to reflect. But equally, it is as important to do what you need to do and go through those different stages.

I think if you start looking inward from a very early age, you are never going to get anywhere because you are going to be so consumed by what people are thinking about you and what you are doing that you are not going to be able to do anything at all. I was talking to a good friend of mine yesterday, who owns her own catering company, and earlier she had been giving out to some girl who works for her, really laid into her saying: "This isn't how we do things around here, blah, blah, blah." She'd just promoted the girl and when she walked out of the building, she started laughing and said: "Can you hear yourself?" We were laughing at that, laughing like schoolgirls, because you don't change and you don't become your work. To stay sane, you have to stay yourself. Definitely.

❖   ❖   ❖

**Then I went to the Dunshaughlin Community Centre.** I saw an ad for a new community centre that was opening up and looking to recruit the first manager to get it up and running. Basically, it was a community centre that was beside a school and didn't have any funding for gym equipment. I decided that I'd apply for it as it was only over the road.

I'd been at the amenity centre a few years at that stage and I knew Paul wasn't going anywhere – he's still there, so that turned out to be a good call. I kind of just had a sense myself that, if I didn't want to be there myself for the next 20 years, I'd need to do something. That's always something that has driven me in my subsequent moves: that I need to move if I didn't want to be stuck in something.

I remember going in for the interview and there were three or four people on the board. I didn't really have any experience with the board at the amenity centre, so this was actually quite daunting, walking in, thinking: "OMG, am I going to be able for this?" I was still young, 23 maybe, but I had done my homework, and I would say this to anybody, particularly if you are young: do your homework! You need to set yourself apart from the crowd a little bit.

I think they also saw energy and they saw somebody young coming in. They saw I'd made the effort to sit down, think about it and put time into it. And it was the first time I walked out of an interview and thought to myself, "I have that", without even knowing if I had got to a second interview.

I did have a second interview. I went through the whole second round interview process before an offer, but I knew after the first one that I had it. And that's what I would say to anybody now, if I was talking to anyone younger or they asked, I'd say: "Figure out what you need to do to set yourself apart and do not go in there if you haven't done your homework. You need to sit down in the weeks beforehand and think about what they are looking for and think about why they are recruiting for this position. What do they want out of you? What can you put on the table that's different?" It was easy to do, but it was different and it was a step beyond: "I looked at your website and I can see that you have …" That bugs me as an interviewer now: it is such a lazy approach. Why not come out and talk to people?

---

*The biggest learning curve is dealing with*
*people and managing a team.*
*All the other things are just tasks.*

---

So I stayed there for four years. We got the place up and running, set up the gym and bought the equipment and got funding. That was my first real learning experience about managing and building relationships. I had to recruit a team, find funding for a team, train a team and keep them motivated and happy. But I found it very manageable in terms of workload. The biggest learning curve was dealing with people and managing a team. You'll always find that the most challenging part. All the other things are just tasks.

❖    ❖    ❖

**Then I went to the Westgrove** in March 2006. The hotel opened for the Ryder Cup in 2006. I was kind of getting a bit bored at Dunshaughlin, it turned out to very samey-samey. And all I had done, if I'm perfectly honest, is replicated what we'd done at the amenity centre because that was the exact same business model, a community-based facility, no competition, grand. I just took their systems and implemented them there, so there wasn't a whole lot of innovation beyond that. But it worked. Then mission accomplished, move on. It's something in me.

The day I was supposed to do my first interview for the Westgrove, my Granddad passed away, so I had to ring and cancel. I remember thinking: "Is that it now? Is it gone?" I got in touch with them a couple of weeks later and went in and did the interview. I didn't think they particularly liked me. I did a first interview with André and got on grand with him. I came back for a second interview with Ian Hyland. I thought Ian thought I was absolutely shite, to be perfectly honest. I didn't think he took to me at all, and in my head, I was thinking to myself: "It's because they are really commercial and money-driven and I've never really been in that environment. There is a gap there in your skill set and he sees it. He sees that you are not going to bring in the big bucks or be able for that environment."

But they rang and didn't give me the leisure centre manager job, they gave me the assistant manager job instead. It was a pay-cut at the time and a big change. But I knew I needed to make a move, so I took it.

Within a week of me starting, the fellow they had recruited for manager left. He didn't buy into the fact that, at the time, the hotel was just opening, so every day was different. You were lifting beds in, you were cleaning the floor, everyone was scrambling together. From March until May, we all worked in a little building outside in the car park, six or eight of us there at the time, and we had such a close bond.

We were a brilliant team. Out of all my work, it is still the one time and the one team that I look back on and say: "That was the happiest and the best team I ever worked with." And it changed, once the hotel opened, because 50 other people came to work in the hotel and we lost that dynamic, but it was brilliant, we had the best fun and worked our backsides off.

Ian didn't replace the leisure centre manager because I had said to him after a few weeks: "Just give me a chance. Don't recruit anyone. And if you think over the next couple of months that I can do it, then let me do it. And if you don't, then work away and hire someone and I'll still do what I'm doing." I got on great. I was definitely helped by the strength of the team.

Certainly when the leisure centre opened, it was probably the hardest I have ever worked in terms of the amount of hours and days and amount of effort that we put into it and there was a real sense of achievement, and it was brilliant.

Then the same thing happened: we were up and running, and I was bored because it wasn't what I wanted to do. The day-to-day spinning classes, gym programmes, just didn't float my boat. This is absolutely no disrespect to anyone managing a leisure centre, but managing a leisure centre in a hotel is not difficult because every day is pretty much the same.

Throughout those first two years, I was on the periphery of the hotel management team because I was leisure centre staff. I think people have a perception about what you do and what you are and what you are capable of. I was on the periphery of the management team because I didn't know hotels and didn't have hotel experience. I hadn't even really been a waitress, apart from when I did a J-1 in America for a while. But over the course of those years, if there were duty manager shifts that Ian needed cover for, I'd offer to do it. I think the general manager came to rely on me or started to trust that if he needed someone I'd do it and that I could do it and that I was a steady hand.

So when the deputy general manager said he was leaving, there were all these conversations in the hotel about who'd go for it. Here comes another bit of trading: I had a conversation with Ian, sitting in the bar, and he asked me would I be interested. I thought we were just having a cup of tea and a bit of a chat, and I said: "Yeah, but I wouldn't know what I'd be doing. I don't have hotel experience, but if you'd be willing to give me a shot, I'd love to give it a go. I'd give it my best shot."

He said he'd think about it and come back to me, and then we had another more serious conversation about it. By this time, my interest was piqued, so now I actually wanted it. I decided this is what I wanted to try. I wanted this job because I loved the hotel and loved the team and at the time, I really, really looked up to Ian, in a big way. He gave me a shot at it – in fairness to him, it was a leap. He didn't even mind when I spilled a full pint of Guinness on the hotel owner and his wife on my very first day!

I did that for another two and half years and the hotel changed, and I don't want that to sound as a cop-out because I changed as well. I loved that role, loved dealing with brides and grooms, loved running the place and loved the fact that I knew what was going on in every different area. I was soaking it up and learning all the time. I just got a real sense of achievement out of it and was as proud as punch, and I thought this was great.

It took a while, when I first took the job, for people to accept that this was really happening. I had to work hard at building relationships and that was probably my first experience of having to earn people's respect. You had to show people that you were willing to work and learn and get stuck. You had to learn from someone who had more experience and let them know you were learning from them and show them that respect as well. But I got there and ended up having a great relationship with the team.

It came to a point, the second Christmas that I was there. Ian was obviously under a lot of pressure financially: the hotel wasn't doing what it was hoped it would be doing; staff were leaving – really good, key people had left; I really felt like I was doing all the crap for want of a better phrase, and Ian was doing his 9-5 and going home. So I felt: "Here I am, in my late 20s, working every day and every night. I'm here until about 4 am every night of the weekend. And it just isn't sustainable."

That second Christmas, we had just done the Christmas parties from the first week in December right through to just after New Year. I had done every single one of them and I was just exhausted. I remember sitting back and going: "You are never going to have a life." Now I'm very work/life-oriented: "You have to have a life outside of work. You have to see your friends and family. You have to get away from work."

Work is work and life is life, and there has to be a balance between the two, even when you love your work. That's why you love it, because you allow yourself that time to enjoy it and then it doesn't become such a chore.

---

*If you are the senior person in an organisation,*
*everyone is taking their cues from you.*

---

I remember at that point looking back and saying: "Maebh, if you don't make a change here, you are never going to meet anybody. You are never going to have a family." I was looking at other people who worked there, who maybe had alcohol problems or were having affairs, their marriages breaking down. I just stood back and said: "Really, is this where I really want to be?"

It was really a hard one to walk away from. With the Westgrove, those of us who were there from the very start felt like we nearly owned a little piece of it, so it was almost like you were breaking up with someone. There was a real separation issue.

So first I took a month off to go visit my sister in Australia. A couple of things had happened also. The relationship between Ian and myself wasn't the same; my trust in him wasn't the same and that had a big impact as well. I think he could probably have talked me around, or I may not have acted as quickly if the trust between us had still been there, but from where I was sitting, it was irrevocably gone and could never be repaired. No apology was ever going to fix it for me. So by the time I came home from Australia, I had started looking for something else.

❖   ❖   ❖

I saw an ad for CEO of ALSAA, the Aer Lingus Social and Athletic Association. Back when I came out of college, ALSAA would have been *the* place, with modern facilities, an aspiration for most. I didn't think I'd even get an interview, because CEO? I was still only 30, quite young. But I got an interview, did my homework: went over, spoke to people, looked around, met a friend of mine, pretended to be a couple, walked around, eating an ice cream, sat outside then, on a lovely summer's day.

I turned up for the interview an hour and a half early! I sat out in the car and then went in and was waiting for ages. This is something else I learned: don't turn up for an interview too early, as you'll see all the other interviewees go in and out, and you can totally freak yourself out because you make assumptions about people.

Eventually, I met the board – three or four people off the board. I felt I just clicked with them. I felt I was different than what they'd just met. I was young, female, had energy, been around the place, had ideas, put stuff on paper to bring into them. I felt that they really responded to that and no more than the previous time that I did it, I felt there was just a good timing issue there. I felt that the person who had been there before me was of a certain generation, certain age, male, and they wanted and needed a complete change – and in I breezed! And because I'd never expected to get an interview, I certainly did not expect to get the job and so I just went in and was myself. I got called back for a second interview and I was told not to come so early next time!

The biggest learning for me at ALSAA was dealing with unions. Definitely in the early days, it was probably the first time I experienced that, no matter what you say or who you say it to, someone's listening. And they are proper listening. Everyone is taking their cues from you. Everybody. So your mood, your form, how you treat people, how you ask things of people, how you respond to people, whether it is staff, customers, stakeholders, if you are the senior person in an organisation, everyone is taking their cues from you. I had to teach myself to be mindful of that.

It's easier if you get an email that annoys you: just leave it alone, don't answer, go for a walk, have a cup of tea, deal with something else and come back to it when you can take the emotion out of it. But if you're just blurting stuff out, you can't undo it and the last place you want to be, if you want to be a leader, is backtracking: "No, I didn't mean it like that" or "I'm sorry I said that". That's the time in your career when you discover whether you are a leader or a manager or an organiser. Whether you can actually lead people and bring people along with you. If you can learn those kinds of skills, then you can be a leader.

I probably realised I could be a leader when I did my MBA while working in ALSAA. I started that a year after I started at ALSAA. I asked ALSAA if they'd support me doing an MBA and they did, in fairness to them. At that time, I kinda had a sense that I was a little out of my depth, maybe in that vision, leadership piece, or maybe it was for my own confidence that I needed it.

I have always tried to push myself outside my comfort zone. The funny thing is that it's not the big things, it's little day-to-day things. For example, I hate talking on the phone, so if I have to ring someone back, I'll put that off until the end of the day, saying: "Oh God, do I have to do this?"

Once I'm on the phone, it's fine. It's the "Hi, this is Maebh ..." I really struggle with. But I make myself do it every day, or if somebody rings that I don't really want to talk to, I make myself take the call. That's pushing yourself out of your comfort zone on a day-to-day level. It's not this huge leap – I don't have to move to Australia to become a surgeon to get out of my comfort zone. I need to just take that call.

❖   ❖   ❖

My older sister Niamh and her husband had twin boys who were born very premature and, as a result, Liam, my godchild, needs full-time care at home. I've seen over the last nine years how they really depended on great charities like the Jack and Jill Foundation, Make a Wish or LauraLynn [Children's Hospice] and it has really opened my eyes to what matters. It has given me, probably all of us, real perspective.

It was over those early years that the seed was planted in me that, if I really wanted to do something good, I'd work for one of those charities. I had finished my MBA, I had good work experience and I had something to offer to a charity that in turn would be able to help families like my sister's. So that's how I first got interested in charities. I didn't really know how to go about it, wasn't sure what the sector was like but I just knew myself that I would love to work in a kids' charity and that I would get a lot from it.

---

*The challenge was getting it up and running.*
*Then mission accomplished, so move on.*
*It's something in me.*

---

My time was up at ALSAA. I knew that both they and I needed a change. And this position at the Rutland Centre came along. I was having a very honest conversation with a person on the Rutland board, who I had worked with previously, and I said to him: "I'd love to get into a charity." I told him that I thought I was going to move on, I was just looking for an opportunity. He didn't say much at the time but he came back to me a couple of months later and said: "Look, I feel I can say this to you now, but there is an organisation that I am involved with, they are looking for someone and I think you would be a good fit for it. Would you like me to put your name forward?"

So we had a chat about the Rutland Centre and what they do and I said: "Yes, absolutely." It sounded like a really good opportunity. I didn't know anything about the sector or about addiction, but it certainly would move me closer to where I wanted to be.

The Rutland Centre is a charity based in Dublin. We provide residential and outpatient addiction treatments for all addictions, so alcohol, drugs, licit and illicit, gambling, food, sex, shopping, gaming, internet, whatever addiction someone might have. We offer five-week residential programmes or a 10-week outpatient programme, plus an aftercare programme, to men and women age 18 and over.

We don't get any State funding at the moment, so we are more like a social enterprise than anything else. Less than 2 per cent of our income is from fundraising. We just survive on what we charge. That's difficult because sometimes in Ireland people equate 'charity' with 'free', but we have to charge. So we do come in for a little bit of flack from time to time, as people think we are elitist or private or somebody is making money. We are none of those; we just couldn't operate if we didn't charge. If we got State funding, that could change.

It is fascinating. Every day here is fascinating and I'm not even at the coalface. I'm not doing what the guys here are doing – they really hear the stories. And even the bit that I am exposed to every day, it makes me thankful, going home to my family every day. You see people change over the five weeks, so that the person who leaves is not the person who comes in.

I'm here 15 or 16 months now, and this one guy, I can still see him vividly in my head, because when he came in, he couldn't look you in the eye. He was a shell of a man, probably not much older than me. But when he left, transformation is not the word for it. He sticks in my head as the epitome of what we are trying to do. And if we can help anyone even half as much as what he got out of it, then what we are doing is worthwhile.

I remember talking to his fiancée or girlfriend at the time and seeing the change in her, and the impact and the realisation of that's why we are here and that's why we should keep doing what we are doing. And that's why, if my alarm goes off in the morning and I feel a little bit peeved or tired or whatever, I think of that, and I go: "Get your ass up and get into work." It's brilliant. If someone wasn't happy in their job, I'd say to them: "Figure it out." That's not a fob-off. The question is: "Is it you or is it the job?"

My outlook is that I'm me. My attitude is to be positive and no matter where I am to put my heart and soul into things and to make the most of them and to see the good and take the opportunities and chances, and so I know I'll be happy anywhere. And if I have my work/life balance right, I'll be happy anywhere.

# GARY McGANN

"I'm a very ordinary guy who worked his tail off to not fail."

*Gary McGann is the chairman of Paddy Power Betfair plc. He is also chairman of Aon Ireland, Sicon Ltd (Sisk Group) and recently was appointed chairman of Aryzta AG. He is the former group chief executive of the Smurfit Kappa Group plc, one of the leading providers of paper-based packaging solutions in the world. He is also a former chief executive of Aer Lingus Group and Gilbey's of Ireland.*

*Gary is a director of Green REIT plc and a former president of the Irish Business and Employers' Confederation (IBEC). In the 'not for profit sector', Gary is a director of Barnardos.*

**I guess I'm a very ordinary guy who got a lot of breaks** both from parenting, through school, through business life, through luck on the one hand and through kindness and decency on the other. Sometimes, tough kindness, tough love. I made my way to whatever I've become or achieved, and there is no question in my mind that there are a couple of things that drove me.

One was my parents, who were west of Ireland people, who didn't spend on themselves at all so everything they had went on us. There were four of us. And then from schooling, when they sent us to schools they couldn't afford, to holidays. They couldn't afford the holidays but we did house swaps or caravan swaps or whatever. My father was a rep for Independent Newspapers. In fact, he was a very talented musician, who made money by night playing music, and by day sometimes did a bit of work for Independent Newspapers. He worked seven days a week, for 15 to 20 years, just to make ends meet, driving all over the country to play 'gigs', as he used to describe them.

When I got to an age where I appreciated what was going on, I never felt any different to well-off children in the school I went to, Coláiste Mhuire. These were all children of the upper middle-classes, civil servants' children, professional people's children. I didn't feel I was any different. That was because of my parents. They didn't let me feel any different. While the other children might go on holidays to Majorca, I might go on holidays to Enniscrone and wouldn't know or care about the difference. I probably still don't!

I learned the importance of hard work very early on also. At the age of 13 or 14, a Christian Brother, Christy Matthews, beat the head off me, told me I was a lazy SOB and a disgrace to my parents, I had more talent than I was using and so on. I never really believed that but I certainly believed in hard work. I had an aunt, who was a teacher down the road from us, who after I had failed my first scholarship exam, getting 4 per cent in geometry and 14 per cent in algebra, kindly explained to me that the geometry mark was for writing my name properly. She was the person who first told me that it was "90 per cent perspiration and 10 per cent inspiration" and we worked and I got the scholarship the following year, thanks to her. So there's an example. Without her, I wouldn't have got it. Or without that Christian Brother who quite frankly scared me into working harder for my Leaving Cert. I did a fairly ordinary Inter Cert, as it was then.

Home was Palmerstown in west Dublin but because my parents were from the west – my father was from Roscommon and my mother from Galway – I spent most of my childhood down on a friend's farm, which was more like a big garden rather than a farm. But great days. We went down to work, not to play. We went down to do the hay, to cut the turf and so on, but we didn't know any different. Sure, that was great craic.

I think the great thing in those days, which is so hard to do these days, is that my parents sheltered us from knowing anything different other than what they wanted us to know and what they wanted us to experience. As a consequence, I never felt inadequate, or as if we hadn't got anything, or that we were denied anything.

Most importantly, as I got into teenage years, I really realised just how hard they were working and, as I became an adult myself and looked back on it, I saw it was a really tough life. Not that different to many people, but that generation just gave everything to their kids. When I think of education, I'm passionate about how we are letting standards slip. Education is the one thing that got me through anything I have done and that was thanks to my parents who gave me the wherewithal to do it.

I did a decent Leaving Certificate. I used to study my tail off because I was afraid of failure. I did a presentation to AIB Private Banking not so long ago, and somebody asked me what drove me. I answered: "Fear of failure." Absolutely no question. Duty to my parents first of all and also pride. Make no mistake about it: I had this horror, whatever about private failure, public failure would be something to really fear. This was later in life. When I was younger, I wouldn't have known the difference between public and private failure.

I hated losing and I lost a lot because I was a decent athlete but not a great athlete. I was a decent footballer but not a great footballer. I liked competing and I didn't like losing but I wasn't a bad loser. But I realised – and I genuinely mean this, this is not me trying to be in any way humble about it – I was ordinary but I worked extraordinarily hard. I've always done that. People who knew me when I was studying in secondary school will know I worked my tail off. My eldest daughter is identical.

Talk about career guidance. My mother was a very successful nurse and I got good marks because I worked my tail off, great marks in chemistry, physics, etc. You had to 'use your honours' in those days. So I decided I'd do medicine. Of course, I walked into medicine with not a clue. I did two months of pre-med until I was asked to cut a rabbit and discovered I'm squeamish about blood. Nobody had explained to me that medicine was about blood. The professor, who was about 70 years of age, about 4ft 11in, said: "Cut or leave." And I remember saying: "I'll leave." So I walked out and went off and joined the Civil Service – the C&AG [Comptroller and Auditor General's office] – and did my degree at night.

---

*Education is what got me through anything I have done – thanks to my parents who gave me the wherewithal to do it.*

---

My father would support me in anything I did. He was unbelievable. He was the cup that never stopped flowing. He'd give you the shirt off his back – and literally did at times. But my mother was a nurse, a senior nurse, almost 10 years older than my father. She always told him through all their married life that they should never have married: "We are totally unsuited, you know."

And she was right. He was in Kimmage Manor [Holy Ghost Fathers] for six years. He was within six months of being ordained and ended up in hospital with a cyst in his neck and had to have a major operation. Who was his nurse? My mother. Straight out of the 'musicals'. He was 23 and she was 32 or 33. He was 24 when they married, 11 months after they met. Totally ridiculous, but a classic Irish marriage. They worked at it, they lived with one another's foibles – and they had many of them.

But she was driven, she was disciplined, and he was away all the time, working his ass off. She really was the one who kind of gave us the backbone, the structure. She was very demanding, very tough and, because I was the eldest and she was quite lonely, I got to know her very well. She was a 'vocationist': a nurse by vocation, then a mother by vocation and it was almost vocational love and I'm sure the family wouldn't disagree with me. I don't think it wasn't love – it was – but it was that type of love – it was kind of, this is good for you. Like the medicine, the pills in the morning. I still remember cod liver oil being shoved down my throat every morning on the way to school. "This'll keep you going."

But at the age of six, I was getting on a bus into town and walking up O'Connell Street. On my own. I went to Coláiste Mhuire from the age of six to 18. It was on Parnell Square and we were living in Palmerstown. I went to Aston's Quay on the 26 bus and walked up O'Connell Street. I've watched my daughter with my grandchildren – nobody walks anywhere now. When they are a bit older, they might get out and cycle down the road, but those were safer days.

**School was all-Irish from the age of six,** so the concept of Irish in the Leaving Cert was a given; we could do that in our sleep. I remember my friends in English-speaking schools worried about failing Irish. For us, it was a walk in the park.

But I also remember every year putting on a pageant in the school. It was a very interesting school, driven by the Christian Brothers at the time. And very good guys. I've nothing but positives to say about them. I mean, the man who beat the head off me at the time: I've mixed views on him but I owe him a lot. He was the athletics teacher as well so we were driven very hard. In fact, my brother was a good athlete: he was Eamonn Coghlan's standard in secondary school. He'd have gone on but he was diagnosed with nose bleeds which they thought were sinister and it turned out a year or two later not to be, so he would have definitely gone on. Himself and Eamon are still very good friends.

But we put on these pageants and we had Tomás Mac Anna from the Abbey Theatre, who was ex-Coláiste Mhuire, and Alan Dukes was in the school years ahead of me. Alan was big, tall and regal, so he'd be some sort of Fionn MacCumhaill character and I'd be some sort of mushroom or tree or something like that in the corner. But I do remember in 1966, the pageant was on at the time Nelson's Pillar was blown up. I was coming down O'Connell Street to go home on the bus and the Pillar had blown. We'd just missed it. Interesting times.

So it was a very classic Christian Brothers' school. Hard, a tough school, but really worked on what was a broad kind of curriculum in those days. We had the obvious: football and hurling. There were two things you could get suspended for: one was playing soccer in the yard and the other was speaking English in the yard. Doing both was an absolute 'mortaller', altogether. And then we had the athletics and the pageants. For its time, the school was actually quite progressive.

We always played football from the time we were kids. It was the school started the athletics and we said: "Why not?" I was a good sprinter and my brother was a good middle distance runner and my younger brother? Well, we never knew what he was good at because he didn't try too hard, though he was probably the most talented of us all. Winter training was always cross-country training in the Phoenix Park – he was always found behind a tree, waiting for the second or third last lap, when he'd join in and come romping home.

Dennis Brosnan was our trainer – he was one tough Kerry man. We used to have to do the Khyber in the Park, up and down, 30, 40, 50 of those. Going up was hard; going down, you'd no lungs left and the legs were running away on you. If somebody fell, he'd kill them.

I think what it taught me was a number of things. I always felt better after it, though I never looked forward to it. So that was the time I realised the value of exercise for mental health, of getting your head into some space other than whatever was going on. Being a man, I could only do one thing at a time and feeling really badly physically because of the running didn't give me time to worry about exams or lessons or anything like that. It was a great teacher of alternative use of time. My mother used to say, "A change is as good as a rest" and insisted, even when we had no money, that Dad always brought us away, even if it was only a couple of miles down the road. We had to have a change of scenery, a change from the normal rhythms of life if you like. And she was right. She didn't have any science behind it, but she had the insights.

I still hate exercise to this day. I always hated it and I still do. I never feel physically better after it, but I always feel mentally better after it. I will tell you what it really taught me – and I see so many examples of the opposite now – the concept of discipline. I know it is an old-fashioned word but the human psyche is lazy by nature. I would happily stay in bed if there was no reason not to. I'd happily sit in a chair.

I have a name for being up very early but I'm not a natural early riser, I'm a disciplined early riser. I'm a disciplined hard worker. It's not an instinctive thing. It doesn't come naturally. With the exception of great natural talent, everybody really is kind of preprogrammed to avoid doing tough things voluntarily. They do so either because it is good for you or you enjoy the rush afterwards. I can remember the six-mile races in the Phoenix Park, the last 300 or 400 metres and I'm trying to figure out which tree I am going to puke behind. And can I do it privately or make a show of myself again?

The mind is all the time battling with itself. The mental battle, even that is important. And that comes from my father: working because he had to. I remember my uncle who was unemployed at the time who would say to my father: "I could never do that." My father would reply: "You would if you had to." You find your strengths and your limits. And where you think your limit lies is usually way short of where it really is. People ask me if I've ever done a marathon and I say: "No, because I hit the wall after two miles!" And I'm not joking. The wall is for getting over and getting around. The wall in anything in life is a self-imposed concept really. It's in your head.

I spent my life 'gaming' myself. I'd say, "I'll do one more lap" and then I'd say, "Ah to hell, I'll do another lap". I'd go on the treadmill and I'd say, "I'll do 30 minutes", then I'd say, "OK, I'll do five more" and then I'm only five away from 40 minutes. I negotiate my way through it and it's all in my head. My head tells my body it's feeling crap but the truth of the matter is that it is all in my head.

It's the same with work: "I'll do another hour." When I was studying: "I'll do another chapter. Nah, I'm too tired. No, I will, I'll start it." Then you start it and then you are halfway through it, always gaming myself, always negotiating. It's your head negotiating with your body because the head is up for it. It's trying to convince the body it's up for it too. If my persona was totally in my head, I'd be in great shape.

I was a sprinter. I was in Ciaran Coakley's era. He was one of the finest sprinters this country has ever produced. He went to Loughborough College, was a great gymnast, but he came off the parallel bars and cracked his skull. He made a couple of Olympics. I was Frank Murphy's era also. O'Connell's School kept Frank back I'd say about three years to win the athletics every year. I was average but we had good relay teams and I won a couple of Leinster medals. My brother won the Tailteann games a couple of times – won the All-Ireland Cross Country. Himself and Eamonn were running for it at the time. Eamonn went off to Villanova and my brother ended up being a lawyer. He still runs where he lives every morning.

---

*I still hate exercise to this day. I always hated it and I still do. I never feel physically better after it, but I always feel mentally better after it. It really taught me the concept of discipline.*

---

Racing was a product of the discipline, not the other way around. It was an expression of the discipline. I've a friend who played tennis up to the age of 80. I was talking to him not so long ago. He is 82 now and he was saying he had to give up tennis. I replied that my ankles went a long time ago and he said: "No, nothing like that. I've macular degeneration. I can't see the ball." His legs hadn't given up at all: that's the discipline. I think the racing and the competitiveness are an output of the discipline, not the other way around. And therefore the discipline survives the passage of being competitive and being interested in competing at the top level or whatever level.

I always had very bad ankles, so I couldn't do a lot of road running, so I did cross-country. But I always think that a marathon is a bit like life. You get found out if you haven't put the work in. You might last five or 10 miles, but you won't do the 26. You'd get found out. In many ways, you get breaks in life but if you haven't actually put the fundamentals in place in a structured, progressive and disciplined way, by and large, somebody or something in life will find you out. And the emperor will have no clothes!

❖    ❖    ❖

**I went to college at night.** I did a BA in history and Irish, which is very important for a businessman! My father, God rest him, would always give us the easy way out; my mother the opposite. Education is education. And to be honest with you, I ended up doing accountancy, and accountancy is not education. Accountancy is vocational. So thankfully, I'd had a bit of education before I did it.

There are all sorts of accountants. There are accountant accountants and non-accountant accountants. There was a great cartoon in the *Financial Times* a few years ago that a friend of mine who was a partner in one of the big firms sent me. It was three pictures of a guy in a bowler hat and long coat and brief case and pinstripe trousers underneath the long coat – three identical pictures. The caption said: "The sad accountant, the happy accountant, the delirious accountant – no difference."

Certainly accountancy doesn't teach you anything about life or people or human interaction or broad-based thinking. It is structured, deep and disciplined. So I'd never encourage anyone to do only accountancy. I'd always prefer them to include something else. There is an element of retrospection here but I did the BA in history and Irish because I was interested in Irish and thought I'd walk through it because I did Irish all my life. I needed to get a degree. You couldn't do a degree at night until you were 21 in those days. You couldn't start a degree. You had to be a mature student. And to be fair, if they thought I was mature at 21, they were definitely mad.

I owe my first degree to my mother and my wife. My mother because I didn't want to let her down and my wife because she wouldn't let me quit – because at 22 and six days, I got married. Interesting. My mother wasn't happy. My father was deliriously happy but my wife said: "You are going to finish your degree." Every night she'd meet me after college to make sure I went. I spent the first 10 years of my married life studying. No credit for the accountancy, so it took me four and half, five years to do it and then I did a master's, MSc Management, in IMI/Trinity. So, when I stopped studying, the kids were confused because most weekends I had been studying. We did nothing. My wife looked after the kids, every night I was home I was studying, so it was a different way of doing it.

My first job was at the C&AG's office. That's where I did a lot of my study. I was lucky. My first boss was Michael Jacob, the father of Michael Jacob, former CEO of Premier Foods and a former president of the RDS. Michael senior was the archetypal civil servant: he could spend two days writing a letter, but when he was finished, it was a masterpiece. Particularly if he didn't want to say anything! A most incredible art. He was one of those people who just didn't offend and, when you are an auditor, you are likely to bend people out of shape from time to time. Michael was very good to me. He used to give me a bit of space. I used to study early morning before work and then again in the afternoon.

I was lucky because you could have been confined to auditing a government department but I was doing commercial audits. So I did all the semi-States' audits: IDA, CTT, Central Bank, Bord na Móna, Bord Fáilte, Shannon Development Company, Shannon Sales and Catering. That's when I met Shannon Hotel School's Dermot Clarke and people like that.

As a young fella, the only time we got a suit was when we got an advance on our expenses for a country audit. We'd go out immediately and buy a suit and then wouldn't have two ha'pennies to rub together for the audit. So we'd beg, borrow and steal in terms of living during the audit, because we had no money. They would put us up but the expenses were to cover our meals and our travel – but we had already spent it, so we'd bum lifts and do all sorts of things. Some of the older guys might have cars and we'd go four and five in a car – we'd figure out a way to get from A to B with no money. They were great days. But it also gave me an opportunity to see commercial life. That's when I realised that I wanted a company car. All of the semi-State CEOs of the time had Triumph 2000s – the Triumph 2000 was the bee's knees. Absolutely the bee's knees and I wanted a Triumph 2000. It took me a while to get there but that was the goal.

I spent nearly eight years in the C&AG's office. The day I joined, one of the bright boys showed me what was called 'the Ladder'. He was able to tell me that when I was 45, I'd get my first promotion, and if I was lucky when I was 55, I'd get my second. Now it wasn't true because he wasn't an actuary, so he didn't factor in sickness, health and people leaving. But I remember realising there was a structure and a sequence and a seniority and therefore, at the bottom of the Ladder, you were going to have to take your turn. So I got promoted to auditor, but an auditor would have been the equivalent to a HEO [higher executive officer]. I just wanted to do different things.

I was lucky with the semi-States in that I got to see business and got to meet smart people like Michael Killeen, Kieran McGowan, Vivian Murray and Dan Flinter. To this day, I would always say to people: "If you can run a semi-State body, you are far more talented in my view than a lot of private and public company CEOs, as you've got the normal business cut and thrust but you also have a shareholder who cannot act like a normal shareholder and is exposed to the whims of society and the media and the pressure of massive union influence." I lived that in Aer Lingus when I eventually got there in 1993 or 1994 and again when I was chairing the DAA.

The semi-States had a lot of really smart people who had come from the C&AG's office: Liam Skelly in Shannon, Dick Scott, who ran Mail Order in Shannon, the chief accountant in the IDA, Joe O'Connor, and Tom Cullen, who was commercial director in Shannon Sales and Catering. They all had a soft spot for the C&AG's office. We were young fellows and they'd bring us out for dinner and show us quite a nice life. So I had new aspirations: a Triumph 2000 and a meal account. It was actually as simplistic as that. Genuinely. It was aspirational and all about 'Hollywood', this was showbiz for me!

I remember the first day I was in Shannon and because we were the auditors we could eat in the silver service restaurant. I didn't know what a prawn cocktail was. I remember that first time I tasted a prawn cocktail, in a big glass, in a silver salver, sitting in ice. I didn't know if I was to eat it, drink it or put it in my pocket! Literally. A new experience: I had to look around to see what people were doing.

Apart from being shown – probably even schooled into – some of my ambitions by the guys I met in the semi-States, I wanted to get into private enterprise. Ericsson was looking for a management accountant. Now, first of all, I still wasn't qualified as an accountant; I was just about to be. So I didn't have the full papers. But one of the guys who was a headhunter at the time had been HR manager at Bord Fáilte when I was doing the audit. I knew him and he knew me and he promoted my cause. He sold me to John Ronaghan, Ericsson's CFO, who gave me a break and became a great friend of mine. Crossing over from the public sector to the private sector was extremely difficult. I was 26 and had no experience. I always described auditing as "doing the exams with the answer book open" against accounting as "doing the exams with the answer book closed".

---

*The principle was one of getting the best and the best generally were people who could build teams.*

---

When I went into Ericsson, we were coming up to quarterly accounts and I was told to do the accounts. I hadn't a clue. I had audited trial balances and P&L to balance sheet, but I'd never actually done them. Four weeks later, I knew how to do it. I got the textbooks out and I worked morning, noon and night.

We were living in Dublin and Ericsson was in Athlone and my wife wasn't initially happy to move to Athlone. I was there for almost a year and a half until she realised I wasn't coming back. I literally went down the first Monday and I didn't get home the first time until the following Saturday week.

It was sink or swim. I hadn't a breeze, but with the help of people, the textbooks and a bit of brain power, I got there and we got the accounts produced and I tell you: that was learning on the job! I thought to myself: "This is it! I've blown it this time." I felt I'd really deceived people and in a way I had, though it wasn't done knowingly. I thought that, because I could audit accounts, I could produce accounts too. Very untrue. I was lucky with the boss. I suspect John knew and he was probably there, when I look back now, as a safety net.

As I got on top of it, I wanted to do more and more and more. I wanted his job and he knew I wanted it. He kept giving me more work, and more and more, and eventually I effectively took his job. He was happy at that point and time. But as I look back, it was real raw, naked ambition on my part. Not due to anything in particular, just to get on.

I remember getting my first company car there. In Ericsson, there were two things important for the guys who were on their way up: the car you were driving and the number of windows in your office. One of my senior colleagues, the production director, told me he was 40 before he had a window in an office at all; he was on the shop floor with no windows. So he advised me to cop myself on. So again, a bit of wisdom from somebody who was a lot older than I was.

It was there I met Vincent Daly who was CEO. John and Vincent made Ericsson, Vincent in particular. He joined Ericsson Ireland in 1964 when the Irish market needed about 400 engineers to install telephone exchanges. By 1982/1983, the Irish market was digital, needed about 10 engineers and we were employing about 800 because Vincent had got business all over the place. He was an incredibly low-key entrepreneur.

Every time I went to leave, because I wanted to move up – and to be fair, John was a young man at the time – Vincent would give me a new job. He was just unbelievable. In a group, Vincent wasn't particularly inspirational (he was shy), but one-on-one he was incredible. I know many people would concur with that view. I went to resign maybe three times in 13 years; every time I'd come out with a new job, a new opportunity, lead in my pencil and ready to kill.

Then, when I was offered the job as group finance director in the Gilbey's Group, he said: "You should take that." If I was to do any more in Ericsson at that stage, I'd have to move to Sweden or go international.

Vincent was the 'big' boss – and he really was – but he never realised the aura he gave off. He was a tall man, austere-looking but to this day, I'm great friends with him and I consider him the most inspirational person I have ever met. He worked his ass off, Monday to Saturday.

Ericsson split the national telephone exchange contract with Alcatel in 1982 when the famous Charlie Haughey did the 'sheep for telephone' deal. We had previously had 100 per cent of the market here; justifying 800 people, they split the market. We got 40 per cent each and they left 20 per cent up for grabs. Vincent had got the 20 per cent before they got out of bed and before we knew it, we had another 20 per cent of their 40 per cent simply because Vincent knew everyone from the doorman to the managing director to the board; he just worked the whole business chain.

He worked every angle of the market, of the business, but most importantly he had an incredible brain, a great contrarian view on how things should be thought about. You'd actually have something all worked out and he'd say: "Do you know what? I think we should do it the other way around." You'd have spent maybe four weeks working on something and he'd say: "That's good, yeah. But let's try it this way." Another example as I say of luck – meeting people like him. Without John giving me a break several times and Vincent being just so inspirational, I'd never have got where I am.

❖　❖　❖

**Then I got to the Gilbey's Group.** Again a headhunter I knew rang me and said they were looking for a group finance director. Gilbey's of Ireland and Bailey's: that was the group. I worked directly for David Dand, again a hugely interesting guy. Ned Sullivan, Bailey's former CEO, is generous enough to say David was definitely the guy to whom the credit goes to for Bailey's because he just stuck with it when people turned him down. Pure tenacity. But Ned is the man who rolled it out internationally. He was the most phenomenal marketer you'd ever meet and a great businessman. He built a team of the best marketing guys I'd ever met. And so I learned a huge amount. As somebody who was in finance and manufacturing, I had no real exposure to sales and marketing.

There was the consummate salesman Tom Keaveney, who would sell sand to the Arabs. Tom was the MD of the Irish sales company. Any hotelier you'd know of old, Tom would have had them as customers and friends. Peter Malone, Rory Murphy, all of the older guys, Brian Murphy and Adare Manor, and Mark Nolan. All of those guys, and David Doyle, and Patrick Guilbaud of the younger generation. Tom would have a significant portion of the wine list and have Bailey's being poured.

Bailey's couldn't succeed if it wasn't successful in its home market. With most products, if you can't prove the concept in your own market, nobody is going to run with it. David Dand would say that if Tom hadn't made it with Bailey's in Ireland, Bailey's would never have made it abroad.

Then there was Tommy Murray, who was head of manufacturing, and who really concentrated on optimising the quality and efficiency of production. One thing I learned was that these companies found the best of the best. Quite often from within, coming up through the ranks. But where they couldn't find it from within, they'd find it outside. The concept of 'good enough' was probably not one they believed in. Instead, the principle was one of getting the best and the best generally were people who could build teams.

The one thing that I absolutely learned all my life is that if you don't know how to play on a team or develop a team or lead a team, you haven't a hope. So other than solo sports, there is no other vocation where being great individually would get you to the level of the success that people might aspire to. Teamwork is the name of the game. Ironically, the best medals I won in athletics were on relay teams.

Frank Fenn also worked in Gilbey's. Frank originally trained as a salesman under Tom Keaveney. Tom used to always say: "All my bright guys, Ned keeps taking them into international. In Gilbey's, they are geese and, in Bailey's, all the geese are swans." One great thing about good performing teams is they are great listeners. It is a skill that is under-practised and in many instances, under-learnt. Some great lawyers have found that, in confrontational situations, they've got out of a hole by saying nothing for two hours and hearing the weakness in the proposition. People like me are busy arguing back and forward – we don't hear the weakness – so listening is a great, great skill.

Martin Rafferty is a wonderful man. He was on my board in Aer Lingus, on my board in Smurfit. Martin very seldom spoke at board meetings. But he had a way of clearing his throat before he was going to speak and then silence would descend and everybody would listen. And it's the old story, it's not the volume, it's the content. His great line was when somebody said, "That's cheap" and someone else said,

"No, that's cheaper", Martin's response was: "There's a reason why things are cheap. You need to figure out is it cheap and nasty or cheap and good."

So that was Gilbey's. I spent from 1987 to 1994 there, so almost eight years. I predated Diageo. Diageo was about two years later.

Bailey's came about in the Grand Met days. One of the magic things about Bailey's Irish Cream was that it was a total Ireland proposition. The grand idea came from Tom Keaveney, David Dand and the team, who sat down for a drink on a Friday evening and said: "Manufacturing tax relief. We're distilling gin and running vodka through filters. But there must be something else we can do, something typically Irish. What better than whiskey and dairy?" But you can't put the two together, as the whiskey curdles the cream.

Nonetheless, a guy called Tom Cullen, who was of Irish extraction, working in the IDV labs in the UK, figured it out. Something to do with the pH factor! The cream needed to be available year-round, which meant you needed cows to calf all year long. Express Foods Ireland, which was part of Express Foods, which itself was part of Grand Met Foods, was run by Bernie Cahill. Express had farms in the north-east, near Virginia, where their cows calved the year around. Problem solved!

---

### Aer Lingus was a totally flawed concept for an island economy.

---

Bernie was running Grand Met Foods in Ireland and David was running the drinks side. Every year they'd sit down to negotiate the price of the gallon of milk or cream, triple cream. I got to know Bernie in those days and John O'Donovan, who was his finance director, and I used to joke that David would go for lunch with Bernie to negotiate the price of milk and come back delighted with himself: "It only increased about 10 pence a gallon on three million gallons or something." I'd say, "Jesus, David, how many bottles of wine did you have?", because Bernie would be going back to Cork with two tails wagging.

❖     ❖     ❖

**In the early 1990s, Bernie was chairman of Aer Lingus**, which had effectively gone into bankruptcy. He got a guy to approach me to see if I'd take on the job and I did. I still remember sitting in Beaulieu Vineyard in the Napa Valley in my last partners' meeting with Grand Met, in 1984, in glorious sunshine, knowing the following week that I was going to be back in a rainy Ireland about to start work in a bankrupt Irish airline, asking myself: "What was I thinking of when I agreed to this?" I had been in government, been in an Irish subsidiary of a European international company, Ericsson, I had gone then to Grand Met, which was a UK company but with an Irish international brand. But here the shareholder was the Irish State, the government at the time. My naïvety, when I think about it.

But I was lucky because Paddy Wright, one of my great, great friends, was on the board of Aer Lingus at the time. Martin Rafferty was also on the board, as was Ted McRedmond, who ran Aon, which was 50 per cent owned by Smurfit at the time. James O'Dwyer was the legal adviser to the board and David Austin, Lord rest him, was there too, as well as Rose Hynes, who came later, and a couple of others. So it was an exceptionally good board. Bernie was a very driven man and had been executive chairman for a while. He was very happy to let me take over so I took the 'Cahill plan' and went at it. I joined in late 1993, I think it was, and stayed until 1998.

Those were very difficult times: telling a State airline that had been an iconic brand for Ireland that it was too expensive and that nobody was prepared to pay for the offer and so they'd two choices: differentiate further on the one hand and/or, more likely than not, take cost-saving measures. Aer Lingus was a totally flawed concept for an island economy. Like most State airlines, the standard approach was to kill off any opposition and while it wasn't done formally, effectively twin-paired routes were carved out so Air France and Aer Lingus would do Paris, and FinnAir and Aer Lingus would do Helsinki and so it went. And then Ryanair came along in my time and changed things dramatically.

But in any event, Aer Lingus was losing more and more money every year in the core business. The ancillary businesses – Cara

Computers, Jefferson Computing, Park Aviation, SRS in Shannon, a robotics company in Canada, and Airmotive, the engine overhaul business – were making money but the airline was making no money. So we sold off most of the non-core businesses, because they were camouflage – and we needed the money, anyway. But they were also camouflaging the fact that we were not focusing on and addressing the core business. So that was a really, really difficult time for people: headcount cuts, pay cuts, pay freezes, massive union warfare.

Team Aer Lingus was an aberration. It was set up so badly by Charlie Haughey's famous letters of undertaking that they had a God-given right to survive, and of course, in time, they almost bankrupted the airline. Sorting that out was the best thing I ever achieved. I had the deal to sell it to FLS, a Danish company, just about done before I left – I had agreed to stay on to complete it – but a certain minister announced on the airwaves that I had no legitimacy left once I announced my resignation. But they got it done, and that was the most important thing, because it was going to kill Aer Lingus. It was so badly structured, union-wise, and so embedded in terms of the resistance.

We had a really good MD running it for four or five years, Donnacha Hurley. He made huge changes to it, but even still, it was difficult as the industry is so competitive. People can shop around, they can go anywhere in the world. I mean, when you are flying an aircraft, you have to fly it to the maintenance yard so it doesn't matter much where you go.

I was working six days a week at the time and we were trying to put a team together. I brought David Bunworth in. I brought in John O'Donovan, from the old Grand Met Foods, who had gone to Carbery Milk Products and eventually got bored. I remember when I first asked him years earlier to come to Dublin to take a job in Grand Met Finance Ireland which I'd set up, he said: "Why would I come to Dublin when I have a Dublin 4 salary in west Cork?" I said: "John, I've no answer to that!" But he got bored and he came as finance director to Aer Lingus and he was great. He was the first guy to tell the unions: "You can either have the milk cheque or you can have the dividend – but you can't have both." They are still looking at him!

One time I had been at a conference and was coming back home on a Sunday, and trying to connect out of London to Dublin. I was galloping across the concourse at Heathrow and Laurence Crowley was at the desk and he said: "Slow down, slow down. There's been a lightning strike in Dublin." I said, "Goddamned pilots again" because I'd had strike after strike. He said: "Sorry. Let me rephrase that. There has been a strike of lightning in Dublin." Lightning had struck the tower and the air traffic control system was down for a few hours!

Aer Lingus involved strike after strike at the time. Some people say they were very difficult people. But they were people who were used to a particular way of life and all of a sudden somebody told them: "You can't have that any more." A lot of these people didn't necessarily do anything wrong. The game had simply moved on. People missed the phenomenal change. They missed the fact we had an international society in the country that needed access and needed to leave this island a lot more cost-efficiently than we were offering. People expected flights to take off and land on time. And so on and so on. The trick was to get that cost-efficiency without losing the interpersonal skills of the front-line staff.

The people who took the most pain in that period were the cabin crew and, to some extent, the pilots. And they were very bitter. Every transatlantic flight I took, I spent most of the flight in the galleys with the crew talking to them, trying to explain that the reason they lost more – they'd have lost a day in layover and were forced to fly more hours – the reason they gave more than anybody else was they had more to give. The crew who were travelling to the States today would have two nights' layover and only travel back three days hence. It was crazy stuff. But if you are used to that and then suddenly somebody throws the switch? We were seen as interlopers. These people were all lifers.

When I arrived at Aer Lingus, I said: "We'll organise a management meeting every Tuesday morning from now on. We'll get the weekend over, calculate the figures on Monday, and I want to know them on Tuesday." I asked my assistant to organise a meeting for the management team in my office where I had eight chairs. She said: "I'll organise the boardroom." I said: "No, organise it for the office here." She just laughed at me. So I went into the boardroom on the first Tuesday morning and there were about 28 people around the table. I thought: "Holy Divine God! How will anybody say anything?" For everyone to get to say three sentences, we'd be there for hours. So anyway, we cut that down.

I had a famous meeting about four months in, when we had started to nail the strategy down. We were negotiating a bailout of £175 million of fresh equity, under the EU rules of 'one time, last time'. The Italians did it nine times, but anyway! People have all sorts of negative thoughts when you mention P Flynn, but without P Flynn we'd never have got it through Brussels. I can understand the negativity but don't underestimate them: Irish commissioners boxed way above their weight. Most of the commissioners we've sent to Brussels worked the corridors, they made friendships bilaterally. Anyway, we'd just got approval for the £175 million.

At this meeting, I had 200 middle managers with whom I was doing a kind of town hall meeting. At the end of it, we did a Q&A session with 200 people in the canteen. I couldn't see everybody. This voice from the back said: "Look, if this doesn't work, as we are taking on a lot of pain, and we can't really take on any more pain, can't we go back and get more equity?" And I said: "Over my dead body will we go back and get more equity." The voice at the back replied: "That can be organised too!" I never found out who it was.

---

*It was all about change, drawing a line under the past, but maintaining the best of the past.*

---

My wife found it very tough. There was a lot of personal stuff, a lot of fairly nasty stuff from a very small minority. The great thing was we formed a team. As long as there are a few of you in the trenches, you can keep one another company and Aer Lingus was just a great brand, a symbolic icon of Ireland, and a great bunch of people. Everybody spoke about the green tail. When you came around the corner from Terminal 7 or Terminal 6 in JFK and you saw the green tail, you felt you were home. So we had a great base to build on and we previously never had real marketing until David Bunworth started to leverage the uniforms and the colour scheme on the planes in 1996/1997 with the front-line team.

We didn't do anything for three years until we were sure we had the turnaround really progressing, and then we started to rebuild the business proposition and work to change the whole psyche of the people. Huge engagement with the staff on the uniforms, cabin crew, the men into uniforms (previously they'd been in black, with one stripe and two stripes), put them into the blues – just refreshed them. Louise Kennedy did it. She was excellent. Then we also did the famous 'drunken shamrock'. Again, it was all about change, drawing a line under the past, but maintaining the best of the past. The colours didn't change, the essence of the Aer Lingus colours didn't change. The principles of what we were about, which was differentiation based on people or service, didn't change, though they struggled to be sustained.

And again, the new guys on the team – four or five of us – now outnumbered the guys who'd been there all their lives. Larry Stanley, who was acting CEO I think three times, was the guy who tapped me on the shoulder and said: "You should appoint Willie Walsh to a senior management role." So we agreed that Willie would go down to run our charter airline, Futura, in Palma, Majorca. We owned 75 per cent and the local management owned 25 per cent and the CEO departed for a bunch of reasons and the pilots were on strike, all of them former air force, a total closed shop – total parity over pay.

Willie went down – himself, his wife and his child – and sorted it out fairly quickly I can tell you. Pilot talking to a pilot about going tech because of a built-in seat 3C – that was when he got his first serious management advancement. He was a pilot negotiator. He was great. Willie had his pilot's licence before he had his driver's licence. He still looks young. He really was exceptionally good. Tom Mulcahy, who was the chairman who appointed Willie CEO, went to the market, looked around and said: "You know what, our own man is better." And he was right. Absolutely right.

❖   ❖   ❖

**From there, I went to Smurfit.** And the connection with Smurfit was Paddy Wright, my great friend. Paddy hadn't quite told me that he had planned to retire early. Michael Smurfit had told him he couldn't retire if he didn't have a successor, so Paddy introduced me to Michael and we got on – but still I didn't know Paddy's intentions. He retired at 59. I was only in about a year then. To his credit, he gave me great advice, landed me well, helped me understand the culture of an organisation that had never recruited at senior level from the outside. Smurfit had grown its own people, through great graduate programmes, great management development programmes. In fact, it acted as a source of management development for other businesses.

I went in as group finance director in 1998. Michael was CEO/chairman. Now I had no promises, but I had indications. Ray Curran, God rest him, was going off to the States where we had just announced a merger between Stone Container Corporation and Jefferson Smurfit Corporation. We had two businesses: Jefferson Smurfit Group, which was listed on the Dublin/London Stock Exchange, and Jefferson Smurfit Corporation, which was quoted on the New York Stock Exchange and of which we owned 43 per cent. Ray went over as CEO and I took over Ray's job here.

Ray was tough love. One of the seriously smart guys. I knew Ray and his brother Bob, who was deputy secretary in the Department of Finance and who was a great supporter of mine – in particular, when I was trying to get Aer Lingus and Team sorted. Bob made enemies. He never got promoted to secretary but probably was the brightest man by far in the Department.

Paddy was Smurfit's COO and when Paddy retired in 1999, I became COO and joined the board and then in late 2001, Michael told me he was planning to move upstairs formally and tapped me on the shoulder, and so I became CEO of Smurfit Group in 2002.

First, I had never contemplated Michael ever retiring, even though he was well into his 60s at that stage. But also I never expected anyone, other than a family or a lifer, to take over. I think Michael basically made the call and what's interesting is Tony Smurfit is now CEO and Tony is CEO purely on merit, make no mistake about that. He was appointed by an independent board of a public company and Michael had no say. Tony had to be better than the equivalent and he is; he's doing a great job. He has hit the ground running, having appointed a new CFO and CEO of Europe, all in the space of about a year.

I think there is no question that Tony and Ian Curley and myself and Michael O'Riordan [company secretary] became a very cohesive executive team. We worked hand-in-glove, and when Smurfit went private in 2002, we had fantastic investors, Madison Dearborn. These guys were very much focused on returns, but really understood how to motivate people and how to support management when they believed in them.

We bought and sold businesses and, in 2005, we did the biggest merger in the industry. We merged the number 1 and number 3 to become by far the number 1. And then in 2007, we 'IPOed' and did a primary listing in Dublin and London. It was the largest fundraising in the sector ever. We IPOed at €16.50 and in less than 12 months, the share price was just short of €21.

And within another six months the share price was €1, as the recession hit – people lost money! And so my greatest memory is that we got all of our top managers into the room, laid out what things looked like, the implications and the need to cut costs, cut back on capital expenditure, cancel the dividend, drive cash flow and basically weather the storm because the business was fundamentally good. And taking 'capex' [capital expenditure] off our men was like taking toys from a child. But we went out of that room with the top 200 guys ready to kill.

I'll always remember meeting a few of them for a few drinks after the two-day conference. Every other business was cancelling conferences, but we had ours. Those days, we were in about 30 countries, 35 now. The only way to get to talk to somebody, and to have the same conversation and dialogue with all of them, was to get them all together.

But also, it wasn't about us talking to them. It was us talking together. And I remember being asked how I thought it went, and I said: "Better than I had hoped for." Everybody signed up, there had been nothing but constructive conversation, challenges and questions, but constructive and quite honestly, I thought there would have been a lot more resistance and negativity. I said: "As a matter of interest, in your view, why wasn't there resistance?" And one guy said: "You did us the courtesy of treating us like adults and telling us what the problem was and laying out the options for a solution and we bought in." I was so glad he said that.

Michael Smurfit is a unique man in my experience. He never looked back. Michael would never talk about yesterday, always tomorrow. Michael's great phrase, which I think encapsulates a whole approach to life, was: "If it isn't terminal, it isn't a problem." Just think about that. Very deep. And if ever I am losing my perspective, I remember that. It was never more apt since the recession. I lost a lot of close friends in death during that period, and it really hit home to me. Absolutely.

❖    ❖    ❖

**A friend of my eldest daughter asked: "How is your dad enjoying his retirement?"** My daughter said: "He got a fail mark from HQ!" I didn't want to stop working. I was lucky, I had been on the United Drug board for about 10 years and was just due to come off when I was approached by Paddy Power to join the board.

The chairman was retiring in about six months, so I ended up as chairman. Then within about three months, the Paddy Power/Betfair merger came along and then I was asked to join the Sisk Board by the family, as chairman. Five generations there, still together, still focused, still positive, weathered a lot of challenges. A brilliant Irish family story. I'm also chairman of Aon, following Paddy Wright again. Aon is part of Paddy's legacy. A wonderful company. And I'm on the Green REIT board with Stephen Vernon and Pat Gunne and then Aryzta came along and Denis Lucey was retiring and the rest is history!

I'm also on the Barnardos board, which is very important to me. The Barnardos people are wonderful and in a very challenging space. The not-for-profit sector has got such bad press; in a number of cases justified, but not all. I'm really struck with them because you have to put something back and this thing needs a lot of work and it's a very serious and difficult space. They are wonderful, committed people.

*My two granddaughters, Zoe and Ava, helped*
*me understand what is really important in life:*
*family, friends and people.*
*Through them, I have tried to erase some of the*
*massive deficit in my work/family balance.*

I need to sort out the management team for Aryzta, which is well under way with the appointment of an excellent CEO in Kevin Toland. Paddy Power Betfair is doing well but will now transition to a new CEO, with Breon Corcoran deciding to do new things. In Peter Jackson, we have found a great successor. Sisk is rebuilding after a very difficult time in Poland and the UK, and Green REIT is doing fantastically well with really smart people.

**On the personal front, I have been married to the same woman for 45 years** – given my business and travel schedule, she reckons it's really only about seven years! I am strongly of the view that busy people with significant international commitments cannot do so if they have children without an incredible support system at home. To remain married to the same woman in these circumstances means one member of the partnership is very special – no marks for guessing which one!

We were blessed with three daughters, who have grown up to be wonderful people in every respect: personally, attitudinally and professionally. I cannot claim any credit (or responsibility) for this outcome as I was 'missing in action' for most of it. They were gifted a great mother who did it all. Despite the fact that I missed a lot of important parts of their lives, my daughters haven't held it against me and I have tried to make it up over the years.

We are a very close-knit family (and extended family on both sides), a family that was enhanced by a great son-in-law and two beautiful granddaughters. As a family, we are fortunate to have our children and grandchildren living close to us and we therefore see them all regularly and make a point of spending a week away together once a year at least.

I believe a critical aspect of my life was going to Ericsson and living in Athlone for 12 years at a formative time in Moira's and my life, as well as that of the girls. Spending a lot of their childhood in the country has, I believe, served my daughters well in character formation and keeping them grounded. A number of our closest, lifelong friends came from our time in Athlone and that remains the case today. Meeting up with them, however infrequently (my fault!), I count as one of the great pleasures in my life.

The last 10 years have had some extremely difficult times for us (and indeed many others). In this decade, I lost three of my closest friends: Paddy Wright, Hugh Cooney and Peter Murray. We also lost two of Moira's brothers and more recently my younger sister.

On the business front, I was a director at Anglo Irish Bank when the crash occurred, causing enormous suffering and pain to many people. I was also CEO of Smurfit Kappa Group, which returned to the public markets at €16.50 per share in 2007, had appreciated to north of €20 later that year and by early 2008 had collapsed to just north of €1, at a great loss to many investors.

I previously mentioned the role of luck and fortune as an important ingredient in most people's relative success. Three factors saw me through the incredibly difficult years of 2007-2010. First, in Smurfit Kappa Group, I was fortunate to have management colleagues across a wide geography who had the confidence and courage to work together to restore the company's fortunes, something that was successfully done. Two of these colleagues now lead very successful large plcs. Allied to that, a critical ingredient for any CEO to survive such a collapse is the support and confidence of a great chairman and board – this I had in spades!

In the context of the fallout, for those involved in the Anglo failure, it was the norm that everyone involved got seriously damaged, most especially the depositors, creditors and investors. Those in management and on the board were also inevitably targeted, some much more than others. I was fortunate that my own chairman and the chairman of United Drug (of which I was a board member and senior independent director) convinced their constituencies to suspend judgment and personally supported me through the extensive enquiries that ensued. Had they not done so, my public company career would have been over. I am eternally grateful to them.

However, the events to which I most attribute my sanity (such as it is!) and ability to come through were the births of my two granddaughters: Zoe in 2006 and Ava in 2009. In walking them for miles as babies during those years, I got a sympathetic hearing from them; they never argued with me or doubted me; and they helped me understand what is really important in life: family, friends and people (and especially grandchildren). Through them, I have tried to erase some of the massive deficit in my work/family balance.

When over the years people asked me what my interests were, I would always answer the classic 'serious' answer: theatre, reading, sport and family. Now I answer honestly: my family, my friends (who, despite neglect, I am still lucky to have), rugby internationals (with my son-in-law and two daughters) and bad golf!

So, going back to the question: "Who am I?" I'm just somebody who literally met the right people at the right time along the way, people who gave me the breaks. I'm probably somebody who worked his tail off to not fail – which sounds very negative – but it's not too far from the truth. There is no substitute for hard work.

# EAMON MORRISSEY

## "I know who I am."

*Eamon Morrissey*'s stage debut was as Ned in Brian Friel's **Philadelphia, Here I Come**. He adapted Brian O'Nolan's writings as Myles na gCopaleen and Flann O'Brien into a one-man show, **The Brother**, and later developed shows based on the works of Jonathan Swift, James Joyce and Maeve Brennan. He starred in the film, **Eat the Peach**, and in the RTÉ series, **Hall's Pictorial Weekly**, with Frank Hall. He currently plays Cass Cassidy in **Fair City**.

'**Who am I?' is an interesting question** for me because being an actor, and a writer of sorts, do I really know who I am? I think that's a question that has always gone through my life. Of course, I know who I am and where I am and all this kind of thing, but there is a kind of duality there: are you the character or are you the real person? I'm fascinated with how people identify themselves.

For instance, Flann O'Brien had so many identities – Myles na gCopaleen, Brother Barnabus, Flann O'Brien, Brian O'Nolan – and because I'm so familiar with his work and doing his work, I have a feeling that he didn't quite know who he was. He didn't know who the real Flann O'Brien was. And I don't think it made him particularly happy. I think it disimproved his life. Thankfully, I don't suffer from that syndrome.

❖    ❖    ❖

**I was brought up in the grey Dublin of the 1950s** in Cherryfield Avenue in Ranelagh, an only child. A late only child, so both my parents doted on me and were very loving and caring. My father was a minor civil servant but he also, as we used to say at the time, 'took a drink'. Nowadays, we'd say he was an alcoholic and that's it. That side of life wasn't particularly pleasant, not that he was violent or anything, quite the opposite, but he'd just be falling around drunk coming up the road.

My mother loved the theatre. She used to go to the Gate in the old MacLiammóir/Edwards days. I was interested in acting from an early age, and I think my mother encouraged me to go to places like Miss Burke's Academy on Kildare Street and later to the Brendan Smyth Academy and so I went through the learning process. So when I eventually decided, from school in Synge Street, which again was Synge Street in the 1950s – not a very pleasant place – that I wanted to be an actor, my parents very nicely went along with it. You were really becoming a bohemian, leaving the tribe, in those days, becoming an actor. These days it's a career. They went along with it. I was 16 or 17.

I never actually finished my Leaving Cert in Synge Street, as in that last year, towards the end of it, I was already working with Brendan Smyth doing stage management and I was asked to go on tour with *The Playboy of the Western World*, so what a launch into the theatre for me! I was stage manager and I remember when we got to Venice, I had to travel with the set when they were unloaded from the trucks and put on to barges during the night and go to the theatre with it, and I wasn't a bit impressed with Venice: "Jaysus, they don't even have roads in this kip." I wasn't good at stage management, I hated it. And then some time in the 1960s, I was so bad at stage management in one show, that Barry Cassin fired me, which was the best thing that ever happened to me because they felt obliged in the next play to offer me a part. That was wonderful and the start of things opening up for me.

Naturally, like many other actors, I went to London to be a star and became a barman. And then back and forward. Television had started. I'd come back on a Saturday to do a sketch on *The Late Late Show* or something like that. So I was backwards and forwards and working more and more here. I did want to work here. It was here I wanted to base myself and then television began to provide a bit more income. Theatre never provided a great income and still doesn't.

I really was very lucky. I happened to be in the right place at the right time. I just happened to fall into acting as a young actor, when Brian Friel came along writing plays – that was wonderful and I was in the first production of *Philadelphia, Here I Come*. They brought it back to the Gate and were to go to Broadway with it, but only four or five Irish actors could travel due to some restriction. I didn't expect to be going, as I was only playing a small part, but apparently when they were on pre-Broadway tour, the guy playing my part had an Arizona rather than a Cavan accent and David Merrick said: "Get the guy who played it in Dublin and we'll get around it legally, somehow." I was in a show at the Eblana and Merrick's manager rang and said: "Would you like to go to Broadway?" I said: "When?" He said: "Tomorrow." So anyway I went and we did a pre-show tour, to Boston and places, and then on to Broadway and it was a huge hit. It came in as a sleeper and took off.

I was there – what a time – in the mid-1960s in Manhattan, free, 23 years of age and the world at my feet. It was just magic. I will never forget the openness of New York, how everything was open for discussion. Even though Ireland was changing in the 1960s, you really still couldn't have an opinion if you were under 40. I just remember the magic of those days.

---

*The 'suits' in RTÉ didn't realise how popular*
*Hall's **Pictorial** was until it was too late.*
*… so the programme survived.*

---

Then we went on tour around America for eight or 10 months, so I saw a lot of the cities of America, good, bad and indifferent. Then I came home and heard that Brian Friel had written another play called *Lovers*, which was going on. I got involved and got a smashing part in that and it went on here. And then we went back to Broadway with it, with Art Kearney playing the lead – [Niall] Tóibín played it here – but he was a huge name in America, and Fionnula Flanagan was the other lover. We were the young lovers. That was another year out of my life.

Ann came with me and we decided to get married. We got married in New York during the daytime and I went and did the show that night. We went on tour with that show, the longest honeymoon, another six or eight months. Then back to Dublin.

**All the time, I wanted to get back to Dublin** because I was learning more and finding out more. I wasn't particularly stupid about what was going on in the country – I knew the history and all that – but I didn't know enough and in order to be the actor I wanted to be, you had to be representing your community, you had to know how to represent your community. And I was basically homesick as well. There were great attractions and temptations, as well, to stay in America, but it really wasn't me. It was a different climate to what I was used to.

When we came back, there wasn't a bit of work. I was a year and a half out of work. Terrifying. We had a terrible time. Then slowly work started to come up more and more. When Joe Dowling took over the Abbey, I became part of his group there – through his years, which were very exciting. It was he who encouraged me to do *The Brother* as a full show. That started it; then I decided I'd do the other giants of Dublin.

I'm very Dublin-based, very Dublin-orientated and there was so much going on in the city apart from all the orthodoxy that was hanging around, but I wanted to do Joyce because I was terribly fond of *Ulysses*. My mother was quite a liberal lady. She gave me *Ulysses* as a 17th birthday present and I never forget reading it. I didn't understand 10 per cent of it, I didn't even understand the dirty bits! But it seemed to be so representative of the city I'd grown up in. I'm still terribly impressed with *Ulysses*. I think it is a most extraordinary piece of work.

There was difficulty with rights and royalties on that, so in between I did a Swift show, the other great giant we had in the city, because I do believe that Swift was the greatest satirist ever. An extraordinary and wonderful man. So I did a show called *Patrick Gulliver*, which worked and has worked and still works as well. Eventually, I got to do *Joycemen*, some of the characters, vaguely telling Bloom and Stephen's story through Joyce and went on to other shows, *Just the One*, a show about drink, and so on. So I was kind of, unbeknownst to myself, carving out this solo slot for myself but also I was doing many other plays as well. I think there is a place for the solo show in theatre but it is just a solo show, and I love the symphony of a huge cast in a great play – it's very exciting.

❖   ❖   ❖

**So then more and more television** and Frank Hall – that was the other huge one – *Hall's Pictorial*, which was only one day a week. We did it all in one day. We had to be out by five or six o'clock or something – quite heavy going. It was all thrown together and you'd go in at half-eight in the morning and they'd have sent you the script the week before and you'd have these reams of stuff. I never learned it – you couldn't learn it.

I was Cosgrave as the Minister of Hardship. They wanted to do this Minister for Hardship. It was during the fuel crisis of the 1970s and at the same time, I was kind of doing take-offs of Cosgrave and his terribly hesitant, careful, legalistic style. I thought I'd love to do him and they had the costume there already, the vest and broken hat. I said: "Can we do this?" They said: "Oh, no. Now wait. Ah, go for it." So that was the start – Cosgrave was the first government minister and certainly the first taoiseach sent up on television.

It just grew and grew that show – and it wasn't all politics. As Frank Kelly and myself used to say, our main object was to have a bit of fun with it. We certainly weren't like some committee writing themes: "What will we satirise this week?" Quite the reverse. The coalition government were always rowing amongst themselves in public, Conor Cruise O'Brien and the likes, and provided great material.

Yes, it was kind of a bit daring. One of the things that helped it was it was never from the drama or light entertainment department, it was actually a product of features. And they were well used to handling the politics of things.

It started as *Newsbeat*. Originally, they got Frank Kelly and meself, just reading pieces to camera of exactly what county councillors or county managers had said and we discovered that, if we put on funny hats and funny voices, provided we quoted them exactly as they were reported in the newspapers, it was chaotic. It was the nearest thing to live, as we had to get it all done in one take. They gave us these kind of sewing-machine things – autocues – and if you pressed too hard, it would go too fast. We had to get it done, as I say, in one take and it was kind of out of that that *Hall's Pictorial* evolved, as it was a chance to be able to do these sketches in this mythical place called Ballymagash – but they were obviously exactly what was going on in the mainstream.

The 'suits', for want of a better word, in RTÉ didn't realise how popular the programme was until it was too late. They couldn't do anything about it. Frank Hall himself was a master of playing the field, so the programme survived.

Eventually it became a parody of itself, a victim of its own success in a way. We began to hear of politicians having dinner parties on the evening that they heard they were going to be on the show. And I think it was President [Paddy] Hillery who had the cloak, wasn't it? We did a programme about him and his cloak. The man in the cloak. It was all Sandeman's Port and that kind of stuff. The next morning, there was a request from the Áras: "Would it be possible for President Hillery to have the cartoons?" So we were becoming popular – you were nothing in Irish society if you were not being satirised on *Hall's Pictorial*.

Eventually, Fianna Fáil took over again and we tried, we spent ages, weeks in the library looking at newsreels, and trying to get these new characters, but they were all grey men in mohair suits. I got to do a fairly passable take-off of Gene Fitzgerald, but people would say: "Who is Gene Fitzgerald?"

So that was its peak. The ratings were massive at that stage. We did have the advantage that we were in a single-channel country – outside Dublin, there was no BBC – so we had almost a captive audience. But I can't get over how people still talk about it. They go on about it: "Oh, as a child, we saw this and that and we just loved it and we all watched it together."

And there is another thing about the Frank Hall show, that he was good at, and I don't know where it came from. They'd be doing the knockabout stuff, but there was also access to information that would be known to only about 20 civil servants. Somebody was feeding bits of things out – I'm convinced of that! It was a completely different and smaller society back then.

**In the 1980s, I would have been one of the first freelance actors to get a mortgage for a house.** It was a huge achievement. I was able to wave some kind of a 13-week contract from RTÉ or something like that to get it. That was a massive commitment.

Then we had the kids. We'd two kids growing up. I spent a lot of my life on the road around Ireland and the UK doing tours. Sick of it,

I never want to see the road again, but that was the way to survive. You couldn't have just one job, you tried to have two or three jobs going at the same time. You'd do the Frank Hall show, then you'd jump in the car and drive to Cork and do a play, then jump in the car and come back and do something else. So hard going, hard times.

Again, I said I was fortunate that I never had long periods of unemployment. Mind you, the work I was doing was Mickey Mouse, no big money in it or anything. But it got you by week-to-week and you kept going some way, so I didn't really have long gaps, and actors can have sustained bad times. Also, if you kind of drop out of the circuit a bit, it doesn't get any better.

---

*I'll never forget the weekend I spent reading*
*At-Swim-Two-Birds. It was huge.*
*Oh, the world opened up to me.*

---

When we came back from America in 1968, the other part of my life is Wicklow, the little house we have in Aughavannagh. At that stage, it was just four walls, no roof. But Ann and myself had planned we were going to build it up ourselves, grow our own and live the good life, because it was only an hour from Dublin in those days. But that lasted about three months.

One, I wasn't competent enough and also I was outside the circuit and suddenly you just were not getting phonecalls about work, or do you want to do such a thing next week? It is necessary to keep yourself right in there and certainly the worst thing you can do is sit around waiting for the phone to ring. Get out and do something, do anything.

❖    ❖    ❖

**I use writing to occupy me.** I'm not very good. I do regret that I wasn't able to do more writing in my life because I love good writing and it's endlessly fascinating for me.

The last solo show I did was *Maeve's House*, which was about the writings of Maeve Brennan who's a wonderful writer. It had a relevancy because she was brought up in the same house I was brought up in. My parents bought the house from her father, Robert Brennan, way back in 1935 or something, so I grew up with all that.

When I was in New York, in 1966, my mother loved Maeve Brennan's writings and she used to get *The New Yorker* now and again. Somebody used to give it to her, it was too dear to buy. And so she knew the writing very well. She encouraged me, so I contacted Maeve Brennan in New York and eventually we met up and had a wonderful afternoon in the Russian Tea Rooms of all places. But she's a spectacular writer. You cannot help being enamoured with her writing because it is so careful, so spare. She could spend a week and a half on a paragraph for *The New Yorker*.

And writing has always been involved in my life. With Brian Friel, again, he is so exact – the work is done. I always remember doing a dress rehearsal with one of his plays, and he was sitting in the rehearsal room and he was going through the script and when we finished, he said: "And yes, Eamon, I'm right here, it's a comma there, not a full-stop!" And he'd be right. So you develop this kind of respect for good writers and a terrible disrespect for bad writers – and unfortunately I've dealt with a number of the second type over the years. There is a unifying thing about writers: they all hate each other!

I'm trying to write now and I find in the past couple of years, I work slower than I ever did, and I always worked very slowly. I know I can't sustain it for more than four or five hours. I get tired. But I just have to accommodate that. And I find the same thing physically. I'm not able for the things I was able for on stage, though you can compensate for that easily enough.

I've no intention of stopping. I don't have the option to retire, you certainly couldn't live on the old age contributory pension! But that's not the point. The real point is it is still very fulfilling.

I really enjoy *Fair City*. It is what it is. It's melodrama, soap, it's all over the place. But it is a great thing to work on and the effect it has on the nation is extraordinary, with 600,000 people a week watching it. It's huge. You do the best you can with this stuff, but I'm heartened by people you meet on the street stopping you and saying: "I love the way this or that worked." It will be some little, small thing you did, like lifting a cup or something, but people are so focused on it. I love when it becomes more human. So that's great.

I've no particular immediate desire to go back on stage and do a huge play. Over the years, I loved rehearsing plays, I just loved that. It's great but then going in every night, and night after night, and then a matinee on Saturday, it can get tiring. And it is very hard to keep the enthusiasm going and you do have to keep the enthusiasm going, you can't just walk through it. It was particularly hard going in the long American runs. Times like that you just had to drive yourself to keep it fresh because each audience is fresh – they haven't seen it before.

When we were away like that, three weeks here and then two weeks somewhere else and four weeks in another place, we were very well provided for in nice hotels with our own facilities. We'd spend our day as I have in a lifetime spent my days: hanging around waiting for the show to start! Because there isn't a lot you can do. Of course, there are things you do. But you can't have a glass of wine even. But that show, right from the very start, that thing you are doing at night, hangs over you and is there to be done and while it can be very rewarding, it is also a bind on you. It holds you. I'm still not fully sick of that. If the right play came up, I'd do it flying.

❖    ❖    ❖

**I was totally fascinated by Myles na gCopaleen.** I'd started to read him in *The Irish Times*, even though at that stage he'd passed his best in the 1950s. But then I discovered all the other things he'd written. It was in the 1960s, I was in London and *At-Swim-Two-Birds* was out of print, and someone loaned me a copy of it in this awful bedsit in Camden Town that I was in, at the top of the house, freezing. I'll never forget the weekend I spent reading it. It was huge. Oh, the world opened up to me.

The man himself was quite an intimidating figure, sitting in Neary's at the counter in those days, with the big hat. You'd have to be careful. But when I came back, I couldn't resist going up to him and I said: "I've just read *At-Swim-Two-Birds* and I've never been so excited by anything." Well, he ate the face off me! "Only a puerile, facile mind would have any interest in that rubbish," he said. I made a hasty retreat.

It was just amazing when I think about it. In the bars I went into – the theatre bars and the likes, though I didn't drink until I was 23 – in these bars you had Behan and Kavanagh, and it was all part of the culture, all around the top of Grafton Street. It was a great honour to be even a tiny part of it. But they were very isolated by the war and lost connection with their European counterparts and the European movements in literature, because Ireland became so isolated, being cut off by the war. They became very big fish in a very small pool. I think it had a detrimental effect on a lot of them.

O'Brien had rejected most of his earlier writing and he was always convinced he was going to write the great one, it was always going to happen. I think he was also somewhat damaged by alcohol by his mid-40s – he was already going down a very strange path. And then losing the job with the Civil Service had a huge effect on him. And he was the most respectable of those writers – he was always in the Civil Service suit, the tie and everything. He regarded himself as a cut above. He is a fascinating enigma of a character.

I tried to get the essence of his writings with *The Brother*, to take something from everything he has written. I put all that together, not just from the Myles na gCopaleen column or from *At-Swim-Two-Birds*, but also *The Third Policeman*, which is just magic. That was part of my aim, to do a representative selection of his writings and, as with all the other writers, one of the purposes, apart from wanting to make a living for myself, was to encourage people to go and get the books and read them themselves. And that was true of Joyce and true of Swift and certainly true of Flann O'Brien. I remember the buyer in Eason's said when *The Brother* was on, sales of Flann O'Brien went up 25 per cent. So it did have an effect, it did get people to read them. And that was one of the purposes of doing it all.

That was always the thing with Myles na gCopaleen: people would say he put too much effort and too much of his genius into writing the Myles na gCopaleen column [Cruiskeen Lawn]. But the column was his genius, 25 years – not all of it top-class, but there is such wonderful stuff in it. And I often thought that he also had such a huge amount of topicality. With *The Brother*: "… can't look at an egg, the egg is barred. Ham, cheese, fish, he'd eat it up and ask for more, but the egg is barred. Problem with an egg is, it never dies." I'm sure that was based on some kind of salmonella in eggs here and I'd love if some university could correlate them with the news stories that were on at the time and I think you'd see matches in them.

Moving off into *The Third Policeman*, and the molecule theory, and it so dark and frightening, that and the other story that I have in *The Brother*, about the skins – the guy who puts on the skins – I mean it's just very, very dark and shows how close comedy is to horror. Just one step more and you are into that.

They are still asking me to do *The Brother*. It opened in February 1974 in the Peacock. I thought it would last about four weeks – it's still going. Then I went and did it in the Eblana and it was packed out there, then the Gate and on tour, and it kept being brought back to the Abbey, because if they had a show that didn't work out, they'd put *The Brother* on again. And it would invariably fill up.

---

*I'm quite happy not to see a sinner for 10 days. And I used to feel embarrassed by that, but now I accept it. Just different aspects to the same person – that is also who I am.*

---

Touring it, to my surprise, it went very well outside of Dublin. I thought when I went to Cork, I was lost, but they loved it and they took to it in a huge way. The last time I had it out was three or four years ago or maybe about four or five years. I've taken out the interval and tightened it down and I don't drink as much as I used to in the original show, but it still works. But they love it in Cork and I've done it four or five times. A little thing appeared in 'da paper': "One of our own is back!" So I've made it! One of their own!

I was always doing something else as well as *The Brother*. I'd be in a play at the Abbey as well or the night *The Brother* closed on Saturday, I'd be starting something else on Monday. In the Abbey, it was very heavy-going: you rehearsed in the morning and did the play at night. It meant you were going, going, going all the time. The danger of that is you slip into a system and it's not good. It is so much better to have time to reflect, to have time to think about things.

❖   ❖   ❖

**I don't think people should retire at all.** I think it can be disastrous for them. If you've been all your life doing a job that you hated, then it's a pleasure to just sit back and do the garden. But if you've been very interested in what you are doing, it's a terrible wrench. I'd hate to be separated from work totally, I'd hate that. Even though we have the other side of life in the little house in Aughavannagh.

It's a little stone house, two-storey, windows each side of the door, that kinda thing. It is my real spiritual home. It is really where I live. Aughavannagh is something about me. I've always loved the countryside, even though I was brought up in Ranelagh and, right from the very start in the Boy Scouts, I just loved the Wicklow Hills. I'm there and perfectly happy. In Aughavannagh, Lug na Coille is just up the road and all around me these vast mountainy forests. I'd put up my tent and live in the hills for five or six days. I would spend a lot of time working things out. Or trying to work things out.

I managed to buy 17 acres when the forestry had felled the area and replanted it and I'm now burning the wood from my own forest. To me, it's the achievement of a life's ambition. It's not because I'm gone all 'green' and that, it goes right back, I always loved to have this renewable source. No one told you life is fair, but I'm not able for the chainsaw any more.

But that's where I want to live. Ann comes down, but not as often as I go down myself. It's been a great workplace over the years. I've written everything I've done and rehearsed all down there, then go out and do a couple of hours in the forest, and that makes a great day.

Even though I've wonderful neighbours down there, I'm quite happy not to see a sinner for 10 days. And I used to feel embarrassed by that, such a contrast to the cavorting around a stage or doing television and then the other half of you that wants to be totally isolated, but now I accept it. Just different aspects to the same person and maybe going back to the question we started with – that is also who I am. No use trying to pretend I'm not that kind of person as well. You get used to the people knowing you and recognising you from *Fair City*, you just get on with it. Gay Byrne used to say: "The only worse thing than being recognised all the time is not getting recognised at all."

I do find it important to me to try to be as close and at one with nature as possible. I think it came from childhood. The more I think about it, the more important I see it. It is becoming more and more acceptable with many writers, that oneness with nature, and trees. This book, *The Hidden Life of Trees*, I'm just starting to read it. It reads like a fairytale and yet it is all based on scientific fact: how trees communicate with each other. You really get that feeling when I'm in my forest in the few acres. There is first of all the silence, and there is this oneness with it. I feel a guilty pride that this is mine and I really shouldn't feel that way as I'm only a guardian – a minder – for the next generation.

The house is great for writing. The perfect times for me would be to get up at 6am, have about four hours writing done and then take a bit of a break and go out and do something physical outside. That mixture in your life is great. Then come home and get a gin and tonic! I can write throughout the year, with the wood-burning stove. Once it gets going, it heats the house quite well. People say it must be a great place in the summer. I don't see it, it's not the point, it's that the place is there, and it's ever-changing over the years. I love being there to hear the first cuckoo. I love to be there when the first swallow arrives and I love to be there to see the last swallow leaving. These kinds of cycles of seasons I think are very important.

I'd write stage work or be learning scripts. Whatever bits of writing I'd have to do, it's a great place to do it. And the fact it's so remote doesn't make a difference. I always remember reading back in the 1970s about this new thing called computers. And how some time after the turn of the century, everybody would have their own personal computer in their house! And they'd be able to communicate through it. I remember sitting in front of the log fire and thinking: "Jaysus, will I ever live to see that?" But now, bloody big satellite dish, broadband, wifi – no signal for the phones down there – but it's amazing the changes that have happened.

❖    ❖    ❖

**I don't know what is next for me.** I don't really know. I've been working and trying and getting frustrated trying to do a new show for myself. I had various ideas.

So I was wondering why haven't I told my father's story. It was a different relationship, but still it has kind of evolved, and it's an almost impossible task, and I want to tell it because young people in particular know so little about what happened from Easter Week to the end of the Civil War. And I want to tell that story without taking sides, which is virtually impossible. My aim is only to tell the story to a whole new generation. As I said, I thought I would have it finished by now, and Yeats would be central to it.

When Yeats was awarded the Nobel Prize in Literature in 1923, Bertie Smyllie, who was the editor of *The Irish Times*, rang him to tell him that the news he'd been awarded the Nobel Prize had come in on the wires at night. Yeats's first reaction was: "How much is it, Bertie? How much?"

That's a good question and a question I have often asked myself.

# LIZ NOLAN

"I'm learning. I'm a student, I
always have been one."

*Liz Nolan hails from Dublin and trained in voice, oboe and piano at the DIT Conservatory of Music and Drama and the Royal Irish Academy of Music. Following a degree in English literature (TCD Hons) and MPhil in Music (DIT/TCD), Liz was appointed academic lecturer and singing teacher at the DIT Conservatory of Music and Drama. A HDip in arts administration (UCD) led to Liz's appointment as education and outreach officer at the Association of Irish Choirs.*

*In 2001, RTÉ lyric fm beckoned. There, Liz has presented a wealth of key shows including* **Classic Drive, A World of Song, Lyric Notes** *and* **Lunchtime Classics.** *She now presents* **The Full Score.** *Alongside her work on radio, Liz has researched and presented numerous acclaimed arts features, which have received international broadcast.*

**My job description is 'broadcaster'**, but I guess I'd have to say I'm learning. I'm a student, I always have been one. I've always been – perhaps driven is the wrong word – tempted by what's out there. The subject I'd pursue, the subjects around it, they seemed to be never-ending. They've been my big challenge or my spur, but they've also been my solace, my big companion all my life.

The biggest gift I was ever given was by a music teacher at school. It was a very nice, middle class girls school in south County Dublin. There was this teacher who was a revolutionary in our midst. She'd insist on putting on operas and bringing us Kodály and Beethoven. I remember one time I was having a lesson with her as she knew I could read music easily. I had a knack for music: I could be put on a stage and deliver a song, whatever you wanted.

Anyway, one day we were sitting together, and she said to me: "But surely you are familiar with the opening chords in Haydn's *Creation?*" I'd never heard of *The Creation* or any of his oratorios apart from the usual bits of *The Messiah*. I remember her being absolutely appalled: "You can't not have heard it, you can't. You stay there. I'm going to make you a cassette tape." It was the appalled response that took me aback, because I was always the good girl, the one that could be relied on to say or do the right thing. I wondered what had I done wrong. But then when she brought it to me, and I heard the first chords of *The Creation – The Representation of Chaos –* those big open octaves and the devastation and the beauty of it ... I remember feeling as if I was personally consumed by that music, that it was something bigger than myself. And I suppose if I had to date my real relationship with music, it would be from that point.

I was 11. I didn't really have a clue about music. I could read music fast, I had pretty good pitch, I had a nice true voice, and I could play the recorder easily, but it was at that moment that I realised that music was far bigger than me being clever clogs and being able to churn out what was wanted. I realised it would become a beloved thing to me, totally separate from just looking for approval from others, but one that would take me on this huge adventure of sorts. It was an extraordinary feeling of freedom.

I was quite an isolated, shy child; the only time I felt at home really was when I was on a stage because then I was in control of things. I could deliver what people wanted. But at that moment, it was like being liberated, like falling in love. I was pudgy and had an English accent; my Dad was English. I was very shy of mixing with other girls, so I'd spend afternoons after school in my bedroom at home, and my Mum let me have my foster uncle's record collection, these really old records – all the big hits, the Tchaikovsky violin and piano concerti, Beethoven's *Sixth*, Mozart's keyboard concerti, lots of stuff.

I never forget the first time I heard Smetana's *Vltava*: all these gorgeous sensuous passages and the story they told. Then Mum bought me my first double album of Callas singing various well-known arias, and I remember being struck by the ugly beauty of her voice, that mix which makes something truly transcendent.

I got into those opera arias and was mouthing all the words – even though I couldn't speak any of the languages, just going by the sound – so it became something bigger than me. It became my consciousness of a larger world, which I couldn't put in a box or control.

In general, I'm a bit of a control freak. I like feeling safe and I like feeling on top of things, but I've never been able to control music. And so, why I define myself as a student is ... because it's my first love. I'll never know enough about music, never. Forget about it. It's vast, it's illimitable, always glorious and unfolding. I meet performers who can walk on to a stage and perform miracles: insights they perhaps wouldn't be able to express in words, although I know some highly articulate and brilliant musicians.

I love that feeling of it being an endless pleasure, a beauty that I'll never ever reach the end of. I do my performances and present things, that's what I do on radio. I can try to be a bridge between the fantastic music and the listener who might not have heard it before; but what I do is for myself, a small part of this huge big sweep, this endless discovery.

My other love is books. I took my first degree in English literature at Trinity College Dublin, following in the footsteps of my brother and my mother. She'd gone back to university when I was 12, so there were three of us in the English department at TCD in quick succession, and that was kind of hilarious. The lecturers didn't know what hit them. But yes, I was the third Nolan to cross the doors there.

When I was young, my mother would sit down at evening time, and her way of getting through her course was to read some of her homework to me. So we'd have to put aside my *Anne of Green Gables* or whatever I had and she'd launch into *Paradise Lost* or bits of Chaucer with me. She'd haul me around the country to visit various monuments, to create a greater awareness of history, of culture, of what was available, what was out there. So I suppose I fell into words then in a huge way, which with the music, all coalesces in my love of song.

Opera is such a great field. It's a wonderful spectacle. It's all sensuous abandon, the greatest fun. All my friends at the Conservatory of Music were heading for big opera careers, but I always shied away from that. I wanted the world of the art song, which is kind of a miniature masterpiece, a perfect fusion of word and music like this distilled essence, a perfume of sound. I utterly loved it. If I had to put a finger on the time in my life when I was happiest, that was the world to be in, a wonderful time.

For my master's, I had a tutor who just let me explore every dimension of my subject. I was studying early 20th century French song. So in my mind, I was there in the cabarets of Montmartre in the 1890s, I was there going around the music halls, studying the great developments of art and music and literature of that time. There is so much. It is difficult to want to surface from that world.

❖   ❖   ❖

**I was brought up in Greystones, Co Wicklow,** back in the days when it was still a rural idyll. A sort of sleepy, little village. We lived in the Burnaby, a beautiful spot. I think we were one of the first Catholic families in that area. My Dad worked in business and was the handsomest guy in Dublin when he first came over in the 1950s. He was a very jovial English man who always watched the *Trooping of the Colour* on the telly and *Songs of Praise* every Sunday. He had a fine baritone voice, and of course, would roar out the hymns. And he had this marvellous selection of naughty pub songs that he used to teach me when Mum wasn't looking. He was a great fan of Benny Hill. Gosh, the more I think of it! The pair of us sitting at the telly, just heaving with laughter. Not the kind of stuff I'd watch today, in any shape or form, but back with Dad, it was magic.

---

*When I heard the first chords of **The Creation** ... I remember feeling as if I was personally consumed by that music ... my real relationship with music would be from that point.*

---

My two elder brothers, who I'm very close to, were away at boarding school, and I was at home. My grandmother lived with us. As a girl, she worked at a bookshop in Galway, alongside Nora Barnacle. And this weedy young fella from Dublin came down one summer, courting Nora – wonder who he was! And Gran and her colleagues used to wonder what was a fine girl like Nora doing with a baggage like that guy ... There you go. Gran lived till she was over 100 years old. In later years, all these scholars used to come and interview Gran about her memories of Nora Barnacle and James Joyce. And she used to give them an earful!

She was the first female journalist on the *Connacht Tribune*. She came up to Dublin with my Granddad. He was a scholar in Greek and Latin, and became a teacher at Belvedere. 'Old Pils', they used to call him. Because he used to say to the students at the beginning of class, "Gentlemen, open your Pils", it became his nickname. They had seven children, and then my uncle Heinz was fostered, during the Second World War. So in later life, Gran came to live with us and we were in this rambling house in the Burnaby.

I was quite solitary from an early age and lived in a dream world. Anything and everything went on in my head – fairytales, cartoons. We had a big garden, where I used to run off and hide and play my games. Because I was surrounded by adults in the family, I grew up very quickly in some ways and didn't relate so much to little girls my own age. Plus my primary school was way up the road in Glenageary, so there wasn't the same opportunity to hang with the local kids as there might have been. When I look back at that time, it's an era that's all golden and gone.

So then secondary school came and I went to Holy Child in Killiney, and it was there I met my music teacher, Mirette Dowling. I scraped through most subjects: I was so enmeshed in my world of dreams that I barely paid attention to what was being said to me. The only person who could penetrate that was Miss Dowling. She was director of the Wicklow and Bray Choral Societies, and she had such an impact on music in Ireland. She spotted that I had this facility. Mum had put me in for various music competitions, singing. I started when I was six, got a prize and went on from there; and Miss Dowling basically took it upon herself to introduce me to the world of music. I was very undisciplined. I hated piano practice and frankly I still do! But I took up oboe on Miss Dowling's recommendation and became a member of the National Youth Orchestra, a fantastic experience. Because to be playing and to be part of this larger sea of sound, to be enmeshed in these chords and harmonies, you don't even question it or analyse it, you're just part of the sound, which is a wonderful thing.

When I was in Trinity, I was living with my brother, who was doing postgrads at NCAD [National College of Art and Design]. We had this little place in Ballsbridge. We lived like two old bohemians, just turning up, eating our takeaways, waving at each other and going off again. We're very alike in many ways. I got my love of 1970s music off him: Talking Heads, The Clash, Elvis Costello, that sort of thing. All the time I was in Trinity, I was moonlighting at the DIT Conservatory where I would be studying singing, drama, piano, répétiteur, and then also at the Royal Irish Academy where I studied oboe. So there was a lot of running around.

I was just starting my finals when I got a phone call from St Teresa's Church on Clarendon Street, where there was a new prior, Fr Chris Clarke; he's actually only just stepped down recently. Fr Chris is a real mover and shaker and was revamping the music in the church, installing a really good choir. He wanted someone to sing cantor for a few Masses, and he told me he'd heard I was a good music reader. So I said: "Yup!" It was my claim to fame. I didn't have the vocal stamina or prowess of other students, but I could intellectualise my way around things.

So with these Masses, I said, "As long as I'm out of there by half past one", because I had my finals starting at 2pm in Trinity that day. I went along, met the organist and composer, Ronan McDonagh, who ever since has been one of my great friends – and that started my association with Clarendon Street church. I was cantor and in the choir there for 15 years. It was my lifeblood.

Under Chris and subsequently under other priors, such as Fr Jim Noonan, the provincial, we sang glorious repertoire: 15th and 16th century motets, classical Masses, plainchant ... The choir is still going strong. I only left when I was pregnant with Seán, and it was too difficult to travel up and down each week. Clarendon Street was central to my life. I'd run in and out all the time.

My 20s saw a mass of different odd jobs. I was working in about six or seven different places, lecturing at DIT, taking on loads of private students, and then in between all that, I'd be fitting in services at Clarendon Street, which was my home, basically. I suppose because of that kind of attachment, artistic and personal, 16th century motets would be one of my favourite music choices ever since. So that took me through that period: choir director, teaching everything from preschool to third level. Just never say: "No." Just keep going.

It was actually a frantic period, if I'm to be perfectly honest. I was terrified half the time. You could say terror's been a great spur in my career! Keeps you sharp. Once or twice I'd find myself in a bizarre situation, where I was still learning how to do whatever the damn subject entailed almost when I was walking in the door to teach it. But the trick, of course, is always in the presentation and always in the pulling of it together. You are the conduit, not the final stop. You are simply the means, and that is how you frame yourself and your subject. It was a million different facets of performance.

I got a scholarship to do my MPhil, which helped me a lot on my way. And the people in my life: my singing teacher, Deirdre Grier Delaney, I owe her more than I can say. Then the lads at Clarendon Street, Ronan and Frs Chris and Jim, they were a constant inspiration. They helped me make sense of it all, because in my 20s, as with anyone, life was a bit crazy. I found myself being all things to all people. Sometimes I felt a bit like Stevie Smith, not waving but drowning. My life would begin at 6 each day, rushing in for the first

8am job, and I'd be home at 9pm or 9.30pm that night. In a sense, it was massively fulfilling.

But I knew I needed some kind of permanence in my life. So I took another postgrad, a HDip in arts administration in UCD, and it ended up with me going down to Cork to become education officer with the Association of Irish Choirs. I found that intensely different: to be doing just one job. I'd go up to Dublin every weekend to sing at Clarendon Street and to see my Mum. Those were the years before the M8 bypass: four hours each way up the motorway, my God!

---

*The magic that happens on stage is founded in utter humanity – the ethereal is a part of what we are and it's just waiting to come out.*

---

I was at sea in my life at that time. My Dad had passed away: once you've been firing on all four cylinders – and then some – for such an extended period of time, and not having to question the whys and wherefores, and constantly having all these stimuli to sustain you ... then to have them taken away and go to the one terrific job – of course, it was great.

But I started questioning myself. I stayed two years in Cork, and I realised I'd never before had to develop a social network. I'd had it given to me – choirs, schools, friends that I knew from all these musical situations – but now, all of a sudden, I was completely alone in a completely vibrant, gorgeous city. I adore Cork. I would just walk around it, gawping all the time, but it was almost as if I had the stage taken away from me. I've always been a loner: is it the flipside of performance? Though these days I've got my little boy with me, so the loner thing is definitely left behind.

❖   ❖   ❖

**In the funny way that fate works,** I was putting together all these outreach programmes – these in-service days for teachers, choral days and this and that – and RTÉ lyric fm had recently started up. This would have been in 2002. I thought: "I'll get some promotion for an event, get something going. I'll ring them up and see what the story is."

So I get put through to this guy Eoin Brady, who's very nice. We have a chat: "You're in Cork? I'm from Cork myself. You've a very nice speaking voice. Did I hear a mini-disc with your voice on it, about a year back?" Now the year before, my friend Ronan from Clarendon Street had seen an advert in the paper, that lyric was looking for deputy presenters. Nothing would do Ronan but that I sit down and make a mini-disc of my voice and send it to lyric. Which I'd duly done and then forgotten about. Eoin remembered this.

His presenter was unwell at the time and Eoin needed someone to fill in for the next day. So he asked whether I could get off work. The next morning, I was in Limerick city, sitting in the lyric kitchen, so terrified! Black spots dancing in front of my eyes and that feeling of the cat sitting on your chest, just staring at the script I'd written. I'd been too scared to worry about whether anybody knew where I was – duuuuuhh!! – and about 15 minutes before the show Eoin bursts in, saying: "Where are you?! Come on!" He rushed me into studio and engineered the controls.

And that kicked off my long and brilliant friendship with Eoin Brady and his fellow-producer and wife, Sinéad Wylde, both my producers on lyric at various points, and who've been the most incredible influence on my life. It was pure luck at that time: between one thing and another, a couple of lyric presenters had to take time off, and there were opportunities for deputising.

And so I'd come up from Cork, and I was starting from the bottom. I've always aimed to be good or polished from the get-go on any project, but this was something else altogether. This is going to sound weird but it's absolutely the kernel of who I am: I have these insane standards for myself. It is very rarely in my own mind that I am really blisteringly good, but if I feel in my heart that I have been good, I don't care what you say or what the entire world says. You could decide that I'm rubbish, but I'll know that I was exceptional, because I've had so many times that I gave an okay performance in this and that, and I'd hear: "Oh, Liz, you were this and that, you were fab..." It'd be kind but meaningless to me.

But there were those rare moments when I actually hit my own bar and I wouldn't care what the world said, I knew it was good. It's so rare that I'm really, really happy when I get it. Mind you, at this stage of the game – with the benefit of maturity – I know when I've done a perfectly good enough job, which is grand. But you only get those incandescent moments of real fulfilment very rarely, and when they come they are wonderful. The world melts away. But it's not a self-orientated thing. If you just get it right, it's the feeling of gladness, the feeling that I did justice to that, I touched it. It is really only just reaching out for that instant – and then it goes. It's worth waiting years, decades for that.

Anyway, I was so lucky. It was just at this period when the station was still evolving, moving in different directions to try out different things – and it was based in Limerick. Back then, anyway, there was still this big hang-up about the Dublin/rest of the country divide, where – in my experience – people weren't that willing to move out of Dublin for arts jobs. So the idea of hanging out in Limerick, on the hope of part-time work, it mightn't have seemed so great for some, but I was still youngish, I had no ties. It was also my great aim to somehow attain this goal of being good on air, because it's quite different from academic music.

Putting together a running order, for example: you don't go along with a chronological congruity, we'll say, putting a Renaissance next to a Baroque composer. It's quite anarchic. But once you get a kind of consonance going on sonically, then it works really well. You've got to know when to be adventurous and when to be reverential. You've got to keep playing with the dynamic all the time and to create your own persona around it, but it takes time to learn how to do that.

During this period – I guess, my apprenticeship at lyric – I was presenting shows right across the gamut from breakfast to late-night shows. I was doing outside broadcasts and concerts. I still went up to Dublin at weekends, but apart from that, there were no other ties. I was literally just parked there.

In fact, I remember my first big gig. I was asked at short notice whether I'd be willing to present lyric's *Breakfast Show* for a month. And so I had to march into my Cork boss and hand in my notice. My brother came down from Dublin because I had to go over to lyric immediately and start prepping. He emptied my flat in Cork and brought my few possessions – mercifully, I'd been a bedsit girl most of my life, so I didn't have too much! – to Limerick for me. I moved into a small hotel in Limerick and hung out for what turned into six weeks.

You know when something is right. There was no question or doubt in all this: stay where I was in a stable job or go for something which had the promise of such achievement in it? I've been so lucky. RTÉ lyric fm is my dream made reality. It's fantastic. I go in to my job every day and it's party time! Okay, there are days when you're knackered, but most days it's just: "How did I get to this? How do I get to do this for a living?" It really is extraordinary. You couldn't have anticipated any of it. It was the biggest fluke in the world. If I hadn't rung Eoin Brady that morning, begging for some promo, it just wouldn't have happened. It's like fate. You simply have to go with this. It's like being born: you can't stay safe in the mother's womb, you simply have to go.

After deputising for about a year, a regular show came up on Saturday afternoons, *The Lyric Pitch*. My head of station, Aodán Ó Dubhghaill, rang me to offer me the slot. I still remember the call and his laughing at my whoops of joy. He's been very good to me.

After another year or so, a colleague moved to Radio 1, and the *Lunchtime Classics* slot became my new home, five days a week. So, whereas up to now I'd still been popping up and down to Dublin, keeping tabs on my previous life, now everything gravitated fully around Limerick and RTÉ lyric fm.

❖   ❖   ❖

**I had to adjust myself in all sorts of ways for a radio career.** Put it this way, up till now, I wouldn't have been picked as the most glamorous of types and was happier skulking around the edges of a social gathering than bouncing up and down in the thick of it. But now I was in this new arena, where the brief was to be personable, to play people's requests, to chat away, go on lots of outside broadcasts where you'd meet all kinds of people.

So, I got the look down, bought some frocks and mastered walking in heels pretty damn quickly. And yeah, I started to cultivate this part of my personality where I'd be chatting to people and became gregarious. It was such an education and a development of who I was – a strange journey from where I'd been.

I was on the lunchtime gig for six years and again, I made some great friendships, all over the country. From concert halls, where people would come up in the foyer saying, "Liz, how are you?", because I was part of their lives. I was in their kitchens, their living rooms, their cars. I'd be like an invisible friend. It was an immense privilege. I didn't feel equal to it sometimes. I'd often have to cut the conversation short with: "Sorry, going on air!"

I'll never forget my first time at the Ploughing Championships, the ultimate education for a townie like me. We were staggering into the RTÉ tent in our wellies, and I pretty much collapsed into Larry Gogan. He looked me up and down and said: "Ah Jaysus, you look perished. Will you sit down here?" He gave me his seat, belted off to find ham sandwiches for all of us, nothing too much for the man. He's a gent. You meet people like him and you think: "This is a great life."

So from there, different shows manifested. I was on the *Breakfast Show* just after Seán was born – that was quite a juggle! Then I was lucky enough to graduate to the *Classic Drive* show, which I worked for about six years. Such a head trip. Eoin Brady was my producer, God help him, for his sins! Sinéad Wylde, Eoin's wife, had been my producer for the lunchtime gig. Generally, I've developed really happy relationships with the people I've worked with.

And I was doing a wealth of features, too, with my research going out on air. I'd run with a whole load of different subjects, from French song to Dorothy Parker, to medieval epics, to pre-Raphaelite art, all kinds of different things. I could bring my ideas to Olga Buckley, lyric's producer-in-chief, and she'd put them on *The Lyric Feature* show.

It's an unbelievable honour and opportunity to be part of that. It's like a sweetshop or a playground in so many ways: the potential for following your inclination or ideas, it's always there. Where does it stop? The music, it bleeds into literature, it bleeds into art, it goes around in this glorious dance. You simply cannot draw the line. It's all learning. I'm a performing junkie, there's no doubt. And I adore broadcasting! Don't ever take me away from that.

*RTÉ lyric fm is my dream made reality. I go in to my job every day and it's party time!*

You have to be well-prepared, because to juxtapose sloppiness with such beauty would be sacrilege. Of course, we all have the capacity to blag and bluff our way. You have to if you're live on air and something unexpected happens: but with music, God knows, you just want to give it the best and most perfect of framings.

That said, we've all been caught out. I remember one time MCing a concert where I marched out onstage to introduce the following piece. Unfortunately, we hadn't been given the heads-up that there was to be a monumentally long pause while some instruments were taken off-stage, some brought on. So, muggins here blithely introduces the next piece, turns around to acknowledge the maestro and sees a guy crouched down beside me, midway through hauling a massive concert harp across the stage. So, while the world seems transfixed around you, in this moment of horror, I remember thinking: "Sod it, I'm still the one who gets to wear the frock frontstage!" I opened my mouth and started pulling it together: "Ladies and gentlemen, a slight delay in our performance, but while I have you here ..." You just find yourself keeping it going and improvising, because at the end of the day, it's all about the framing and presentation.

You cannot begin to realise the dedication of musicians and singers. Marvellous understanding: they'll fit themselves into an endless variety of situations. They'll be there, they'll deliver, professional in the face of so many changes, technical demands ... And the repertoire they tackle week in, week out is extraordinary. They're decent, nice people, who you can meet in the pub afterwards and talk about films or holidays or kids at school or any normal concern. But to have that juxtaposed with extraordinary achievement, where the superlative is an everyday job – there's a heroism in that. You realise how the magic that happens on stage is founded in this utter humanity, that the ethereal is a part of what we are, and it's just waiting to come out. It is mundane moments like that which kind of complete it for me.

I was lucky even when I was at the Academy of Music. My teacher and inspiration, Deirdre Grier Delaney, she'd let me stand up in French song class and just talk to everybody about the meaning of the verse behind the song. She'd say: "Now, Liz is going to speak for a while." The others must have been so pissed off with me! Having that platform, that licence, to express in different ways, I suppose it gave me the bit of latitude to hop on to other moving vehicles and to expand the brief. And to gain a little confidence when I realised I wasn't crashing and burning in all the projects I took on – that I could keep them going. It's a necessary part of music, it's a necessary part of the arts: you have to have that ability to keep jumping, keep learning as you move.

RTÉ lyric fm is an absolutely central part of my life. And if lyric wasn't there or if life were to evolve to a point beyond lyric, music and learning would always take primacy with me. I suppose I'd build on what I've learned over the years in terms of presenting, flexibility, and a kind of alternative take on organisational skills. Not what you read in magazine articles on organisational skills! But simply on organising our perception of what's around us. It's rather like these commedia dell'arte characters: somebody who comes up with these displays of artifice, which you know not to be real, but at the same time they throw a new light on actual reality. That's how I sometimes feel my job is. They know I'm there as a performer, but at the same time I try – through my presentation, how I put together all the different elements of music – to offer a different slant on what it is. To provide a moment, a 'click', a glance of illumination in that way. So I always want to play with words, always want to play with music in whatever life or job I would go for. That's something I adore, a benign manipulation.

I think the 'celebrity' aspect of the job is something more geared to other branches of working in media; it's certainly not something I'd relate to myself. I don't think it's part of me at all, I wouldn't even know where to begin with it. Put me on stage, I'll do whatever needs to be done. But in real life, God no! Come on, I'm not a celeb. I don't eat quinoa or do Instagram, or whatever the clichés are.

I'm just lucky to work where I am. I have opportunities I could never have dreamed of back when I was starting out. In my case, it was almost like fate. I knew there was a huge likelihood that nothing would have come after those six weeks back all those years ago in

Limerick, and I'd have to start all over from scratch, but there was no option but to do it. I couldn't turn away from it. I had to follow it through.

❖  ❖  ❖

**In my future, I'm thinking maybe of another postgrad.** I'm very privileged in what I do because my job encourages me to balance my life as a professional with further research – as well as being a mother. The greatest single regret I have is that I gave away all my books when I was pregnant with Seán. It was kind of a difficult period and I thought I had to change myself in some way, to commit myself to a whole new set of strictures.

I was also living in a very small house, and the books were just falling out. But that would be the most searing regret I've had in my life. I know books are things and we shouldn't regret things, but it's what they represent. They represented decades. I used to save up my waitressing money for the Arden Shakespeare editions – at £2 an hour, it took a lot of hours to buy a book.

A career is a wonderful thing. It's quite a grown-up thing, if I can use that term. I've never really considered myself as having fully grown up. I can navigate my way in the world, but all there really is beneath the day-to-day distractions is learning.

I think maturing lets you know your fields of interest. There are so many things that I regard as magnificent fields of study, but they hold no personal passion for me. I know the areas I simply would love to immerse myself in, and in another year or two, it'd be great to go back and juggle more learning alongside my work. I want to explore art this time because I feel that feeds into music and literature perfectly. It's pure consonance. There isn't any real line of distinction as I see it between them all. So yeah, if I can possibly juggle something, I will.

I'm going to be dashing off after this and taking Seán for a Friday treat at McDonald's – not every Friday, by the way! He's eight now, he's grown. It's wonderful to see him at this stage, very different from me at that age. We're a good team.

He pretends to be mortified at my antics. I was on *The Late Late Show* for the centenary celebrations last year, plugging a concert I was going to present, Mozart's *Requiem*. So, myself, Miriam O'Callaghan, Martys Morrissey and Whelan, Seán O'Rourke and a couple of others were dressed up in these antique clothes from 1916. We had a photoshoot first, then we all went on *The Late Late*, arriving onstage in a vintage car. God bless Seán's teacher from school, she recorded the show and played it for his class afterwards. You can only imagine his reaction: "Ohhh, mother!!!"

# ROBERTA O'BRIEN

"I'm a mother of three beautiful children, a wife, a daughter, a sister and a friend."

*Roberta O'Brien was one of the first two females to be awarded a Naval Service cadetship. She is now a senior officer – lieutenant commander – in the Irish Naval Service with over 20 years' experience. Her sea rotations have included navigation officer, gunnery officer and fisheries officer onboard the LÉ Niamh and executive officer (second-in-command) of the LÉ Emer. In 2008, Lieut Cdr O'Brien took command of the LÉ Aisling, the first time in the history of the Naval Service that a woman was appointed to take command of a State ship.*

*She has also been the Naval Service's health and safety adviser and senior staff officer for the flag officer commanding the Naval Service.*

*Lieut Cdr O'Brien enjoys team sports, having played competitive Gaelic football, hurling and rugby, and now enjoys keeping fit and running.*

**What am I? I'm a mother of three beautiful children.** I'm a wife. I'd like to think that I'm a loving, caring and understanding daughter, friend and sister. These are the kind of words that jump into my mind when I think of what I am.

I hold the rank of lieutenant commander in the Irish Naval Service. I'd say I'm dependable and hardworking. I expect a lot from others, but I expect a lot from myself also. I'd consider that I'm fair and approachable. Am I tough? It depends on whom you ask! I suppose I'd be tough, but I'd be equally as tough on myself. I remember somebody saying to me just that: "… but Roberta, you are as tough on yourself as you are on others."

And possibly I've mellowed over the years. I suppose it's due to age and less of a sense that I've to prove myself. Certainly when I was younger and as a female working in a male-dominated organisation, you do feel that you have to be that bit better and not give anyone grounds to say anything negative about your work ethic or towards you. I'd be a firm believer that you must walk the walk yourself as a leader. I wouldn't believe in hardship for the sake of hardship either. There is a time for putting the head down and doing the hard work required of the job, but there's also a time to have fun as well, which is also an important aspect of the job.

**One of my earliest memories is of my mother coming home from work,** which was a very unusual thing at the time, and she had a present of a tennis racket and ball for me. She had gone back to work in the bank after having to give up work when she got married in 1972 – you weren't allowed to work when you got married in the 1970s. I remember she went back when I was about four or five (in 1982/1983 for a year or two), because my brother was two or two and a half then. I thought it was great to get presents. I didn't see the fact that my Mam wasn't at home all day as a bad thing, especially as I was benefiting from it. I remember that she did seem very happy at the time to be working in a profession that she really enjoyed.

Growing up in Aherlow [Co Tipperary], I do remember we didn't have a lot of money. But it was a reflection of the time also – very few people had money in the 1980s. My parents had the beginning of their married life in Dublin but, due to a tragedy – my father's sister died very young, at the age of 30, leaving four children – Dad and Mam decided to move back to Aherlow.

My mother was always very outspoken and a real feminist and always said: "Don't let the fact that you are a woman stop you from doing anything – you can be whatever you want to be."

My whole family were always into sports. I used to play hurling with the older brother outside in the yard and my mother would say: "Why don't you play with the local team?" The headmaster in my primary school at the time used to coach hurling and football with the boys at lunchtime. My brother encouraged me and said that I should go up and join them, that I was well able to play with him. So I did and played hurling on the under 12s, up to under 14s at home.

I was the only girl on the team. I was accepted once I proved the first one or two times that when the lads would 'puck' me a ball, I could catch it and hit it back. You'd always get the snide remarks at the matches from other teams who didn't know you – "Ah, it's a girl you're marking" – but then once play began, that was the end of it. I would have gone to school with a lot of those guys on the team, so I fitted right in.

Overall, I'd a very happy childhood. Mam loved us all and was a very good stay-at-home Mam, but she was a very active person in her adopted community and always got out and about doing drama and meeting friends. Back in the great era of the Munster hurling final matches between Cork and Tipp, Mam was not afraid to don her home county colours of Cork and show her support for her home county despite living in the Glen of Aherlow in Tipperary. She wasn't a shy person – "Don't accept your place" – and she'd have always said: "Go for whatever you want to be." I remember a busy house, with a family of seven and having younger brothers and sisters, where you had to change nappies and do bottles as a kid. I used to say jokingly that I think that it was my mother's way of making sure that we were fully aware of the responsibilities that go with parenthood.

Pivotal moments? Good and bad? I suppose good ones would be family milestones, such as Communions and Confirmations. For such events, I remember, we went to my Granny's house in Bishopstown in Cork. At age 10 or 11, I remember cycling five miles with my Dad back to the small farm we had for a brief period to feed the cows. I remember enjoying the time spent helping out between feeding the calves, saving hay and setting the potatoes.

At the age of 12 or 13, I remember playing Scrabble with my mother and sometimes my older sisters late into night at the weekends. I used to love that time with her and my siblings, having fun, while also learning new words. She was a really bright woman, who loved crosswords and excelled at them, especially the cryptic ones. She was always trying to teach me how to solve them, explaining that they were like bad jokes. I'm still nowhere near her ability, try as I might.

---

*The ships interested me because of the navigation, the chart work, the plotting of the courses, all that and the freedom and getting away.*

---

And then not so nice memories: getting bitten by a dog at the age of four. The family had been visiting friends. My siblings, my cousins and I were playing outside when their dog attacked me. I remember my Dad beating the dog off me. I had to get stitches and still have three scars on my right leg from the bite. After that event, I didn't speak for a few days, which highlights how traumatised I was – especially for me not to talk! To this day, I am nervous around dogs but I try not to show it, especially in front of my kids as I don't want them to have that fear of dogs.

I was always wanting a BMX for Christmas and each year wondered why I didn't get a BMX – and the realisation when you get told that Santa doesn't exist and there is a reason why your stuff isn't the same as other friends in the community.

Again, there are seven of us. The eldest in our family is 45 and the youngest is only 26. My Dad says I'm in the middle of the two families, the baby of the older family and the eldest of the younger lot.

Where I grew up, it's lovely. I love going home, but when you are a 12- or 13-year-old teenager, living in the middle of nowhere, it's different. Our house is about three-quarters of a mile up off the road at the top of a passage-way. We are at the foothills of the Galtee Mountains. When my colleagues came to my mother's funeral, they were saying: "You do live in the middle of nowhere!" But what connects the family home to the big cities is the fact that we are so close to the motorway.

❖  ❖  ❖

**When I got to Leaving Cert, I was trying to think about what I'd do** and I was big into sport and study, so I looked at PE teaching. And on another trip that I'd done, in fifth year, we'd gone down to the Port of Waterford and one of the masters of the ships was talking to us, and I was really interested. I asked him what you had to be good at and he said you'd have to be good at maths – and I loved maths. So I was there: "Okay, right." So that kind of sparked it the first time.

I then looked into the Army but I quickly realised it was not the career for me. The ships interested me because of the navigation, the chart work, the plotting of the courses, all that and the freedom and getting away. If you ask any of my friends, growing up, I always wanted to leave home and I was always counting how many days I had left in school. To be able to get control of my life in order to achieve and get what I wanted – and I know there is more to life than money – I was very conscious that I didn't want my life to be a struggle.

My younger brother was big into the FCA and all that. I've a lot of family in the military. My Grandad was a warrant officer in the Irish Naval Service, my uncle served in the Naval Service, another uncle is currently serving in the Army, my younger brother and sister are currently serving in the Army, my brother-in law is in the Navy and my husband is in the Army.

Granddad, my mother's Dad, was also a warrant officer in the Naval Service, so the family had a house here on Haulbowline Island. Back then, Haulbowline was like a little community. Between Irish Steel workers and Navy personnel, their wives and children, all grew up on the island, so you used to have a post office and a primary school here on the island. Then the children went to secondary school in Cobh. My mother would have grown up just down the road so I didn't even tell her that I was going for the Navy, as I didn't want her to get over-excited.

When I was doing the research and didn't want to say too much to Mam, my uncle was in the printing press in the Army at the time, up in Dublin, and he had a lot of access to leaflets and booklets about the Defence Forces. So he sent me a big wad of stuff and I began reading up on it. I'll never forget reading the part about the Army: there was a piece by a lieutenant about when she was when in the cadet school. Reading her job description, I said: "No way, I wouldn't like to do that."

The Navy appealed to me more, despite the fact that they had no women in there at the time. It was just what they did – the navigation, seamanship, going out to sea, doing fisheries. I said: "Yes, that's what I'd like to do."

I put in my application and got called for an interview, and that's when I told Mam that I'd gone for it. She was thrilled. I knew she would be. When you are from a big family, the slagging happens – I still get slagged: "The golden one because you joined the Navy!" So Mam organised that I got a tour of the island and I got more of an idea of the Navy. Everyone thinks that because you are in the Navy, you must have known how to sail or that your Dad must have been in the organisation, it wasn't like that for me. You learn all that stuff on the job when you come in.

I captained the under 13s Garda Cup Final. They decided they'd make me captain for that match and it made the local *Nationalist*! In another competition, the final of the Féile na nGael, our team got the opportunity to play in Semple Stadium in Thurles. There was a girl on the opposition team, and the manager of the team wanted us to both mark each other and I remember our team manager saying: "No,

that's not Roberta's position. She plays wing back." He didn't see the
need to make the girls on the teams mark each other.

I viewed this as a positive measure of my ability and I liked it. My
perception was why shouldn't I be allowed to play. Because I went to
school with the lads, I was very lucky, I fitted right in and I was part
of the team. In relation to being captain for the Garda Cup Final, I
think there must have been discussions. They made a bit of a deal
about it, they must have seen I'd made the effort, but they said they'd
decided they'd make me captain. I had a photograph taken before the
match when taking the toss – it was unreal. Looking back, it was
probably the dedication I showed and love of the game that shaped
this moment. It was a small parish, everyone was delighted, none of
the lads were giving out or anything like that. I got on very well with
the whole team.

I went to secondary school then in St Anne's in Tipperary Town. I
was only there a few weeks ago, by invitation, to present awards for
leadership, academic ability and contribution to the community to the
pupils of the school. I was also asked to give a talk to the 300-plus
students who were attending the awards ceremony. It was nice to be
asked. They gave me a brief to talk about what the students are getting
their awards for, a bit about leadership, a bit about what I did. I
remember writing the speech. My initial draft was about 23 minutes
long. When I emailed the principal, she said: "It only has to be about
five or 10 minutes." So I edited it accordingly.

Thankfully, they were delighted and I was glad that I had made the
effort in preparing the talk. My key point was, yes, we've come a long
way with equality but there is a bit to go yet. In this generation, women
are told that they can do anything; however, as a parent, I notice
certain subtle messages in the media that still define the expectations
put on both men and women and how they should behave.

I have these healthy discussions with my Dad, but my key message
that day was that it's not that you are better than a man, or vice versa,
it's that you have to be the best you can be and to aspire to being the
best that you can be. Don't think that you can't choose a career or a
job just because somebody says you can't. Yes, there are challenges
but don't look at what other people are doing. You must do what's
right for you: that was my message to them. You can't be comparing

yourself to others – so-and-so does this, they've a great life – you have to look at yourself and what is right for you and what works for you.

In order to maintain my continuous personal development, I did a higher diploma in management and marketing in UCC and we did a practical weekend down with Pat Falvey. I thought he was brilliant; he is an excellent motivational speaker. We had to do these different tasks where they broke us up into groups. Somebody else was tasked with taking charge of the exercise and we were getting nowhere. So in the end, I took charge and we completed the task in a few minutes. I saw that sometimes people are very reluctant to jump in, but when things aren't working out I've no problem taking charge. I hate doing it if it is going to annoy people so you've got to strike the balance. You could get people's backs up within the group and I think that is about bringing people along with you. It can be situation-dependent.

---

*You have to be the best you can be and to aspire to being the best that you can be.*

---

As a ship's captain, there are times that you have to be autocratic, such as fighting a fire or bringing a ship alongside, but at other times when trying to implement change or policies, you have to bring people along and make sure you are talking to the key influencers on board, explaining your rationale. You can have a briefing every day from the ship's captain but you need to do more as a leader when meeting people onboard every day and getting your message out subtly.

I bring my people skills back to home. As I said, I came from a family of seven, with an age span of almost 20 years, and I was stuck in the middle, so I guess that I saw myself as an arbitrator between the older and younger batch of siblings. I did feel that, because I was in the middle, I wasn't fully in either batch so I always tried to ensure that we all got along. And this entailed developing listening and understanding skills that formed the foundation of my people skills.

As a family, all of us get on with one another. Aunts and uncles would say we are very close but even back then, I realised the importance of people skills.

In secondary school, I was big into wanting to be a PE teacher. It's funny, Mam wouldn't have discouraged it but I remember her saying: "It'll be very expensive ..."

My Gran lived in Bishopstown at the time and the parents financially were trying to gear us all towards UCC. But, in fairness, she didn't put me off it. However, the fact that there weren't a lot of jobs in PE teaching at the time was a factor also. So you can even see at that early age, it was important to me to get a steady job. A steady income would have been one of my driving forces.

Funny, I'm jumping now, but another pivotal moment, and I do remember this, going in the car in the school with my mother, I think I was in first year or second year, and Mam going: "This is most important now. People think second year isn't important at all, but it's like the foundations of a house. If you don't start to do your study now, you won't reap the rewards." Both Mam and Dad were very much about education – education was the way out. I had a conversation with my sister – she's a teacher now – but she said: "I don't remember that conversation at all." But I'm sure Mam gave it to all of us. It was just how I took it, the importance of education and having a good work ethic in that regards.

I didn't get PE in the end. I didn't get the points but I was awarded a cadetship in the Navy even before the CAO offers came out, and I surprised myself at how excited and thrilled I was to have gotten the Navy. I was working in Bansha Castle, a B&B nearby. I had a summer job and I used to cycle in five miles, do the work and cycle home. I nearly crashed the bike with the excitement on the way from work and, in fairness to the owner of the B&B, she popped a bottle of champagne to say congratulations.

❖    ❖    ❖

**So I joined up in 1995. They'd never had women before in the Navy,** so myself and another female, Orlaith Gallagher, also a lieutenant commander now, were the first. The Naval Service were trying to decide if they were going to send us to the UK to be trained or if they'd train us themselves. We were being told: "Oh, have passports. You are going to the Royal Navy to do your training." Then it was: "No, we'll train you ourselves." Orlaith is now working in Dublin in Defence Forces headquarters. She's had command of a ship as well.

We came here to Haulbowline first for two weeks. We joined on September 18th, 1995. My parents brought me down and we were welcomed to the place. Everyone was as nice as pie, then we got to the cadet's mess and it was like, "Right, get changed", and the seriousness started. I had left home. I was excited. It was going to be two weeks here and then the Curragh and I wouldn't get home for the 12 weeks then until Christmas. I came down to the naval base a bit anxious, to be honest: "What if I'm not able to do the seamanship?" I decided to take it one day at a time, chip away at it.

I remember we went to Dún Laoghaire and did sail training for the day. Then we went out onto the *LÉ Eithne* for a week and I loved it, but I was wrecked tired. They put us into the watch system straightaway, so you are up at 3.30am and you don't get to the bunk until 12 the next day and then up at 3.30pm and you might get to the pit then at 10 at night and back up at 3.30am. We were just being shown the navigation, but actually doing understudy lookout with the other ranks.

We were also given the mundane tasks required at sea, such as scrubbing the decks, cleaning the heads [toilets] and showers and cleaning the mess area [dining area]. As a junior cadet, you are down in the ratings mess, and you carry out all the tasks of a rating and junior NCO [non-commissioned officer]. Hence you work your way up and know what work your future subordinates have to carry out. When Dad picked me up at the train station at the end of the week, I was still swaying.

Then we went up to the Curragh for 12 weeks, which I hated. I didn't like the experience, though I know there is a need for it. It's to introduce us to military life and to militarise us. I was not permitted to leave the Curragh camp without permission and weekend passes to Newbridge had to be earned. There was always a curfew, even at weekends.

The first three months of induction training are long days, as everything is new – from the foot drill to rifle drill, physical training, military writing and courtesy and etiquette. You are up at 6am until

11pm at night, polishing boots, ironing shirts and completing cleaning details of the section rooms [training classrooms] and lines [area around the accommodation]. It's changed a bit now, but we were picking leaves out of drains and dumping them in fields, sweeping roads.

I never heard the word Brasso before I entered the cadet school. I remember feeling very sorry for myself on my 18th birthday, 'brassoing' a plate on a door, going: "What am I doing here?" But it was all character-building stuff. It is amazing how being put through these tough times really causes a class to bond.

There were three other girls with me, Orlaith who I mentioned, Lorraine and Caroline, both of whom were in the Army. We are all the best of friends to this day and meet up regularly. We always had music on when doing our cleaning details in the accommodation area, or 'the passage' as it is called. The line from a song by the Rembrandts – "So no one told us life was going to be that way ... I'll be there for you ..." – springs to mind when I think about my time in the Curragh and the great friendships that began there. It was the camaraderie that kept us going. The friends that I made in those three months were for life.

When we started off in the Curragh, there were five Naval cadets, 20 Army and 10 Air Corps cadets in my intake. During training, we were split into sections with a mix of Army, Air Corps and Naval Service cadets. It was important for the team and unity to mix with everyone else, so that was good. We had a great class and we all got on. So when you are having to get through stuff, whether running or academic work or cleaning leaves out of drains – 'details' as we call them – you are all in it together. That is when you see the importance of working together to get through the difficult and mundane. The flipside of it, when you see somebody who doesn't, who just goes off and does their own thing, you can see how detrimental that is. It affects the outcome.

I think because my mother knew I didn't like the Curragh, she wrote to me every day. It was really nice to receive a letter every day and a big boost to my morale. Of course, back then you didn't have mobile phones and the only means of communication with home was a phonebox down the other end of the lines where the guys were – and you had to ring a bell if you wanted to go up the stairs to use the phone. Due to the large class, it was difficult to get the opportunity to use it. Therefore the 'letter in the pigeon hole', as we used to call them, was like: "Yay!"

The training was very intense. I love running now, but I found it very difficult back then. I'd say it to anybody joining: "It doesn't matter if you are last, the important thing is to just keep going." I've a cousin who's just recently joined and I said to her: "Look, we all have our strengths and weaknesses. Nobody will excel at everything. The important thing it to do your best. It's the collective ability of the individuals is what makes the team." But, of course, you'll have the people who think you have to be able to carry a 36kg pack to make you a brilliant leader or officer – it doesn't. The Albert Einstein quote always comes to mind here: "If you judge a fish on its ability to climb a tree, then it will live its whole life believing it's stupid."

---

*I was really lucky I was the navigator for the*
*LÉ Niamh when it was tasked to go to Asia.*

---

There are other attributes you can bring to the table. But when you are 18, and a minority in a male-dominated group and you are going running every day and coming last all the time, yes, that was tough to manage, even psychologically. So the first three months of the militarising was very tough in that regard. And when I look back, the running wasn't that hard. It was just the fact you knew it was going to be something outside your comfort zone, and nobody likes doing something they are the worst at every day. But keep going and you'll be fine.

It's not what we do every day anyway. It's more to do with your mettle, your psychological ability to push yourself and not give up. That's how I'd see it and that's the rationale behind it because, certainly as a naval officer, I don't need to be able to run marathons. But having a certain level of fitness, stamina, ability to climb up the side of a trawler and maintain a certain level of fitness for your own health and well-being is important. I did find it tough and, on the other side of things, I wasn't into the tactics and that, getting 'camoed up'. I thought this isn't what I want to do. I want to be out at sea.

I couldn't wait to get to sea; even a few of the instructors used to be slagging me when I was in the Curragh. I worked hard and got on with it and at the end of the term the head of the school asked me if I wanted to transfer to the Army as I was doing so well. My class officer jumped in, "No, she doesn't."

I subsequently trained a cadet class – you go up there with your class to keep an eye on them. And we do the courtesy and etiquette side of the house, so straightaway the banter between the Army and Navy and Air Corps gets going – you have those nuances as well.

I finished at the Curragh and came down here to Haulbowline. I was lucky to get through in the end because the week before we were due to come back down here, I broke my wrist. Fortunately I had completed my military training at this stage.

I came down to the naval base and it wasn't as great as I thought it was going to be. Initially, we were up early doing our morning activities and running, with academic classes in the evening, instead of picking up leaves, so it had its challenges as well. I did find the academic aspect of my training challenging but I did enjoy it. I enjoy studying.

I really enjoyed when we went out to sea. We went out to the *LÉ Emer* for three months and I really enjoyed that. You basically put into practice the subjects you have done in the classroom. The patrols were three weeks out, two weeks in, but you were slotting in as part of the crew. I loved it at sea.

And then we went back into the classroom and did more academic stuff. Then you'd go out on your own as a senior cadet. When you are a junior cadet, you are doing the work of the ordinary ratings and the non-commissioned officers (NCOs) – in the rank structure, you've the officers, NCOs and other ranks – so you are in the ratings mess. When you go out the second time, you are actually doing what an officer would be doing up on the bridge, the chart work, filling out the logbook, etc.

I did have my doubts and discussed my future career with my parents. In fairness, I remember Dad saying: "Do you enjoy what you are doing?" I said: "Yes, but the politics ..." I could see it at that stage regards people and this and that, the politics, management structure and who gets on and how they interact and interplay. I said I couldn't deal with that for the rest of my life, and my father said: "But Roberta, you've that everywhere!" That's the way he said it to me. So I came back here and I was so much happier. I'd made my decision.

A classmate asked me if I was leaving, and I said: "No, I had a chat with the parents." And while they were quite happy for me to leave and go to college in UCC, after the chat with my Dad, I thought: "No, he's right. You are going to have to deal with people no matter where you go." People ask me if I enjoy going to sea and I'll say, "I love it" but it very much depends on who you are at sea with.

I loved my training on *LÉ Emer*. When we got sent to NUI Galway to do a science degree, we were very fortunate, because this meant that we were going to college with our Army colleagues and it gave us the opportunity to rebuild connections that I believe benefited both services.

This was before the National Maritime College of Ireland was built here. There were only about four years where they sent naval officers to Galway, so it was a fantastic experience. I was sent there from September to May [1997-2000] and then came back here for the summer to work, but you were on a salary while you were in college. My sisters, who were on grants, said I wasn't a real student. Which I wasn't, especially when I was getting a salary. However, I did have to sign an undertaking of 10 years' commitment to the Naval Service on completion of my degree.

When I used to come back to the naval base during the summer, I found that very hard although I loved the sea-going aspect of it. I remember a particular tough, old taskmaster saying to me: "I'm tough on you because you are a woman." He made life so very difficult for two summers that I almost packed it in. But look, you have to get through these things.

What got me through it? Friends, people in the organisation, other officers on the ship who would say: "That's just him." He was the ship's captain at the time. He used to keep me on my toes when I used to be up on the bridge – he gave me my own watch, before I had my watch-keeping certificate – but yet, I'd be there thinking: "He's going to come up now. What's he going to ask me? He'll try to catch me out with something."

You are what's called the captain's representative on the bridge for your watch for four hours and you need a certificate, similar to your driver's licence, but during these summer months while I was at college, I still hadn't got that piece of paper, and I remember dreading him coming up. I still would not be an advocate of his approach to mentoring or his teaching methods but it made me want to be sharper, making sure I didn't get caught out.

Look, you have to be positive. When I was going for the lieutenant commander interviews, he was very good. I went and spoke to him and he gave me great advice regarding the interview and all that.

I enjoyed Galway, loved it, but by the end of it, I couldn't wait to finish up, to get qualified and start into my first sea-going rotation. I was sick of being the trainee, as we'd done two years as cadets and three years in Galway. I could have done four years, but I'd no interest in doing geology for a fourth year.

At the same time, I just wanted to get back and start into the job. I regularly have this conversation with my husband Peadar – that's the part of the job I love, being at sea. But because things have changed at home, it's harder to justify it. And, if I stay, I will be going out to sea, because if you are in the Navy, it's part of our job and the part that I really do enjoy. It's the mix of people on board, the mix of what you are doing as part of your job, the variation in activity at sea – from sea fishery protection to search-and-rescue operations to naval boardings, fire fighting, etc. It is like a little family onboard ship. As I put it to somebody before: "Can you imagine having to sit down and have dinner with your boss every night?" You learn to develop your diplomacy skills at a very early stage in your career. I always felt that I couldn't let my guard down.

When I finished the three years in Galway, I came back here, did more navigation exams, refresher, rules of the road – like driving a car, you've the rules of the road for driving a ship – and then you have a practical exam. You go out onto a ship for a week. You get assessed in navigation, visual and blind anchorages – where you advise the ship's captain on what courses to steer to bring the ship in safely to anchor and actual ship-handling it. So that is a nerve-wrecking week. You are out getting assessed for the week, with the final day being the ultimate assessment.

Orlaith and I were the only two executive branch/operations branch cadets in our class – and we had to navigate the whole way up into Limerick. My friends came down from Tipp to wish me the best of luck. It really meant a lot that they came to visit and it spurred me on more to succeed.

Even though you do get a pilot going into Limerick, in the Naval Service you have to have your passage plans prepared regardless, as the ship's captain has ultimate responsibility. Therefore, as the navigator – we were trainee navigators – we had to have the passage plan and the 'nav' notebook and the visual aids we were going to use to assist and advise the captain. Yes, the captain listens to the pilot but s/he always likes to have the navigator as well and the passage plan prepared. So that was what we practised and then you do your three-point fixing along up the river. It was a tiring week but it was worth it in the end. Getting the watch-keeping certificate was a milestone in my career.

❖    ❖    ❖

**I was delighted to get my first appointment** – on one of the new ships back then, the *LÉ Niamh*. I was really lucky I was the navigator for the ship when it was tasked to go to Asia. The ship was away for three months. It was 2002, the cusp of the Celtic Tiger. The objective of the deployment was to promote Ireland and Irish products abroad, and the voyage was very much linked with Enterprise Ireland, the Navy, the Department of Defence and the Department of Foreign Affairs.

Trying to get a foot into the Asian market was apparently very formal, very hierarchical and required a significant level of protocol. Hence the concept of the Asian deployment was developed and marketed from the point of view of "Look, you are stepping on Irish soil when you come on to the Irish State ship", so we were at our busiest when the ship was alongside. When alongside, a marquee was set up and a number of receptions hosted. We were working non-stop and were tired at the end of it. Strange as it may seem, our down-time was when we were at sea.

*Training the cadet class, I was my own boss,*
*and I enjoyed the autonomy this afforded me.*

It was an amazing experience. Prior to the deployment was stressful as I was the navigator. When I found out we were going, part of me was delighted, but at the same time I did have an appreciation of the significant workload required to get the passage plan prepared and executed. This was solely my responsibility, so there was a certain amount of trepidation on my part in this regard.

The ship stopped in Malta first, in Valletta, for refuelling. Then we went through the Suez Canal, an amazing experience. We stopped off in Eritrea because the Irish troops were over there and to refuel. It was a tough experience to see a country so devastated by war.

Then we went down to Cochin [Kochi] in India and stopped off there. The ship had a link with Fr Raja, a priest who had a charity shop in Schull. We were bringing clothes over for him to collect and he was something like 200 miles from this port. But when he got there, due to the bureaucracy and politics, the port policemen would not allow him onboard. So our guys put the bags over their backs, and said: "Where is your car, Father, and we'll go out and escort you and go with you." Again, I hadn't been to India before – my first time seeing the distinction between the haves and have-nots.

Singapore was our first big event per se. We had to put up the awnings and hosted on average two events per day. Singapore was where we had one of the largest events, with about 200 guests onboard, all on the upper decks under the awnings on the ship. It was phenomenal – we were like a floating hotel. Singapore was very busy.

But there were some lighter moments. We were in Hong Kong for St Patrick's Day, so we got to go to the Hyatt Hotel, where there is a large St Patrick's Day ball, and a couple of crew got invited to it. As we were moored, we had to get the boat taxis ashore for the black tie event. I had a dress, but I wore Adidas runners with the blue stripe matching my dress for the boat taxi journey. Now I had the high heels in the bag, but I was winding the captain up, saying: "What do you think of my shoes for tonight?" He didn't know what to think. So when I eventually got ashore, I told him not to worry, I had a pair of heels in the bag.

Then we went up to Shanghai – again, we were there for four days with one or two events each day and at least two or three corporate lunches. The corporate lunches were in the ward room, the officers' dining area, so that had to be all set up. We had five officers – six, including the captain. There were always two officers on: one on duty by day, one on duty for the whole night.

Across to Incheon in Korea – it was the year of the soccer World Cup, 2002 – and then Tokyo and Penang in Malaysia and then back up to India, Eritrea, the Suez Canal and Palma. A truly amazing experience.

On the ship, the crew were training, resting, and keeping the ship going. When we got to Tokyo, everything was prepping for the next few days: food, logistics, cutlery, cleaning linen, party packs, big screens for briefings. You'd different companies, different crowds coming down to make their pitch to important businesspeople on board, so really we had to make sure that everything was plain sailing and went off smoothly.

Tokyo to Penang was the longest trip at sea. It was seven days and we got beautiful weather. We crossed the equator, about 20 or 30 miles south, just so we could say we crossed into the southern hemisphere and we did the whole King Neptune thing and doused everyone with the guck they make up (flour, milk and eggs, etc) – some tradition that they paint the bullring blue and that kind of stuff.

So you did things to bring a bit of lightness to the journey. I enjoyed getting the break, not having to do receptions and hosting the whole time. Despite being in different parts of the world, there was very little down-time. Hence the seven days at sea was just what the crew needed. You did your twice daily four-hour watches, but then when I came off watch, I'd enjoy going for a run on the treadmill and a bit of reading. I love reading. I don't get to do enough of it now. It's a nice hobby to have.

Promotion from sub-lieutenant to lieutenant is fixed-term once your annual appraisals and recommendations are given by your commanding officers. The first time you'd actually go for interview for promotion is lieutenant to lieutenant commander.

After a year and half at sea, they asked me to go in to train the cadet class but I wanted to finish off my two-year stint on the *LÉ Niamh*. I went in the following year to train a cadet class. I really enjoyed training them because the cadet master pretty much left me to get on with it. I was my own boss, and I enjoyed the autonomy this afforded me. The syllabus of training is very structured and rigid. I had to get through it and I had to train a class – you saw a beginning, middle and an end to it. I started with 16 and I finished with 10. I would be confident in the ability of the officers commissioned under my watch.

I suppose that the class would have considered that I was tough on them but there are certain standards that must be met and I was unwilling to compromise these standards. I did ask a petty officer (PO) I'd sailed with before on the Asian deployment to assist me with the training as I had identified him as someone who I wanted to be the link between me as class officer and the cadets.

My PO was a well-seasoned leading hand and a very hard worker, but not tough for the sake of it. He was the epitome of 'firm, fair and friendly'. I remember him saying, when I was a year into the training: "Ma'am, they all think that you are a wagon!" I had no issue with that. It was not my job to be their friend; it was my job to make sure that they first and foremost met the required standards of the Naval Service and second that they would be conscientious, hard-working officers. I led by example – for instance, I always joined them for their physical training. Like my PO, I was firm, fair and friendly but I also had to ensure that they were competent and develop their leadership capabilities. I subsequently served with two of them, and one of them said they didn't realise how sound I was. I said: "You weren't meant to!"

Then I went back out as second-in-command of the *LÉ Emer*. As always, I enjoyed my time at sea: two years as XO [executive officer]. There was a great crew and my boss at the time, the captain, who is retired now, was a brilliant mentor. Again I doubted my career choice, but my ship's captain told me: "You definitely have the ability, so you should stay for ship's captain anyway and then make your decision afterwards."

He said from personal experience that being captain was the best appointment in the career of a naval officer and this inspired and spurred me on, because you always go through doubt. "Do I have the ability?" Yes, I can do nav and I can do XO, but ultimately being responsible for a State ship and the lives of your crew was something that I didn't take lightly. There is such a sense of accomplishment in being able to manoeuvre a 65-metre vessel into a tight berth and I must admit, while I am always apprehensive in doing this, I do get a great sense of achievement from getting it done.

You'd be sitting down beforehand jotting down the way the wind is blowing and planning, but you have to stay calm while it is happening. I got great guidance and exposure to ship-handling as a second-in-command of the *LÉ Emer*. The captain was brilliant. When I said this to him subsequently, numerous times, he'd say: "Oh, you are just saying that." I'd say: "No, if I'd have come across a different type of captain, I may not have stayed."

The crew we had were also excellent and this added to my time at sea. A two-year sea rotation can be made feel infinitely longer when the crew don't gel. Due to the fact that the *LÉ Emer* was the oldest ship in the fleet at the time, people had a perception that she could not perform to the same extent as the other ships. However, the captain did not use the age of the ship as an excuse. He demanded high standards of his crew and he led by example.

---

*There is such a sense of accomplishment in being able to manoeuvre a 65-metre vessel into a tight berth.*

---

A junior officer in the Naval Service normally does two years ashore and two years at sea. When I was a year in after my XO stint, I got the opportunity to do a relief on the *LÉ Aisling* as lieutenant. It was only for three days but I was going to be in charge, so that was fantastic. I brought the ship back into the basin, so that was my first time ever on my own with nobody giving advice. The basin entrance is about 19 metres wide and the *LÉ Aisling* was only about 10.5 metres, but it is still quite tight. That was a fantastic experience.

I got a call a few weeks after my promotion, asking if I wanted to go out to sea ahead of time, so I said: "I will." I loved it, really enjoyed it. I had a great crew. The coxswain onboard, the most senior NCO, had been a leading hand when I was out on the *LÉ Emer* as a cadet. The Navy is small and I was also at sea before with the bosun, who is in charge of all the deck work, and I know him to be a fantastic guy. Equally with the officers, one or two I'd been at sea with before and others I hadn't but it was great. I just really enjoyed being in charge and making the decisions and going with that.

You get your sailing orders, and 'command' directs you on where you have to go and what-not. I really enjoyed the fact I had control of where the ship was going to be. Once the work was done, I had the control to bring the ship in. I always gave shore leave – if guys just wanted to stretch the legs to go for a run or a walk. It is often nice to get off the ship and clear the head. I'd learned from another ship's captain: "Offer them the time off the ship, whether they use it or not." Of course, if the weather is horrendous, it may not be safe to grant it.

I saw the importance of communication skills and realised that the way you give/deliver news and orders to people is equally as important as the news and orders themselves. My two years onboard the *LÉ Aisling* were extremely rewarding and an enjoyable and challenging experience.

The relief I was supposed to do onboard the *LÉ James Joyce* was cancelled. I want to go out now as a relief, to get a handle on what the new ships are like to drive. The crew size hasn't changed even though the ships have got bigger, because the technology has advanced as well. The ships are out for longer as well and are expected to stay out in rougher weather, so the ships are a lot more comfortable for the other ranks in particular. As an officer, you'd have always had your own cabin; the other ranks share and would have had cabins with four berths, as we'd call them, whereas a lot of them now are two berths.

A ship gets what is called a 'sailing order' from ops command. The 200 nautical mile limit out from the coast is broken up into zones of 1 to 10, so you'll be told you'll have to carry out patrols in certain areas. When I first joined, you'd be hoping to find a trawler but now we have a vessel-monitoring system that gives a live feed to the ship on where the trawlers are. If a ship comes across a trawler, you can go and check on the system how long it has been operating in the area, previous boardings carried out, etc.

One of these ships costs about €70 million. But the many lives on it are more important and the captain is responsible for all of them. I look forward to taking command of one of the new ships.

❖   ❖   ❖

**What does the future hold?** I've had phenomenal experience and such exposure to a large variety of roles and responsibilities at such a young age. It has been daunting at times but amazing too when I look back. To get promoted to the next rank, I did my senior command and staff course.

It was funny: before I went on the course, I was pregnant with the twins and my boss said to me: "So, Roberta, what is your plan when you come back from maternity leave? It's not that I want to get rid of you here in naval headquarters, but you are here about three years and it is very important to get the variation in your range of areas of expertise."

I said to him: "Well, sir, I'm planning on doing the senior command and staff course." He said: "Who is going to mind your children, Roberta?" I said: "Sir, thankfully, I have a fantastic husband who is willing to share the joy of rearing the twins, touch wood, all going well." He said: "You should have a contingency plan."

That was because I was going to be away Monday to Friday. It still surprises me that this is still the mindset of a certain generation. I know he meant it in the nicest possible way, but women are in the Navy 20 odd years now and I was thinking: "Would he have asked that to a male colleague who intended on going on a command and staff course whose wife was due to give birth?"

I love the Navy and I see it as a great place to work, but there are huge morale issues within the service and the Defence Forces in general over pay and conditions and I would find it difficult to stay in the Navy if I wasn't in a position to make it a better organisation. But this is where the leaders step up to the mark; they can acknowledge the fact of it and then persist and try to get improved pay and conditions.

In the meantime, there are other areas where you can try and make it a better place to work, as you have to be constantly changing and improving with the times. So if I stay, I'd hope to get promoted, but it's dependent on the organisation and where it is going as well. The promotion is really about another challenge. I sound big-headed but I could do the job at this stage, so yes, it is really about another challenge.

# PÁDRAIG Ó CÉIDIGH

"I'm a person who loves
challenges."

*Pádraig Ó Céidigh is the founder of Aer Arann and Aer Lingus Regional. A former recipient of the EY Irish Entrepreneur of the Year award, Pádraig was nominated for World Entrepreneur of the Year in 2003 and has twice been invited back as a judge. He is adjunct professor of entrepreneurship and business in NUI Galway, chair of the Business School Advisory Board and an alumnus of NUIG and Harvard Business School. Pádraig is a former board member of RTÉ, Croí, Bord Iascaigh Mhara and Fáilte Ireland West and chair of the National GAA Research Board. He is also founder of other companies in publishing, music, aircraft maintenance, outsourcing, homecare and internet marketing. Pádraig is currently an Independent Senator (nominated by the Taoiseach) and chair of the Joint Committee on the Future Funding of Domestic Water Services.*

**My parents were from Connemara,** my mother from Ballyconneely, my father from Spiddal. Both of them left school by the age of 10 and neither went to secondary school. Life then was all about hard work, with a bit of fun thrown in from time to time. My father grew up speaking Irish. He had to learn English as a second language.

They met in an Irish dance hall in Cricklewood in London, and came back to Ireland to raise a family. My father worked on building sites in Galway – actually, he was one of the labourers building Galway Cathedral back in the day – and then he used to drive a truck for Údarás na Gaeltachta. During the summers, while in secondary school, I worked with him, carrying blocks and cement and labouring on building sites.

At age around 12, I worked in a local factory in Spiddal on Saturdays, making Crolly Dolls. Those dolls used to be exported all over the world and were in high demand. Hugh McFadden from Donegal was the manager there. Outside of the GAA pitch, this was the first time I saw and began to understand teamwork in action. Hugh was a very good manager. He was firm but fair.

I was always challenging myself: "Can I do it faster?" I'd time myself. "Can I do it better? Can we, as a team, improve?" There was probably eight or 10 of us on the production line, each person doing their own thing along a conveyor belt, but part of the overall process with a common goal. If you were at the start of the belt, you could dictate the speed, so I always wanted to be at the start of it. I was always testing to see where there was a bottleneck. "Can we change this a little bit? Can we make the production line more efficient?"

I enjoyed that challenge. And when we were going up to the bog cutting turf, carrying it in wheelbarrows or on our back, I'd be thinking: "Is there a faster, better way of getting this out to the boreen? Is there a better way of doing this?" I didn't come up with a better way but that was the way I was thinking. I was 12.

I attended Coláiste Iognáid, the Jesuit secondary school in Galway, which was kind of unusual at the time because not many people from Connemara went to 'the Jes'. My parents knew very little about the Jesuits, other than going to Mass there from time to time. To be honest, I went there because a friend of mine was going there. We travelled in and out of the city to school by bus. I was always very keen on sports and played a lot of Gaelic football and hurling at home in Spiddal. So, when I went to the Jes, I found myself training and getting on school teams in Gaelic, rugby and soccer. This helped me settle into this new and very different environment. I found it really difficult there for a while because it was very different to the rural, Irish-only school I had come from. I found it very strange at first but, reasonably quickly, I got into it and really took to it.

In the Jes, Paddy Lydon was my first maths teacher. Paddy and I later taught together and we are still good friends today. I built a really good relationship with the teachers. I bought into the Jesuit ethos and philosophy. This is a cornerstone of who I am today and how I live my life. I found the Jesuit education absolutely phenomenal – it brought me to a different level of thinking, reflection, understanding and engagement with the world. Little did I know it at the time, but the Jesuits became a significant and a very positive influence on my life.

❖     ❖     ❖

**After the Jes, I studied commerce and business in UCG.** It is amazing the influence great teachers can have on a young person's life. Michael Holland was one of those teachers. I enjoyed university life. I played hurling, football and rugby and had plenty of craic with the lads.

When KPMG came to the university interviewing students for jobs, I was keen to do the interview but didn't have a suit. A friend came to the rescue, as he allowed me to borrow the suit he had worn for the same interview an hour or so earlier. The interview was going fine, or so I thought, until one of the two KPMG interviewers smiled and said: "Did I see that suit before?" And I said: "You did." The suit was owned by a fellow a bit smaller than me, so it was a bit obvious. I thought: "I'm not going to get this job. I don't even have the proper clothes to wear." However, to my surprise, they offered me employment in their offices in Dublin or Limerick.

I spent that summer working on building sites in London. I decided to come home for the graduation, mainly because of my parents. As I was the oldest of the family, it was a big thing for them. After graduation, I worked with KPMG for a while. Over time, I realised that accounting and audits were not my sweet spot; they did not excite or motivate me. Yes, I could have kept going and created a nice career in this area, but I knew that this was not my passion. Having said that, I didn't know what my passion was, though I knew I enjoyed meeting and working with people in a team environment.

---

*Each student was valued for who they were and the talent they possessed. We all worked together as a team to support the development of this talent. I had discovered my passion in life.*

---

Then, on a wet and wintry Saturday afternoon in Galway city, I bumped into the headmaster at the Jes, Fr Paddy Tyrrell. We went for a coffee and a chat. I remember Paddy saying: "I think you'd be a great teacher. Would you consider teaching?" I wasn't married at the time and some of Caitlín's sisters were teachers, so I said: "I might." I returned to UCG to study for the HDip and I was back in the Jes, this time as a trainee maths teacher.

Again, I focused on becoming the very best teacher I could be. I wanted to learn about how the best teachers taught, how they interacted with students, how they effectively transferred knowledge to their students. Over time, I recognised that my role in the classroom was not to teach but to facilitate learning, to create the environment in which people learn.

When I started, I said I was going to model myself on great teachers I had had such as Michael Holland, Paddy Lydon and others. Then after a while I realised that I had to create my own teaching style which I was comfortable with and in line with my personality. So I started doing that.

Then I said: "How can kids learn more effectively?" So I used to get my kids to write their own Leaving Cert maths book. I started teaching mindfulness, though at that time I didn't know what it was called. I used to get the students to do yoga at lunchtime. I introduced 'mind maps'. I started to teach them *how* to learn, rather than *what* to learn. All very left-field stuff. And it worked. The students were enjoying the classroom learning zone. Each student was valued for who they were and the talent they possessed. We all worked together as a team to support the development of this talent. It was powerful. As you can see, I had discovered my passion in life.

However, over time, I felt more and more and more in a straitjacket situation. I was getting increasingly frustrated as I did not have the flexibility to explore new ways to teach, to learn and to discover the world. In fact, the frustration began to affect my health.

❖   ❖   ❖

**Then one day Caitlín said: "Take a career break.** You could go back and be an accountant." I said: "No. Been there, done that." "You are a solicitor as well. Open a law practice." I had studied law at night in UCG and got an apprenticeship for about three years with Billy Loughnane, who had a law practice in Galway. Billy is from Clare, a great sportsman in his day. So, I set up a law practice in Galway city, with no business plan, little idea of what I was doing and no clients.

I also set up a music school with Carl Hession, a fellow teacher in the Jes. I had an office in Dominick Street for the law practice. So the office doubled up as a music classroom at night and a solicitor's practice during the day. At 4pm, I'd put away all the files and the law office became a music school. At 9pm, the musical instruments were put away, I'd take out the files and it became a law office again, ready for the morning!

Still waiting for clients to come in, I decided to do a short programme on Raidió na Gaeltachta and discuss principles of everyday legal issues. I also answered questions from callers. The programme producer thought it was a great idea and asked me how much money I wanted to do it regularly. I said: "I don't want any money for it: you can give it to a charity. It'll be publicity for me." So I went on every Tuesday at about 2 pm.

One time I was up in Kinnegad – no mobile phones at the time – and I went into Harry's to make my call to Raidió na Gaeltachta to answer questions. Somebody was on the phone in the foyer, and the receptionist wouldn't let me use her phone, so I had to go into the kitchen and go on the radio with the kitchen staff making burgers in the background and me talking about legal problems with people from Connemara in the Gaeltacht areas. But it went fine and helped me build the practice.

❖   ❖   ❖

**In the early 1980s, an Irish summer college in Spiddal closed.** I was chairman of the parish council and we tried to get someone else to take over running the school as it was a very important part of Spiddal's economic and social life. As we could not get anyone to run the summer school, I decided to take on the challenge, so I went into partnership with another teacher. That summer, about 300 students attended the Irish courses; within three years, we had it up to about 1,000.

This increase in enrolment was due to two simple strategies. We created a first-class and unique experience for students to learn Irish in the Gaeltacht. The students became our best salespeople as they experienced our Irish courses first-hand. We also built a strong bond with their parents. Then we created a database to communicate with all Irish teachers in the students' schools back home.

The 80/20 rule is incredibly important for leadership in my view. I thought there must be at least four teachers of Irish in each of the schools that each of those students came from. So I did out a little sheet, got the students to give me their names, the name of their school, the address of the school and the names of four teachers – their own Irish teacher and then some of the other teachers in their school. Using the database, I sent out a letter to the teachers, saying: "Conor was in Coláiste Connacht last summer. You are teaching him. He got on really well. If you want to ask him about anything, he'll tell you all about it. And by the way, here are 50 brochures you might give out to your classes." And that triggered it. Little things like that made a huge difference. If you provide a first class service, your customers are your best salespeople.

❖   ❖   ❖

**That gave me the financial start I needed to get involved in another project,** which was to shape the next part of my life: Aer Arann. This was a totally new and different adventure. Again, I had no roadmap and little concept of the airline industry.

It has just dawned on me now that, as we reshape business, business also reshapes us. It's only when you look back on life that you see how strange or opportunistic the manner in which things happen and shape your life. It was Christmas Day 1992 and I went for my usual long walk along the sea shore in Cornaron. It was early evening and a heavy mist was rolling in across Connemara from Galway Bay. I stumbled across this partly finished airstrip running parallel to the shoreline. This was mystical, magical and amazing. I thought that the people behind this project were either crazy or brilliant – and I know that there is a thin line between both. I said: "Wow. Some day, I'm going to have an involvement in this because there is something unique, something special, something spiritual here." Spirituality is very important to me; it has a lot to do with my Jesuit education.

I became more observant of what was happening in relation to the airport and the airline. Soon, it was clear that the company wasn't going well. It was owned by a guy called Tim Kilroe over in Manchester. I'd never met him but I managed to get his phone number and met him in the Four Seasons Hotel at Manchester airport and ended up buying the company with Eugene O'Kelly. I couldn't afford it myself. I mortgaged my home to buy my part of the company.

At the time, I knew nothing about aviation. I never had any interest in airplanes. To me an airplane is just a bus with wings on it. But we developed the airline and turned it around into profitability reasonably quickly.

Then one Sunday, a colleague phoned me at home and told me that a senior executive from Aer Lingus had just flown to the islands and was asking if he could meet me. I said: "Great, yes." So I met Larry Stanley, who asked: "What are your plans for this airline?" And I told him: "To keep doing what I'm doing and making a profit." He asked if I'd any thoughts about growing the airline. I didn't at that time, to be honest. I was very focused on steadying the ship. Aer Arann had never really made a profit until then. Then I realised that, even though he didn't say it directly to me, Larry Stanley thought that this airline could be part of something bigger. This chance meeting with Larry inspired me to investigate the possibility of growing the airline past the service to the Aran Islands.

---

*There is something special, something unique in bringing people together and building a dream together. Believing in people is crucial.*

---

I became aware that the Department of Transport issued a request for tender every three years for European-registered airlines to tender for passenger routes between Dublin and the regions of Ireland. We decided to tender but were unsuccessful on the first occasion.

However, shortly afterwards, the airline that was awarded the Donegal/Dublin contract got into financial difficulty. The department called me and asked if we would be interested in tendering for the route as it was going back out for retender. I only had a few weeks to create the tender submission.

I called Tim Kilroe, who sold us the airline in the first place back in 1994. He now operated Jetstream 31 aircraft out of Manchester airport. I leased one of them from him. In those days, the schedule was as follows: at 7am we would do a position flight from Manchester to Dublin with no passengers, then Dublin to Donegal and back to Dublin again (the contracted route) and finally back to Manchester again later that evening, as Kilroe needed the aircraft for some night work there. I was paying for the Manchester/Dublin and Dublin/Manchester leg. It wasn't making money so I had to do something fast.

I became aware of a Short 360 airplane based in Dublin that was doing very little flying. I found that it was owned by BAC in Gatwick. I met with David Robinson, BAC's CEO. Basically, that airplane was flying on contract from Dublin to the Isle of Man and back again in the morning and doing the same thing in the evening. David was keen to lease me one of his Short 360 aircraft; however, I was only interested in the one he had based in Dublin and I wanted to operate the Isle of Man route as part of the deal.

The combination of the contracted route to Donegal together with the Isle of Man business made us profitable, albeit marginally. I quickly realised that I needed a back-up aircraft, so I got a second airplane from David. This was the start of building a small regional fleet and operation.

Again, call it faith, luck, opportunism or whatever. It was St Patrick's Day and I was in Croke Park for the All-Ireland club finals. I happened to meet a guy there and we got talking. I discovered that he owned a freight company and flew freight from Dublin to Coventry and return every night. By the end of the chat, I had agreed a deal with him that we would fly his freight on this route. I always try to strike while the iron is hot.

So, around 7pm, after the Isle of Man flight, we would unscrew the aircraft seats, store them in the back of a HiAce van, put freight on to the plane, take it to Coventry, come back with more freight and at 2am or 3am, whenever it was back, take the freight off the plane, vacuum it out and put the seats back in. We had a roster between ourselves to do it. We did whatever was needed to make it happen. It was hard work but, great craic.

Soon we had three or four planes in our fleet so, as we expanded, we decided to tender for some other contracts. However, I wanted to build the airline to the point where it wasn't dependent on State or EU contracts. My biggest challenge was that I didn't have the money required to invest in the growth of the airline, which meant I couldn't recruit senior experienced executives from Aer Lingus or Ryanair or anywhere else. I did not have the financial resources or the level of industry experience to attract them.

However, around this time, a charter airline called Transair, based in Dublin, had just gone bust so I headhunted those staff. When I told the bank manager that I was headhunting staff out of Transair, he said he'd heard it all now and told me I was bloody crazy. "What are you doing that for? That company failed." I said: "That's the very reason why I want those staff: they know what failure is." It was one of the most important and best decisions I ever made in my life – to get those people – because, my good God, they did not want to fail a second time.

The company was growing fast but it was all instinctive. I started Galway/Lorient because my sister was driving me mad. She was married and living in Lorient in north-west France and she couldn't easily get back to Galway. She said there were a lot of people like her out there, so I visited Lorient and met with airport and local chamber of commerce officials. That's how Galway/Lorient started – and it worked really well.

The Waterford/Luton service started when I met a couple of businesspeople from Waterford who wanted a service to the UK. They didn't have a structured business plan but when I saw their passion for their community and region, I said: "With passion like that, I'm going to do it." And it worked. Some routes worked better than others but the company was flying it.

My problem then wasn't the growth; it was how to manage the growth. I had people employed in engineering, operations, pilots, HR, finance, commercial – all doing their own thing. I thought: "Hold on, there is something wrong here. This is just not right." So I said: "Guys, I'm going to bring you all to Galway for a three-day workshop. I want each of you to prepare a report to tell us what you are doing in your own area and you'll have five minutes to present it to the whole group, senior and middle management, about 35 of us. In your report, not only tell us what you do, but who are the other stakeholders in the company that help you to do your job and how they are important to you in achieving your objectives."

We did three presentations in an hour and at the end of that hour, I divided everyone into groups for a 45-minute breakout session to analyse the three presentations and prepare feedback. They really got to understand what everyone else was doing and how important their role and other people's roles were and what pulled them together. It was incredibly powerful. The engagement was powerful. We all became aware of the gaps and how to fix them.

I needed an experienced chief engineer, so I recruited Tom Colgan who had just retired from Aer Lingus. Probably 63 years of age, a very quiet, gentle, big man, Tom was with us for about a year and half to two years. One Friday night, Tom was leaving after a few pints in a bar beside the airport. He came up to me, put an arm around me and said: "Pádraig, I've been 34 years working in Aer Lingus and I'm two years working with you and those two years were more enjoyable than the previous 34." I said: "Wow, Tom, why was that?" He said: "When

I was with Aer Lingus, I was fixing airplanes. When I was with you, Pádraig, I was building an airline!"

That brought it home to me that there was something special, something unique here in bringing people together and building a dream together. Each of us knew that we were part of that dream and we had to play our part in order to realise that dream. This we did. Believing in people is crucial.

❖    ❖    ❖

**I have given a lot of my time to supporting entrepreneurship and judging entrepreneurial and business competitions,** such as the EY Entrepreneur of the Year, on both a national and world stage. I have met with and reviewed business plans for over a thousand companies over the years, and I've never seen a company grow in my life, only people grow. And that was my key theme all along. So when I won the EY Ireland Entrepreneur of the Year award, I was invited out to Monte Carlo to represent Ireland in the World Entrepreneur of the Year finals. Representing my country and carrying my country's flag is one of the highlights and proudest moments of my life.

A few days before the event, I contacted some of the staff and said: "We are after leasing a new ATR aircraft and it will arrive in Dublin Airport on Thursday next. Use this airplane and come out for the weekend with me and bring your partners. We will party in Monte Carlo." They came out. We certainly partied and had great craic.

The following year, I was a judge for the World Entrepreneur of the Year award and Greg Ericksen, the partner in charge at EY, asked me: "Pádraig, I've seen entrepreneurs come out here with their partners, business partners, some with wives or spouses. You brought your whole family – not many bring their whole family, that's very unusual. But you brought half your staff out with you too! That's really unusual. Why did you do it?" I said: "Greg, if you gave me that trophy for World Entrepreneur of the Year, and I couldn't bring my family or my staff with me, then you could keep it. I didn't build that airline. I'd only one role to play in it. I don't have the ability to build an airline." As Tom Colgan said: "We all built it." I made that very clear to the staff and I demonstrated it to the staff time and time again.

---

*The company has a role to play in my life, but it is not me, it does not define my life or who I am as a person.*

---

One of the best shows I have ever seen in my life was *Tom Crean*, the one-man show. It's brilliant. Aidan Dooley, the actor, is from the Claddagh in Galway and I had the great pleasure to meet him in Freeney's on High Street in Galway one Saturday evening. When we won European Regional Airline of the Year, I brought all the staff and their partners out to CityWest Hotel to his one-man show. Tom Crean was an unsung hero explorer at the turn of the 20th century who hailed from Kerry. He was a man who never gave up, even when faced with the greatest challenges. This, to me, reflected our team in Aer Arann. It was all about endurance: despite the challenges Crean faced going to the South Pole, he kept going and kept going and kept going.

I remember telling my staff: "If there is anything I have ever seen that epitomises all of us as a group, that's it. Because the measure of any of us is not the distance we get kicked down into the ground or the failures; our measure is how quickly we bounce back up again and the distance we rebound – and that's how I measure myself."

I know I'm going to fail. I have failed. I will fail again, just the same as anybody else. But that endurance was epitomised in our company and in our challenges and struggles in fighting for each other and with each other. God knows, we didn't have much but we had that. It's what kept us going.

In 2006, my health was suffering, because I was working so hard. I was travelling up and down from Galway to Dublin on the first flight every morning and back down again at night. I did not want my family to move to Dublin so, in order to spend as much time as I could with them, I travelled daily between Connemara and Dublin to do my work.

Despite the health warnings, I thought I was fine. I was looking after myself physically. I was running New York marathons and half-marathons on the Aran Islands. I regularly went to the gym and generally took care of myself. I didn't want to tell anyone about the health issues because I knew it would be an issue due to the high-profile media attention around me and the airline at the time. Anyway, I was looking at buying Manx Airlines, which had 600,000 passengers.

In 2006, I pulled out of running the company on a day-to-day basis. We got a recruitment company to help get us a CEO. But critically, I said to my senior management team: "I want you to interview your next boss." This gave my management team an opportunity to get actively involved in the process and not be just passive bystanders. They brought a unique line of questioning and assessment to the process, and it also illustrated to them that I valued their opinion on this critical appointment. Overall, it worked really well.

It was not hard for me to step back. It was a pivotal thing in my life at that time when I asked myself the question: "Am I the company or is the company me?" The company has a role to play in my life, but that's it, it's a role to play. It is not me, it does not define my life or who I am as a person. I know people who unfortunately have committed suicide because they couldn't create that distinction. The company, no more than a car, has got a job to do to get you from A to B. You have got to look after it. You've got to maintain it properly – and even then it may break down, through no fault of your own. But it is no more than a car at the end of the day. It is not you. You are only the driver of the car, not the car.

Also, I asked myself: "Why would I stay in as CEO of this company?" I made out a list of reasons: control, ego, power. They were the only reasons. It was my call, I could stay there: control, ego, power. But I said: "If I were working in this company, would I want as my leader someone whose characteristics are driven by control, ego and power? No!" To me, control, ego and power are not key characteristics of a good or a great leader. What good leaders do – and what I've been trying to do all along, even when I was teaching in secondary school – is to create the environment within which people can actually be leaders.

You don't block leadership, you don't create leadership, you enable leadership. So I stepped back for all of those reasons.

My mistake was that I probably stepped too far back. I went effectively totally non-executive. And I've talked to a number of entrepreneurs since who did something similar and they all said the same thing. Entrepreneurs very often do one of two things in situations like this: they don't give up control or they give up too much control. It's either one or the other. Very few of them take the middle road. I had a great board of directors and I would listen and yet I went too far the other side. But that's fine. There is really no such thing as balance in life. You are always working on creating balance in life one way or the other. Leadership to me is a see-saw, the balance between on one side caring and the other side daring – and you are always swaying between the two. It is within that sway and the extent of that sway that you can in hindsight truly measure the level of risk – and I emphasise *in hindsight*.

**When I stepped back, I set up** *Foinse,* a weekly Irish language newspaper. I was appointed to the board of Fáilte Ireland and I also involved myself in other community projects.

One evening, while walking on the prom in Salthill, Caitlín told me that Crumlin children's hospital were organising a group from Ireland to run the New York marathon as a charity fundraiser for the hospital. She suggested that I consider training for this event, though I am not an athlete and certainly not a long-distance runner with over 15 stone weight to carry. However, as a person who loves challenges, I decided to contact Eamonn Coghlan, who worked with the hospital's fundraising arm. Eamonn convinced me that, with some training, I could run the marathon and that I would not get a heart attack in the process. Well, that was enough encouragement for me. I got a few friends, including Myles McHugh, from Galway to go raise money and run the New York marathon with me.

This gave me the inspiration to set up our own half-marathon weekend on the Aran Islands, whereby the net profit would go to

Crumlin hospital. I also ensured that all funds were managed and controlled by the hospital directly.

The Aer Arann half-marathon also served another important purpose. I wanted the Dublin-based staff to understand the spirit, the ethos, the core of what we are all about, where we came from and what is our essence. What we were about was the Aran Islands and ordinary people, decent people, working hard to make a difference for themselves and their families. And I wanted us to realise how fortunate we are. There are parents with sick children, fighting to live, maybe to be able to walk, to breathe properly, to have a normal life. Fine, we are working and growing an airline and winning these awards, but big deal – big deal at the end of the day. Let's really see who we are and what is important to us.

I think we've raised altogether approximately €1.8 million. We have raised money for Our Lady's Hospital for Sick Children in Crumlin, Temple Street Hospital and other local charities. Next year, the profits will go to Pieta House. I think the biggest challenge we have – and we are not even aware of it – is stress and depression amongst people, especially young people. I believe it is the single biggest factor that will hold us back as a people, as a nation, as a community, as families: the level of unwarranted stress in our lives. Forty or 50 years ago, people were smoking – it was the thing to do – and it took a long time to realise the serious damage it was causing to our health.

❖    ❖    ❖

**If you look at my life, community was always very much an integral part of it.** Even the businesses I have grown were about connecting communities.

Therefore, it is not a surprise that I created Casla Homecare, to support and look after elderly people in their homes in Connemara. I am also involved in GAA at national level. This is a deep passion of mine, as I realise how much the local GAA club gave me as a kid growing up in Spiddal and how much this wonderful organisation gives to communities throughout Ireland and further afield.

Seanad elections take place every time there is a general election and I decided to contest the Seanad election on the NUI panel. There are three seats and I came fourth. I remember my family saying: "Now that's out of your hair, let's move on." I was very comfortable in moving on and concentrating on growing businesses.

> *I once thought that, if I was successful, I'd be happy. I now realise there is a difference between happiness and success.*

However, a few weeks after the NUI election results, I got a phonecall from Micheál Martin, who said he'd like to suggest me to then Taoiseach Enda Kenny to be one of the Taoiseach's 11 senator nominees. I said: "I'll definitely think about it. It's a huge honour to be asked. I'll talk to my family about it." Micheál explained: "An Taoiseach has to announce it on the floor of the Dáil tomorrow. If he is going to appoint you, he'll phone you beforehand so you can talk to him." I did not get the telephone call from the Taoiseach and so I assumed that he was not appointing me. Instead the Taoiseach announced my appointment from the floor of the Dáil that Friday evening. I became aware of my appointment from my son who lives in Chicago and from other well-wishers who called me.

I'm in An Seanad now about a year. It is a big change. What did I discover? I learned that politicians do work hard and put in long hours. It is not an easy life. I discovered that they really do get involved for the right reasons, the people I've met anyway. They are also focused on getting re-elected.

I enjoyed my role as chairman of the Oireachtas Joint Committee on the Future Funding of Domestic Water Services. This was a real challenge and I enjoy challenges, especially the ones that provide no guarantee of success.

In my view, the Civil Service system needs overhaul. There are a lot of really good people in the Civil Service, who want to engage, are as passionate about our country as anybody else but they are incredibly frustrated. They want to contribute, but the way the system has built up and layered over the years makes it very difficult to create meaningful progress in a timely manner. It slows down effective decision-making. It is at the opposite end to entrepreneurship and building business. I believe that all civil servants from principal officer upwards should be afforded an opportunity to be seconded for a three-month work experience in private enterprise. They then can use this experience in reflecting on the work processes in their respective offices.

I introduced a Bill before An Seanad last November to help assess the effectiveness of our State and semi-State bodies. The Bill, if supported, would set up a public review body, working with the Department of Public Enterprise and Reform. This public review body would be independent and would review the effectiveness, the corporate governance and fitness for purpose of each State agency at least once every seven years. But when I brought that Bill in front of An Seanad, Fine Gael, Fianna Fáil, the Greens, Labour, Sinn Féin and all the Independents voted against it. Every one of them. It was a coalition. It's probably my biggest claim to fame in An Seanad.

**The future for Pádraig?** It is only now in the past year and a half that I've managed to grapple with this, but I once thought that, if I was successful, I'd be happy. I now realise there is a difference between happiness and success.

Leadership comes from the inside out. You cannot be your best at leadership unless and until you lead yourself first and you have got to know, when you are leading yourself, what are your motivators. What are your drivers? What is holding you back and what is allowing you to go on? You have got to learn to understand how you think, how you reflect and your decision-making process.

I have had a great life so far. I am truly fortunate and grateful for all of those experiences and in particular for the wonderful people in my life. I'm still a student at heart, doing a PhD – on my life!

# BRENT POPE

"I'm forever ever-changing."

*Brent Pope is a former professional rugby player and coach, who hails from New Zealand. After a successful playing career at the highest level in New Zealand, Brent arrived in Ireland in 1991. Since that time, he has been a mainstay in RTÉ's rugby coverage over two decades, as well as featuring in numerous crossover television programmes.*

*Brent has successfully published six children's books for various charities and, in 2012, wrote an award-winning autobiography, **Brent Pope: If You Really Knew Me**.*

*Brent is an ambassador for many of Ireland's leading mental health charities and is a regular guest on television talking about positive mental health. He is studying for a master's degree in psychotherapy and writing another book to be called **Win Success in Sport and Life**, due out in 2018.*

**I'm forever ever-changing.** I think that's probably the best description of me. I don't think I can ever pare down at any one time exactly who I am or who I have become.

I suppose I try to be my own person. I guess that's all any of us can be, isn't it? But I'm ever-changing or certainly trying to be. Things have changed in my life as to who and where I am at a particular juncture. It's like a journey really and while we like to use clichés "like people will never change", I don't think that's always true. We are forever discovering things that make us who we are. If you ask most people who they are at different stages in their life, they are probably different people. Like that, that we are forever moving forward, evolving and finding our purpose in life.

❖   ❖   ❖

**My childhood kind of defines me** and I really take stock in that. As children, so much learning and development are done or not done at an early stage in life. Realistically, I had a fabulous childhood. Physically, I didn't get off to a good start and ironically later in life my physical wellbeing was never an issue, though my mental health was.

I was born a very sickly child with double pneumonia, bronchitis and the umbilical cord wrapped around my neck. My mother always told me I was destined to do something with my life because I was lucky just to survive birth. But it also made my first couple of years pretty tough, in the sense that my parents didn't know if I had various diseases or not. I was always sick and weak. At one stage, up until about eight years of age, the doctors thought I might have cancer because I was so ill all the time. I have remained someone with bad blood most of my life and I pick up infections pretty easily.

Even though I've been involved in sport all my life, I always seem to take longer to heal. I was always getting infected scrapes from the rugby field, often having to scrub my wounds after a match with a scrubbing brush so that they would not become red and infected. I was also a bad asthmatic as a young child and I remember having to go and see a breathing specialist every week; I think her name was Dr Heather Thompson. I have memories of having to take days off school and visit her, carrying out all sorts of breathing exercises with cotton wool.

But I was lucky: I grew up out of the asthma by living in the countryside, working a lot of my school holidays on farms and working with animals, always running around on various Huckleberry Finn-type adventures. Those were the days when you were told by your parents to "get out of the house" early in the morning and at the weekends encouraged to "go out and exercise" or "go out on a little adventure on your bike or on your horse".

So in some ways, coming from New Zealand and always being close to nature, the sea or the mountains was idyllic as a child. Most of my young memories are going around to my friend Richard Taylor's place and having swimming races, playing cricket and rugby all day every day – always active. I think all that helped my general physical health. So physically, an idyllic lifestyle of sport, nature, animals and adventure: all good.

Psychologically, things were a little bit different for me. I suppose it is funny now as I look back, but my father once said that a school teacher came down in the first few years of primary school and said: "Brent has psychological problems." Dad kicked him out of the house, saying he was the one with psychological problems. I loved that about my father.

But I think I was always a happy kid on the outside, in the sense that I was the class clown and a cheeky chappie with a big smile and a chubby freckly face, ripped pockets and skinned knees, Billy Bunterish. I was cheeky, but that masked a lot of unhappiness for me even at an early age.

I remember my first panic or anxiety attack when I was about 14 or 15 years of age and there was this overwhelming sense of failure, even though I didn't have anything to fail at at that age. Everything was good, there were no major pressures in my life. I just felt this overwhelming fear that I would fail at everything in my life and I would never amount to anything, that I would be a complete failure. I remember it was a Sunday night, bath night for some reason, as in those days I often had to have a bath after my brother to save hot water.

To this day, I remember this dark mist that suddenly came over me, which I recognise now, even in my 50s, and there was just an overwhelming feeling of sadness for some reason. After just sitting in the water that became ice-cold, I couldn't breathe. I was shaking, unable to see what was happening to me, a frightened, alone child. I went back to my bed that first night and I curled up in a ball and cried for the rest of the night. I knew then that there was something wrong with me. It is funny how you have a gut feeling about whether something is normal or not. I knew it wasn't a normal way of thinking. I just knew it wasn't, even at that age. People might say, "Aw, you were just young and naïve", but everybody has that innate thing in their life when they know what is best or worst for them. Doctors can't tell you; nobody else can tell you; you can only tell yourself.

I just knew from that moment on that it wasn't the normal way a teenager would be thinking. And that started the self-doubt, the lack of confidence, the lack of self-esteem, even though on the outside I was the kid who had all the jokes and was good at sport and good at most things. Despite all this, I had no self-belief in myself at all. And what little I had could be stripped away from me quite easily. If the teachers or somebody said something negative about me, I would always – and I still do today – believe it to be true. People with mental health issues often do. You believe that one negative thing out of 10 to be the thing that defines you; 'they' said it, therefore it must be true.

*Don't carry any shame like me. Be happy with who you are: that's the real secret.*

And I continued having panic attacks throughout my teenage years on a regular basis but I hid it well – tears of the clown. I was ashamed that I could control my physical health but I couldn't look after my mental health. I could go around the back of the bike shed and give somebody a belt on the nose or I could play rugby at a high level and use that sub-personality of aggression to benefit me. But I couldn't look after my own mental health.

There was no one you could go to for help in that generation. Men were seen as having to be the strong, silent type, the 'John Wayne syndrome' as I nicknamed it. Men don't show emotions. All I ever heard as an answer to my problems was to: "Man up, toughen up, real men don't cry." All those things played a huge part in my life.

Why was I so different? I was deeply, deeply ashamed of who I was, of who I had become. I was told to go back to the gym, run another lap, all was okay, but it wasn't. "Who do I talk to, who can help me?" Nobody, alone and ashamed. Now, much later, that I have found some purpose in my life, I talk to people about being happy in their own skin. And that's a good thing. I wasn't, I just wasn't happy in my own skin. I was a fake to myself.

So that's a summation of my early years: physically fine; psychologically, I just knew that I was a square peg in a round hole. Yes, most kids go through that self-doubt at some stage, they just don't tell anyone about it. They should.

I never knew that you can give children confidence. I don't blame anybody; it just wasn't the generation when we were told what we couldn't do rather than what we could do: "You can't do that", "You won't do that", "You are destined for that". And you didn't question authority in those days, that was not your place.

There was a pecking order in society which was your parents, the family priest, the doctor and the school teacher. And perhaps the policeman was thrown in there somewhere too. Your view of the world was: "Don't get in trouble with the principal or the police", "Go to the doctor, he knows best, him and the priest". And all those things tied up into who you became.

I was brought up as a highly religious person. Dad and Mum were very involved in the local church, so there was that side of things too, being brought up a strict Catholic and having those views on religion and spirituality. They played a big part in my life later on.

When we look back, we can all see things in our lives as defining moments. I think we can either use them powerfully for us or against us, and I think I decided early on that I wasn't going to subscribe to other people's views of me. I was determined – internally, not always externally, because I wouldn't show it – I was determined to be good at sport. I was determined to succeed at study. I was determined to make something positive of my life, even though I may have been told that that wasn't a realistic option for me. So I just worked harder at achieving it.

I was a goal-setter very early on. I wrote down goals. I looked at goals and said: "No, I'm not going to tell anybody. I'm not going to brag, but I can do that." And when I put my mind to it, it was a very powerful force. To always prove the doubters wrong.

I've been doing that all my life really, and it has been a huge motivator for me. I was told at school, "Brent has poor report cards"– my report cards were mostly always filled with Ds and Es – or "Brent is easily distracted and distracts others" – that was a favourite one from my teachers. Despite all that, I knew deep down that I was intelligent. I knew that about myself. Maybe not necessarily always the top of the class, but I worked harder, I was street-wise. I knew qualifications would not come easily to me like my brother, but I had a drive. I would study late at night, sneak study books home, get up early. I worked harder than anybody else in my teenage years. I wouldn't tell anybody, it was just about studying under the covers to achieve something for myself.

Even as a rugby player, I'd say to myself: "I'm going to prove you all wrong." If I thought somebody else was training on the roads five miles a day, I'd be doing seven miles a day. And that's what would push me. I'd be saying to myself: "You know what? If I want to get where I want to get to, I'm going to have to do more than the next person." I won't give up and I never have.

Nothing came easy for me. I did have to work hard, even at exams. But I also learned at an early age to focus on what I was good at, rather than what I wasn't good at. I knew I had strengths and weaknesses, in school work and even in sport, but I said: "Hold on a minute, let's not dwell on those for too long. Accept the major weaknesses but, hey, these are my strengths." If I wasn't good at one subject, I wouldn't necessarily park it but I would focus my energies on the ones I was good at. In university, I won a full scholarship based on what I was good at. My grades in subjects that I was good at – English, history and geography – were some of the best in the school, while other subjects like maths, I was hopeless at.

Looking back in later life, I'm a wee bit disappointed that I always did things to prove people wrong, rather than to prove myself right, if that makes sense. It was always about: "Well, you said I couldn't do this, I couldn't make this rugby team, or I couldn't achieve an honours degree. You said it, so I'll just prove you wrong." And I don't know if later in life that has prevented me from actually enjoying my achievements along the way. I've always been known as 'Project Pope'. I'm very project-driven. I'll get that done, and achieve it. Bang. Done. Now. Wait for the joy. Okay, it hasn't come. Move on. Do something else.

So I don't know whether sometimes, while that ability to say "I'm going to do this to prove you wrong" drives you, it actually also denies you the happiness of having achieved something along the way. Sure, you've got there, but for me it's very hard to sit back and reflect, pat myself on the back for even a moment and say: "Heck, yeah, I did it." That's why books like this one are inspiring to me. It's about getting something on the shelf you can be proud of rather than making the top 10 best-seller list or making millions. To me, it's always been about giving something back, the pride of doing something to the best of your ability, never about accolades or money.

I think what I have learnt from the success of businesspeople – people like Ireland's own Denis O'Brien or the likes of Bill Gates and Richard Branson – I can't speak for them but, in the end, I think that making money is only a small motivational factor in their success. It's about: "I have achieved something great." I presume Denis O'Brien doesn't sit back, count his money, pat himself on the back and say: "Haven't I done brilliantly?" Why? Because I don't believe that's what drives him. What drives him and people like him is to succeed in everything that they put their minds to, to create something, to build empires, that is the joy of their success. If it was just about making money, it would eventually become unfulfilling.

For me, it's always about this now, not did I make a difference in my life but did I make a difference in somebody else's. That's what motivates me. That is more important than anything I may have achieved on the rugby field or television. When I have panic attacks now as an adult and I think that nobody will love me when I am older or visit my grave when I die, I want someone, somewhere to say: "Brent helped me. In some way, Brent Pope made a difference."

❖     ❖     ❖

**Who are my influencers?** The funny thing is that the answer to that is no one specific. I'd like to be able to list a collection of great people but it was mainly me that influenced me. That's certainly not an ego trip, because it changes over time, I think, who and what motivated me years ago may not have the same effect now. It is just that, internally for me, I was always at war with myself – that was the battle only I could win. The first book I ever bought as a teenager was *When Will I Be Happy?* How sad is that? But it proved one thing: that even then I knew I had trouble finding that in my life. But I had a determination that would always say: "Okay, I know that you believe that I can't do this, but I know enough about myself and I'm going to show you I can." I was probably average in a lot of things, but I knew deep down that I had resolve, that I had real determination.

---

*I've always been known as 'Project Pope'. I'm very project-driven. I'll get that done, and achieve it. Bang. Done.*

---

There have been a few influences when I look back now: a good teacher, some good advice from my parents, my brother Mark, a good mentor, a good rugby coach. It only takes one single moment to change a person's life. I remember when I was at school, I was a good writer and I loved to write. I especially loved to write creatively: poems and short stories. Like a lot of people, I think I was slightly dyslexic; sometimes I couldn't make out the words properly, still can't at times. I remember a teacher, Ms Stapleton, who I adored, saying: "Brent, let me worry about the grammar and the spelling. You just write." I remember it to this day; it is quite emotional for me, not because I loved to write but because someone believed in me enough to encourage me to be myself, warts and all.

The following year, I got nominated for an essay award for the best young writers in New Zealand – she had sent it away secretly. I didn't have the confidence to be able to write well because I was so embarrassed by my sentence structure but she just kept saying: "You are a fantastic young writer, just let it flow." I'll always look back on that moment and although it was just one part of my life, the creative side, that one bit of confidence years ago has allowed me to go on and write a collection of children's books, an award-winning autobiography and become a sports journalist.

It was something I later used when I went into rugby coaching. For too long, I was bullied by coaches: make a mistake and you're dropped. I even remember a coach telling me that forwards were never to kick the ball after I had made a fantastic kick; it was not the done thing. Again, "Don't do this, don't do that", stripping your confidence, highlighting your weakness rather than telling you that you can do anything if you apply yourself.

I changed that when I became a coach. Sure, I was not the most technical of coaches but I was a good motivator and I always got the best out of players. I made them succeed. And it was just through that lesson: encourage them. Rather than point out what they did wrong in a match, I would encourage them. I would often say to my players: "Hey, you are a great player. Don't always worry about the technicalities too much. Play to your strengths. Play what you see. The rest will follow." I love to tell people good things about themselves. Why not? Why not, when given any chance in life to empower others?

People have such difficulty in this country in telling other people the good things about themselves. They're embarrassed, but why? Only a couple of weeks ago, I was in the Dundrum Town Centre and this lovely girl served myself and my girlfriend, Orla, who had a serious leg injury at that time. It was a thankless job, I imagine, but she was kind and thoughtful to us. Even after serving us, she was back cleaning the counter, taking pride in a job that others would think beneath them. I went back and said to her: "I think you are fantastic at what you do." She started crying! The whole emotion of somebody telling her that she was doing a good job and was appreciated. She said nobody had ever come to her before and said that she did a good job.

How powerful are words! To me, leaving a €10 or €20 tip would not be the same, because she wouldn't have known what somebody else had actually thought of her, that all her efforts meant something. I was at a seminar when they played a video of a man who cleaned toilets in South Africa. He spoke with pride about how those toilets were so clean and welcoming. For others, it was the worst job in the world but for him it was all about pride. I so admired that man. When was the last time you told someone at your workplace or at home that they are doing a great job or that you love and appreciate them? When I ask this, I hear: "Oh, they know." I say: "No, they don't always know."

That realisation comes from mentors along the way who were kind to me and who also knew that I was a bit different. Because I felt different. I went off to a stereotypical New Zealand university where I was labelled as 'a rugby guy', but I always wanted to be different. And that was another thing that I did when I was younger: I befriended people who were different as well. Some of my friends were into sport, some of them weren't; some of them were into art, some in bands, some creative, not accepted by the norm but accepted by me.

I was never a bully and I'm proud of that. Being different myself, there was always something in my personality that stood up to bullies. Often at school I stood up for the oppressed, those that others picked on. I was physically strong and aggressive and I was popular because I was good at sport, but I never isolated anybody. I would always include others not so popular, maybe because I knew how I felt and I never wanted anyone to feel that way. Even to this day, I try to judge people on character, not where they come from or what they do. Maybe I get it wrong sometimes but I try.

Because I was different inside, I was different on the outside as well and I would always dress differently. I often got slagged going to college or rugby training because I'd have white shoes or rolled-up trousers, so different from the regimented rugby-type guy. But because I was good at rugby and aggressive, people always accepted me after a time, but I always thought that was shallow. I was lucky enough to gain respect in a macho way, but what about those who couldn't?

Going back to the lack of self-belief and self-esteem, I probably just wanted to be noticed. I never even liked the way that I looked. I know a lot of teenagers feel that way but I felt ugly. I know I felt very nervous around girls, even though I would bluff it again, and people would think I was confident around women. But I felt very nervous about the way that I looked.

Funnily enough, now people ask me why I'm in the fashion trade and have my own POPE shirt and shoe brand, and I'll say: "You know what? This dream really started from a really unusual place. It started from the fact that I always liked to dress well because I felt that empowered me and made me feel I could look better. If I looked good, I might feel good as well. Because I always thought that I was just kind of average, that I wasn't anything great to look at – I wasn't the 'Elephant Man' but I wasn't handsome. My love of clothes started because I wanted to look the best I could and not from an ego point of view – far from it – but because I just wanted to feel okay about the way I looked." And that remains today, and it all stems from a lack of self-confidence. It's strange how things shape you, isn't it?

When I look back on my life, all those things came together to make me. I was always pushing my comfort zone, finding it hard but also coming to terms with the fact that I was a bit different. All those things go to make up the answer to that question: "Who am I?" Those parts of the jigsaw, good or bad, made me who I am. They made me move to Ireland after a tough period in my life, when I needed change, and I often thank this country for saving me. If you had said to me, coming out of secondary school or when I was a trainee quantity surveyor in Dunedin in New Zealand, "At some stage, you'll be working on TV in Ireland, with children's books, a fashion brand, a published autobiography", I'd have said: "That's an impossibility. That's not even on the radar." So it's funny how life changes.

No matter how I got there, people need to take stock of, for good or for bad, this is who I am and this is where I am. And that certain things in my life have shaped me – again, for good or bad – and I just accept that. I've made plenty of mistakes and I have regretted them painfully. I have never set out to hurt a soul but have hurt myself; my issues around love and loss always hurt.

When things became more difficult for me psychologically – and they still do – I did realise deep down that we all have the ability to change, that we can start to look at ourselves more positively and that hopefully brings a positive outcome.

*I love to tell people good things about themselves. Why not? Why not, when given any chance in life to empower others?*

So I learned from a relatively early age, as I suffered through catastrophic anxiety attacks, if something was going to go wrong with me, it was going to go wrong spectacularly. Even now, if I'm having a panic attack, it's about that I'll be homeless, unloved and that nobody will attend my funeral, that I'll die alone, and it frightens me. I think that is what will happen seriously. It's irrational! But it's rational to me at that moment. People who have extreme anxiety know that feeling when you feel like saying, "Don't give me that old stock line that everything will be fine", because the way I feel at that moment of anxiety is that it won't be. It's real and it's going to happen: I'm going to be in a sleeping bag on Grafton Street, people walking over me, nobody remembering me, dying alone. All those things seem like they will happen to me.

You can't apply logic where there is no logic sometimes. The nicest thing I ever heard said, which was quite moving for me, was when I was talking to a girl who was in St Pat's hospital. I was there as an ambassador for Walk in My Shoes, a mental health initiative they run. She was a fabulous young girl with so much going for her on the outside. Her mother was always trying to push her into doing things – it was her way of loving, I guess – but, at one stage, she said, giving the girl a hug: "I don't get it, but I get you." I thought that was beautiful. Her mother meant that she didn't have to always understand, but that she loved her daughter regardless: "I don't get it, but I get you." Wow!

When people try to get me, especially on down days, I say: "Look, you don't need to. You just need to understand it is real for me at that moment. It's not a reality for you and I get that, and I get that you see that I'm not going to end up on the scrap heap of life, but, for me, just now, that's my sad reality."

I've gone on to study various forms of psychotherapy and counselling and I travel Ireland talking about mental health. It's my purpose. I don't want others to have gone through the pain and shame that I have. It saddens me when someone is in despair. I want to grab them and say: "It will be okay. Let's just get past this stage and keep moving forward." It's hard to do when I struggle too, but that's my purpose now.

The physical side has served me well all my life, so I don't worry so much about my physical well-being. I'm not someone who trots off to the doctor's every day because my body has been good to me by and large. Yes, I've had breakages and numerous injuries, but generally where other people are fixated on their body, I'm the opposite. It's just that my mind hasn't served me well. That's what needs the constant work – the mind, not the body.

But so what? Why is it easy to walk into a doctor's and say, "Fix my broken leg", yet the shame long-associated with opening up about mental health is stigmatised? It frustrates me. We must make it easier for this generation and those that follow to realise that at times it's okay and natural not to feel okay, that we all have our crosses to bear and that all people's lives are hit with some bumpy roads at times. The secret is to make it not only acceptable, but positive to seek help. I didn't have that chance. There was nobody I could talk to. I was seen as weak, half a man, and as a result I carried shame for too long. Why? Just because I was a little different.

I just know that at times I have to work harder than the next person, but like that teenage boy who said, "If the other player is stopping after five miles, I will do seven", that's what I have to do. Just find a way, box clever, fight the good fight. I know I will always suffer anxiety, always make mistakes. I'm human but it's how I learn, how I put one foot in front of the other and say: "It will not define me. My weakness is maybe my strength too." And I have a choice, to accept or not.

The most liberating thing that I ever heard was to write down the things that you want to do in life at any age and then put the word 'choice' underneath them, because we all have a choice, you know? Do you want to leave your job? You may say "Yes" or you may say "No", but you always have that choice, to change the 'in' to the 'out'. You could leave your job tomorrow if you really wanted and travel the world, you have that choice. Everything in life is a choice – everything – and once you realise that, you say: "Okay, I've made that choice for good or bad, but it was my choice." So make some choices, change the 'in' to 'out'. It's never too late.

❖  ❖  ❖

**My first defining moment in my life was gaining self-belief.** And luckily I found it in rugby. I knew deep down that I was a good rugby player because I'd been selected for representative teams even when I was very underage. I find it so stupid now but I wish I knew what I should have known then: that I was a bloody good rugby player.

It's just that that I never wanted to appear egotistical. When other people were pushing their own skills, telling coaches how good they were, I didn't. I stood in the background and I let a lack of self-belief and low self-confidence question why I was even there, why I was even selected on this team, worrying that I wasn't good enough to be in their company. I was shy, and while I would be hurt and disappointed I never let it show. I made out that it didn't bother me, but it did.

Later, when I was invited to train with, say, Canterbury, Otago or New Zealand teams, with or against players who had been pin-up idols for me, once I got to that stage, I'd say to myself: "Hang on, not only am I as good as these guys, I could be better than them." That was a long time coming for me and I wish it had come earlier as I missed out on a lot of teams along the way. When I'd be on the verge of making national teams, I would go into my negative space: "These things don't happen to me, good things don't happen to me."

In 1985, as a young rugby player, when I made headlines that I would be selected as a wild card for the All Blacks, I was the only player in the world who was on their knees praying to God that I would not make it. Why? Lack of confidence. "Who was I to play with these players, a small town kid from the sticks?" I would talk myself out of things rather than into them and that has haunted me in a lot of things. Even in relationships I would think: "How can she love me or find me attractive? She will leave." I was good and kind and loving but never felt good enough.

Up until I was about 26, as a rugby player I don't think I thought I could make it, even though I'd get numerous Player of the Day awards or numerous national accolades and all those things bestowed on me. One year, I was voted as one of the top three players in New Zealand but looking back now I don't think I gave myself the best chance of being the best I could be.

And that annoys me even now, as I look back. It annoys me because I still find it very hard when people ask me about certain rugby players who have gone on to be some of the greatest the world has ever seen and that I played with or against, I'm expected to say the right thing. And yes, they were brilliant, but give me a chance again against those guys and I reckon that it could have been me. And that will haunt me into my grave, that feeling that I didn't achieve what I wanted to simply because I lacked confidence at key moments – not in my ability, I don't believe I was ever outplayed by anyone despite who they were – just because I never put myself forward.

❖   ❖   ❖

**Another defining moment came when all my sporting dreams were shattered in a matter of seconds.** That was a turning point for me. To have a dream that I had all my life: "Hey, I'm going to prove them wrong. I'm going to be the only All Black from my school. You all think I can't do it, but I'm going to be there, in the All Blacks, in the World Cup." That picture of having an All Black jersey in the corridors was one I held as a young man, the dream that I had gone where no other player from my school had been. I'm still probably the most decorated rugby player in my school, having played on a lot of teams, and I was good enough to play for my country. But it's the one thing that I'll always regret: a World Cup winner's medal.

On good days, I say: "Brent, you did the best you possibly could." I prepared myself that year in 1987. I felt so fit and in all the All Black training squad fitness tests I was right up there. Before rugby was professional, I trained at the gym before work, ran the beaches and hills of Dunedin at lunchtime and swam hundreds of lengths of the pool at night. I was ready.

I played in an early season game and scored three tries. I was everywhere that day, Brian Lochore, the All Black selector, was at that match, saw me and so I was included in the All Black trials, South Island team and the training squad leading up to the start of the first World Cup. In one of the games I remember outplaying a guy who would later become a great friend, Paul Henderson, who went on to captain the All Blacks. He came up to me after one game and said: "Man, I'm not at the races. I can't compete with you." And he went on to captain the All Blacks ...

*One year, I was voted as one of the top three players in New Zealand ... but looking back now, I don't think I gave myself the best chance of being the best I could be.*

I was poised to achieve something great, which was winning a World Cup in your own country when people had said I couldn't do it. That was going to be the greatest moment of my life, but five seconds before the end of the very last warm-up game – after I'd just been announced as the Player of the Day – days before the World Cup started, my whole world came tumbling down. I pushed for the try line – looking back, I didn't need to, but I did – I got my arm caught and another All Black, Andy Earl, fell on it, by accident, of course. But my elbow smashed out of its socket, my arm gave way and I broke it in numerous places, my arm was just hanging. As the other players walked from the field, I was rushed to hospital, often blacking out with the pain of a dislocated elbow that would remain out for hours and compound fractures that broke my skin.

That affected me psychologically because I'd nothing to fall back on. It still hurts now. I came back the following year and again I battled my way back; it was about resilience. They told me at the time of my World Cup injury that I might not be able to play the same again due to the extent of my injuries. But I came back, I trained hard and I ended being Player of the Year for Otago.

Then there was another All Blacks side going to Japan and I was sent out all the sponsorship letters, saying that I had more or less made it without actually saying I was in the team. My mother even got a phonecall from someone in the Rugby Union who had overheard the team being announced and said I was in. The front page of the *Otago Daily Times* read: "Pope a certainty to be named in the All Blacks tomorrow." After just a horrific injury, I had made it back.

I later heard that the Japanese, fearing the might of the World Cup-winning team, cut the games by one, which meant the All Blacks would only tour with 25 players, rather than 26. I wish they knew what that did to me, that they could destroy my resolve. Psychologically, the damage that was done at that stage was just about irreparable. I'd had to battle all my life. I'd come from a small, rural township. I'd fought my way up, always battling the odds, always giving my best and more. I'd got into these teams on merit. I'd got to be one of the best players in the best rugby country in the world. And to get to that stage where I deserved to be there and ... bang, you get one knock and then another one! It's devastating for life, because had they given me a chance and taken just one more player or given me another chance, who knows?

In 1992, I was asked to come back from Ireland to play in the final All Black trials. My provincial coach in Otago for nearly 10 years, Laurie Mains, had always told me that if he ever became the All Black coach, he would select me. In 1992, he did, but I was loyal to my Irish team, St Mary's, and they had a game to stay in the first division so I stayed and never said a word. Looking back, maybe I should have gone back, but in many ways Ireland had saved my life and I owed my Irish team that much.

In the end, two of my team mates from that Otago team, Arran Pene and Jamie Joesph, made it. Somewhere deep down, I had been hurt so many times that I couldn't face it any more; it had broken my will. I know I deserved to be there, I know it. And yes, I was lucky to have a long and great career and to wear the black jersey, but it doesn't change things. How good could I have been, I will never know.

After that World Cup and Japan tour – and I'm not ashamed to admit it – I went through a very low period of uncertainty. Anybody who doesn't think that taking away your goals like that doesn't affect you just doesn't understand. It may not affect you then and there, but it does down the line: everything comes crashing down. I hit an all-time low and I went into full-blown depression, a nervous breakdown. I left my job, gave up rugby, locked myself away from friends and family and wanted to give up. Again, I had lost my self-belief but worse, I didn't even feel that I wanted to prove anybody wrong. They were right: I had failed, not in anyone else's eyes, but in my own. The prophecies had come true: I was what others had thought all along. My drive had disappeared.

Getting within inches of the peak and failing, suddenly the slide down was longer than I anticipated and I became depressed, which now I look back on and say: "Yeah, that's okay. Why wouldn't I?" I didn't see it that way at the time. I alienated myself, shut the door on life and I couldn't talk to anyone. I'll always do anything I can for the Samaritans because then at that time of all-time low, when I didn't know who to talk to and I really was in desperate need of help, I thumbed through the telephone book one early morning and came across a helpline number for the Samaritans, for people suffering with depression or thinking the darkest of thoughts. I had both.

I remember to this day the voice that greeted me there on the end of that line; it changed my life. I wouldn't go as far as saying it saved my life – that's a bit dramatic – but it changed it. And it was just this warm gentle man saying, "Hello, what's wrong, my friend?" or something like that. This guy wasn't my friend – I didn't even know him – but he was kind and gentle with me. We just talked for hours, and the next day on his advice I set about making some small changes: just to tidy up the apartment, to get back training again, to look after my physical well-being. This coincided with a phonecall from Italy at about three o'clock in the morning to go and play rugby over there; at the same time a call came from Ireland to play for St Mary's in Dublin.

And that was another defining moment in my life. I made the change, to go to Ireland to start my life again, to do something different, to change the 'in' to the 'out'. I only intended to go to Ireland for three months or so but I loved it. But it wasn't about coming to Ireland to play rugby really. It was about taking a job up in Tallaght and delivering drinks to inner city places that were so far removed from what I had known as a commercial property valuer. I needed to start again and it was a non-stressful job for me, because while I was trying to repair, I needed something that was low-key to build my confidence. Geoff Coman of Coman's drink company will never realise what he and St Mary's did for me, and I will always be thankful. And I loved that job, it changed my life too.

I made new friends in Ireland who did not know my past, who would not judge me. I was enjoying rugby again and the sadness was lifting. And while I had again missed my chance at becoming an All Black, my mental health was what mattered most now. I made the choice to make myself well, to heal from the inside out. It was lonely, of course, because even in Ireland there was nobody I could really talk to, but I was in a new environment where nobody knew my past either.

Look at my life now. And that's what I want people to believe: that I had a choice. And my choice was to stay in Ireland and make something of myself. I could have gone back and got the ultimate achievements and probably have a few caps sitting up in my wardrobe but I look back and think that, just when I had finally found a place of happiness and contentment and was enjoying new friends in a new place, and overall really enjoying my life, I could have done what? Plunge myself back into what may have been a short-term fix for a long-term problem? So I did my stint at Mary's and was well-regarded as a good player and I loved my time there.

❖   ❖   ❖

**Then came another defining moment of my life.** Ireland were playing New Zealand in 1995 in the first game of the World Cup and Niall Cogley, then head of sport at RTÉ, Fred Cogley's son, rang me and said, "Brent, you know a lot of the New Zealand players", which I did. He went on, "You also know a lot of the Irish players", which I did too, as they came out of the club scene in those days, so I'd have played them week in week out. So he said: "Would you do commentary on the game?" I said: "I don't think I'll be able to because I'm going back to New Zealand to see Mum and Dad and I have paid for the airfare."

I remember it being something like £500 at that stage and I said: "I can't really do it." So he asked if RTÉ paid the cancellation fee, would I stay on another day. I ummed and ahhed about it. In the end, I cancelled the flight.

Afterwards, the panellists on that day – the late great Bill O'Herlihy and Mick Doyle, who have sadly both passed away, former Irish captain Ciaran Fitzgerald and myself – went out for dinner that Saturday night. Bill O'Herlihy said: "The switchboard has gone mad about your inclusion. Brent, would you please consider staying for the whole tournament?" The agreement was that RTÉ would look after half my airfare, which seems funny now when I look back and realise that I probably worked for 10 weeks on TV for an airfare. That was it: there was no pay.

That was in 1995. People forget that George Hook or Tom McGurk didn't come on the scene for about another five years. So I'm the longest-serving rugby panellist: 22 years, not having missed a year since then. That started my transition into media.

It also coincided with a move that again was good for me coaching-wise. Victor Costello was thinking of going up to St Mary's and I was at that stage 31 or 32 years of age, so I went to Mary's and said: "Look, you've a chance to get a fine young player who's playing for Ireland. Take him over me. I'll go off somewhere and learn a bit of coaching and I'll come back to Mary's at some stage." And that's just how it panned out.

---

*It's always been about stretching who I believe I*
*am myself and who others believe I should be.*

---

I loved my time at Clontarf. It gave me new direction in my life to really achieve something with a bunch of great players who wanted success. We climbed up the ranks and along the way were promoted from Division 3 of the AIL, won Division 2, made it to Division 1 where they had never been before and still remain to this day. We won the Leinster Senior Cup for the first time in decades and won two Floodlit Cups – not bad for a team that started at the bottom of Division 3. St Mary's approached me in 1999/2000, their centenary year, and said: "Come back to coach. You always promised you would."

Well, we won the AIL League, the first Leinster team in history to do it, so that was really full circle for me. I then coached Leinster A.

I was then offered a number of professional coaching jobs in Ireland and abroad but I chose to stay in the media. I believe now, looking back, that I could have gone on to become a good coach and to be maybe a Warren Gatland or a Joe Schmidt. After all, they started at the same level. It's just they made the choice to go down the coaching route and look how successful they have been.

I just decided that I loved the media more, the writing and the TV. And also I loved the fact that I had become somebody in Irish people's lives so I could walk out in the street and people wanted to come up and talk to me. And that's never been about ego for me, it's been more about: "Well, I'd done something. I've proved people wrong. I've done something right in somebody's eyes."

Even writing the children's books and doing the charity work and the shirts and the books: it's always been about stretching who I believe I am myself and who others believe I should be. I know I use all those quotes but the best things in life really do happen outside your comfort zone.

In life, there is a lot of luck involved. When people become unemployed or redundant or change their lives, they freefall – and then suddenly they see opportunities that they may not have seen before. I think I was more open to change when I came over here first.

I think all these things help shape us. And when you look back on it like that, it becomes a kind of destiny of change, but you don't know it at the time. Things come to you, you think out of the blue, but actually, they are not. And if I look back, I was first on TV here in

1993 in a programme called *Rugby after Dark*. I just made one showing, but obviously Niall Cogley thought enough of me, but I had taken a chance too: risk and reward. And if they had not, I may not have worked on TV and my life would be different now.

Good or bad, we all continue to change during our lives sometimes due to luck or circumstance. We might think: "How did that come to me?" Okay, there is a certain amount of luck involved, but people make their own luck too. It's about taking the opportunities when they come along, making the right or wrong choices when they appear, but also understanding that it's all part of the shaping process. We are really just the sum total of all our experiences, good and bad.

❖  ❖  ❖

**Work for me is all about purpose now.** What is my purpose? I always had a strong work ethic, physically, like my father. I admired him greatly, because he was a hard-working, decent man. And he was scrupulously honest. He'd do eight or 10 hours and he'd do it to the best of his ability – always. I always had to work and I always work hard because I don't think you get anywhere in life if you are not prepared to work. And again, that's the whole luck thing: you make your own luck through hard work.

But work has a different meaning for me now. It's where I want to work on my life, where I think that purpose is, and for me that is about educating myself and educating others to being able to achieve their dreams. That's my legacy and my purpose now in a sense. I live a lot of my work in that mantra. There is a movie called *The Bucket List*, with Morgan Freeman and Jack Nicholson, where one of the lines is: "Ask not whether you've made a difference in your own life, but whether you've made a difference to someone else's life." I think it is a lovely way to live my life.

I don't know that I'm a particularly religious person, but I'm a Christian person and I want to make other people's lives great. Whether that's a smile, whether that's giving people the time of day, whether that's talking to older, lonely people or whether that's giving something back, that's what I regard as my life's work now.

If I'm asked to talk at an event, I always say: "Please don't make the mistakes that I have made." That's not being cruel on myself, but I just don't want the people in front of me, young or old, not to know that they have a choice. In life too. You don't have to go to a great rugby school, you don't have to make the first team or be a stick-thin model to be attractive. All you have to be is who you are and be happy with who you are. To be happy in your own skin is the secret to a happy life.

I continue to fight the good fight, and there are days I slip and fall. Even months ago, I despaired at a choice I made that was wrong; it forced me back to the days of depression and it took all my will to make myself better. But I have the tools. I am no longer fighting this alone. I can go and seek professional health.

Last week, I lost a friend who tragically took his own life. On the outside, he had everything but, on the inside, he was dying. It is irrational to those who have not been there how anybody could feel this way, but we never know what is going on beneath the layers. All I know is that we need to encourage sufferers to get help, to change and to lead wonderful, productive, happy lives. That is all I have ever wanted for society and myself. I will have taken the long road if that happens but I know that, like all things in my life, it took hard work. Nothing comes easy in this life.

Don't carry any shame like me. Know that we are all different, that we all make mistakes, that we are human. Learn to forgive not only others but yourselves at times. Give back. But, most of all, be happy with who you are – that's the real secret.

# INDEX

# OAK TREE PRESS

Oak Tree Press develops and delivers information, advice and resources for entrepreneurs and managers. It is Ireland's leading business book publisher, with an unrivalled reputation for quality titles across business, management, HR, law, marketing and enterprise topics. NuBooks is its recently-launched imprint, publishing short, focused ebooks for busy entrepreneurs and managers.

In addition, Oak Tree Press occupies a unique position in start-up and small business support in Ireland through its standard-setting titles, as well training courses, mentoring and advisory services.

Oak Tree Press is comfortable across a range of communication media – print, web and training, focusing always on the effective communication of business information.

## OAK TREE PRESS
E: info@oaktreepress.com
W: www.oaktreepress.com / www.SuccessStore.com.